Harvard East Asian Series 39

THE FAILURE OF FREEDOM
A Portrait of Modern Japanese Intellectuals

The East Asian Research Center at Harvard University administers research projects designed to further scholarly understanding of China, Korea, Japan, and adjacent areas.

057017

The Failure of Freedom
A Portrait of
Modern Japanese Intellectuals

Tatsuo Arima

Harvard University Press / *1969*
Cambridge, Massachusetts

Distributed in Great Britain by
Oxford University Press, London

Preparation of this volume has been aided by a
grant from the Ford Foundation.

Library of Congress Catalog Card Number 74-82292

SBN 674-29130-1

Printed in the United States of America

To my parents

Preface

This book deals with the dominant modes of thought in prewar Japan, primarily in the Taishō era (1912–1926), and with the intellectuals' failure to grasp the simple fact that such ideas as freedom and emancipation—which many of them enthusiastically espoused—are basically political and social categories. I have tried to explain some of the reasons why these so-called Taishō intellectuals could not see the virtues of a constitutional form of government, however clumsily inaugurated it may have been in Japan.

Needless to say, there were some intellectuals, among them Yoshino Sakuzō, Minobe Tatsukichi, and Hasegawa Nyosekan, whose lives and works were committed to the preservation and promotion of constitutional government. Yet the Taishō intellectuals on the whole failed to support these thinkers in their efforts to perpetuate that form of government, known as "Taishō democracy," which might have guaranteed their intellectual freedom. My interest in these intellectuals first arose from a concern with the problem of why this happened, why these men, seemingly so opposed to the more baleful forms of nationalism, in fact took no socially effective action to prevent its emergence and subsequently became its victims. Thus the main theme of this book concerns political indifference, ignorance, silence, or even cowardice. It would, of course, be grossly misleading to imply that the anarchists and Marxists dealt with here were ignorant of or indifferent to the political issues of their time. I have, however, tried to show the degree to which they were ignorant of, or even hostile to, what one might call constitutional politics. In short, this book is an examination of the anticonstitutional strains among intellectuals in prewar Japan. I have chosen some literary figures and groups whose writings might at first sight seem irrelevant to the actual political events of their time. But I believe that their novels and literary theories provide telling evidence of the various attitudes the Japanese intellectuals assumed toward society, of the kind of emotional and intellectual problems post-Meiji Japanese had to cope with, of the conflict between old and new values—a constant theme in modern Japanese intellectual history—and, above all, of the prevailing image of man, which is always crucial to an understanding of the intellectual atmosphere of any age.

I should like to emphasize here that my purpose is neither to assail the intellectuals' lack of social and political commitment nor to speculate on what they ought to have done. It is rather to examine the relations between thought and action, the intellectual structure of anticonstitutionality, and the pattern of political behavior that it assumes, and, consequently, to understand the intellectual setting or climate of opinion in prewar Japan.

During the years this book was in preparation, originally as a doctoral dissertation presented to the Department of Government, Harvard University, in 1961, I received many kindnesses from teachers and friends. First of all, but for the constant encouragement and wise counsel of Professor John K. Fairbank, I should not have completed this work. The debt I owe to my teachers in the Harvard government department is very great indeed, particularly Professors Carl J. Friedrich; Harry Eckstein, who is now at Princeton University; and Dr. Judith Shklar, who introduced me to the history of political thought and provided many valuable insights into the kinds of problems I was trying to solve in this book.

Professor Edwin O. Reischauer, while he was still Ambassador of the United States in Tokyo, read the entire manuscript, pointed out its errors, and gave me critical but kind comments. I was especially grateful for this because I, more than many, knew how busy he was. Professor Albert M. Craig of Harvard University also helped me to improve the manuscript at various stages.

In addition, the following people read the manuscript and gave me valuable suggestions: Professors Masao Maruyama and Takeshi Ishida, both of Tokyo University; Professor Robert N. Bellah, formerly of Harvard and now of the University of California, Berkeley; and Professor Ernest P. Young and his wife, Marilyn B. Young, both of the University of Michigan. Professor Shōzō Fujita of Hōsei University gave me helpful comments on Chapter Two.

It is to my thesis advisers, Professor Benjamin I. Schwartz of Harvard and Professor Sanford Lakoff, formerly of Harvard and now of New York University, that my keenest appreciation goes. Professor Lakoff went over every detail of the argument with painstaking care. I do not believe that he and Professor Schwartz know how much I have appreciated their attention and friendship.

I am also grateful to Dr. Glen Baxter of Harvard Yenching Institute for his kindness over the years I spent at Harvard. I should like to express my gratitude to Mrs. Elizabeth M. Matheson and Mrs. Anne T. Harby for their excellent editorial work, and to Mrs. Yasuko Dower for bibliographical assistance. My wife Fumiko helped to prepare the bibliography and glossary.

Needless to say, any errors in fact and judgment that remain are mine.

T. A.

1968

Contents

I THE REVOLUTIONARY
RESTORATION   1

*The Meiji Restoration / Nishida Kitarō:
The Epistemological Character of Taishō
Japan*

II UCHIMURA KANZŌ: THE POLITICS
OF SPIRITUAL DESPAIR   15

*Uchimura and Nationalism / Mysticism:
Religious Individualism / Uchimura's
Concept of Personal Ethics / The
Doctrine of No-Church / Eschatology:
Uchimura's Doctrine of the Second
Coming / Uchimura's Social Teachings*

III THE ANARCHISTS:
THE NEGATION OF POLITICS   51

*The Antiparliamentary Mentality /
Ōsugi Sakae*

IV JAPANESE NATURALISM: THE
LIMITATIONS OF EXPERIENCE   70

*Shimazaki and Tayama: From Society to
Libido / Critiques / The End of the
Rebellion / Social Roots: From Concern*

to *Alienation* / *Art and Reality: The Nature of Experience*

V   THE SHIRAKABA-HA:
    THE TYRANNY OF ART   99

Aristocratic Origins: Family and Generation / *The Politics of Aesthetics* / *The Benevolence of Nature* / *The Genius and Social Alienation* / *The Image of the Family* / *The Shirakaba-ha's Contribution to Art and Letters*

VI   ARISHIMA TAKEO: BOURGEOIS
     CRITICISM   128

A Bourgeois Self-Critic / *Japanese Naturalism Examined:* Aru onna / *The Loneliness of the Intellectual* / *Instinct and Morality: Love as the Social Principle* / *The "One Manifesto" Controversy and the Self-Execution of a Bourgeois*

VII   AKUTAGAWA RYŪNOSUKE:
      THE LITERATURE OF DEFEATISM   152

The Lost Freedom / *The Politics of Satire* / *Death as an Intellectual Choice*

VIII   PROLETARIAN LITERATURE:
       THE TYRANNY OF POLITICS   173

The Paradox of Intellectual

Impatience / Tanemakuhito: *Not as
a Servant but as a Collaborator* / *From
Collaboration to Servitude* / *The House
of the Left Divided*

CONCLUSION   214

NOTES   221

BIBLIOGRAPHY   259

GLOSSARY   273

INDEX   289

The Failure of Freedom

I / The Revolutionary Restoration

A common preoccupation of Japanese intellectuals today is the study of their predecessors' experience with the ephemeral experiment known as "Taishō democracy." Eagerness to avoid the repetition of an experience that was so brief and yielded so soon to the pressure of anticonstitutional forces leads these intellectuals to speculate on what might have been done to prevent the atrophy of the constitutional form of government in Japan. Many of them single out the intellectuals of the Taishō era as partially responsible for the failure of the experiment. Ironically, it is because the Taishō intellectuals were interested in such moral precepts as "freedom," "individualism," "emancipation," "the dignity of the individual," and "the perfection of the self" that they have now become so susceptible to this retrospective criticism. All the criticism shares the assumption that the Taishō intellectuals could have participated in the political and social processes of Taishō Japan if they had correctly understood the circumstances.

Be that as it may, the fact is that the Taishō intellectuals were incapable of seeing the problems of their day in terms that would have enabled them to play a responsible and active social role. The primary purpose of this book is to analyze and explain the intellectuals' inability to express abstract concepts in concrete social terms. Beyond the immediate causes of this inability, which lie in the very structure of human thought and consciousness, broader forces were at work. The autocratic governing circles suppressed any overt deviation from the given social or political norms, and this encouraged the intellectuals' inherent tendencies toward acquiescence and social alienation. Still another cause for their failure lies in the very nature of the Meiji Restoration, and we shall begin, therefore, with the background of Taishō Japan.

The Meiji Restoration

The use of the term "restoration" to indicate one of the most radical social transformations in the history of any nation demands some explanation. Although Japan experienced after 1868 a series of changes which, from the point of view of an outside observer, can properly be called revolutionary, to the Japanese who lived through the four eventful decades of this transformation the changes did not signify a simple departure from the past. Rather they were seen as a perpetuation and restoration of what was best in that past: although the old order was often laid aside, the passion and the spirit of the new order were symbolized by the elevation of the imperial system from obscurity to political sovereignty. To initiate the change, the conception of the emperor as a symbol of traditional unity was resurrected. The unwillingness to make an abrupt break with the past was paralleled by the peculiar role, both conservative and innovative, played by the traditional elite caste, the samurai, and by the traditional social codes derived primarily from Confucian ethics.

What is paradoxical but extremely important to an understanding of the Meiji Restoration is that these traditional forces were often working against one another. It was because the samurai early recognized and responded to the need for social, economic, and political changes that Japan was able to assume the burdens of the modern nation-state which foreign powers thrust upon her. The samurai dissolved the caste system, although through it they had maintained their professional and ethical supremacy in Japanese society. By introducing a system of universal conscription, they deprived themselves of their traditional role as the exclusive guardians of society. In the change, however, the ethical code of the samurai, *bushidō*, at once retained its force and ceased to be a class ethic. As the samurai created new social realities, they naturally had to acknowledge the inadequacy of inherited ideologies. But they could not be content merely to adopt European ideology. Proud of their association with the Japanese past, they thought of themselves as the heirs of a great tradition and as the shapers of its modernization. Thus, whereas the typical European social revolution pitted the old against the new, proposing a transvaluation of all values and compelling groups in society to make a choice, in Japan the past was not only made congruous with the future but was even invoked to legitimize its emergence.

This is not to suggest that the metamorphosis was accomplished without pain; and it is particularly in the realm of intellectual history that we see the difficulties of the adjustment. The patent inability of traditional thought to account for and evaluate the realities of change led Japanese intellectuals to follow all kinds of untried paths, where they were besieged with difficulty and anxiety. It is with the consequences of this intellectual experience, or in other words, with the imprint made by this *revolutionary restoration* upon the Japanese consciousness, that I am concerned. There is no better record, no more telling evidence, for the understanding of Japanese history in the twentieth century than the intellectual experiences that grew out of the Meiji era. The failure of Japan's effort to extend the emotional experience of emancipation beyond the level of the philosophical, the religious, and the aesthetic into the realm of social reality is part of her general failure to preserve and foster the constitutional form of government.

To Japanese who wished to take a concrete stand with respect to the emotional experience of emancipation, the choices were never clear-cut. It was impossible to choose between the old and the new, for both played conspicuously effective roles in the change that ignited the sense of emancipation in individuals. Nor was there a clear choice between East and West. Even the imperial throne could invoke both German idealism and Confucianism, neither of them indigenous, to reinforce its legitimacy. The hybrid and inarticulate nature of the new system's political symbols made it extremely difficult for the intellectual either to embrace or to reject its social manifestations.

In the absence of God and Church, many a Japanese rebelled against "family," thinking that only his ties to this venerable institution stood in the way of complete emancipation. But in this respect as in others, the difference between Japan and the West is striking. For if in the West religion and the Church for centuries frustrated the intellectual, emotional, and social emancipation of the individual, the part the family played in Japan after 1868 was an extremely ambiguous one. The projection of the traditional image of the family onto the very framework of the modern Japanese state meant that even this bulwark of the traditional order was being profoundly identified with the work of change. The Imperial Rescript on Education of 1890, which prescribed the character training for children until the end of World War II, emphasized the moral identification of one's loyalty to the family and to the nation. More often than not, the reason given for the promotion of efficiency in commerce, industry, and government was couched in terms of obligation to the larger family. Since in certain circumstances the image of the family was highly useful in carrying out necessary changes, to refute the family, both as an institution and as a symbol, was to remove one factor contributing to change. The same could be said of the warrior's ethical code, Confucianism, the Imperial Household, and many other traditions.

The function of the family as an agent for change, however, did not safeguard it from attack. The rebellion against family was a common preoccupation of the intellectuals and it ended in an inconclusive truce: no one could go so far as to say, "Family is dead," for it never died. As Akutagawa Ryūnosuke says, "There are many reasons to kill God, but there is no god in Japan who deserves to be killed." [1] This indeed is a pregnant aphorism. Once the changes heralded by the Meiji Restoration were set in motion, not a single institution, ideology, or religion seriously raised a voice in opposition. Maruyama Masao refers to this as the absence of tradition.[2] From his ironic description of what was presumably a strongly traditional society, Maruyama concludes that, to the Japanese mind, history has usually meant a mere accumulation of recollections. That is, Japanese history has not experienced the dialectical principle, no conscious opposition to what has gone before. The negation of the past has not been necessary, for there has been no tyranny of the past as in the West, where Christianity and the Church stood as a bulwark against change, frustrating the individual's social emancipation or his freedom of thought. Before a nation-state could assert itself in Europe, the idea of the Universal Church had to be disposed of. Secularization in general entailed the expansion of the liberty of conscience, and this meant that the individual consciousness had to confront directly the Christian dogmas it was in the process of rejecting. Again and again such active confrontations took place, on the intellectual level and on the level of social institutions. And these two levels were closely related. Filmer and Locke, the Leviathan and the Thomistic concept of politics, or Bodin and Althusius were real alternatives for thought and action. It cannot be overemphasized that Japan did not undergo any such experience, either with respect to ideologies or with respect to such institutions as the family or the monarchy. Since these ideologies and institutions had all the flexibility of the undefined as well as the tenacity of the functional, there was no reason to apotheosize any one of them in order to kill it.

How then was the Japanese intellectual to make the kind of break with convention that would symbolize his emancipation? A number of alternatives suggested themselves. One involved a total flight from society on religious or aesthetic grounds, placing the ultimate hope of the individual outside society, either in eschatological anticipation or in artistic creation. But the flight from society could also be expressed politically, in the radical belief that society could achieve ultimate regeneration only through the total negation of immediate reality. No less escapist was the striving for perfection of the self, to be pursued without concern for, and with the ultimate aim of freeing the self from, the trivialities of one's society. This socially quiescent philosophical attitude, seeking a harmonious unity of sentiment and thought, may be contrasted with the uninhibited expression of individual sentiment glorifying diversity, a sentimentalization of the individual experience, as it were, which was yet another alternative. In this process, the individual creates his own cosmos. It may be characterized either by melancholy or by optimistic hope for the self, but in either case the self has no clear conception of its relationship to others. Here freedom is most painfully confused with social irresponsibility and aimless defiance against convention. It goes without saying that none of these alternatives was ever simple or unambiguous.

What characterized all these alternatives was a turning away from existing social reality and a striving for emancipation that never came to grips with the realities of the socialized self. They all contained a kind of impatience with reality as a possible source of hope, and it was this impatience which prompted the intellectuals' social alienation. Worse yet was the fact that, with a few significant exceptions, the intellectuals pursued each of these escapist alternatives with no notion of their inadequacy. On the contrary, they all shared a confidence that full emancipation would eventually be achieved. None of them seems to have anticipated that in social terms their attempts at emancipation might prove futile and even catastrophic. They were in essence trying to go beyond the revolutionary realities and the ideology of restoration. Social realities eluded their grasp: the emancipation of the self was to be sought outside actual social processes.

*Nishida Kitarō: The Epistemological Character of
Taishō Japan*

No one made a more profound attempt to emancipate the self and to actualize his individual aspirations beyond society than Nishida Kitarō (1870–1945). Unanimously, histories of Japanese philosophy single him out as modern Japan's most creative philosopher.[3] His metaphysical system reveals many intellectual elements which he shared with less articulate Japanese. Although it would be an exaggeration to suggest that his philosophy underlies the whole intellectual pattern of the Taishō era, some knowledge of his thought is indispensable for understanding the basic intellectual and emotional problems confronting the Japanese of his time.

Between 1894, the year of his graduation from Tokyo Imperial University, and 1909, when he came to Tokyo to teach at the Peers' School for a year, Nishida taught at two local higher schools (Kanazawa from 1896 to 1897, Yamaguchi from 1897 to 1899, and then again at Kanazawa from 1899 to 1909). It was during these years that he established the basic structure of his philosophy. In 1899 he wrote to his closest friend: "What do you think is the means by which we might attain what you name the unity of thought? I believe the method of Zen is the shortest way to attain this end. If we could not get to this unity of thought through Zen . . . no other means would do. Therefore, regardless of the actual outcome, I intend to discipline myself in the ways of Zen throughout my life."[4] His diary and correspondence show how persistently Nishida meditated in Zen temples. "It has been already a few years since I started to sit at Zen. Progress is slow. I have gained nothing. I feel fully ashamed of myself."[5] Again he writes: "Although I sit [Zen terminology indicating meditation], with the recurrence of such miscellaneous thoughts as the wish to be a college professor or to go abroad to study, etc. . . . somehow I cannot purify myself."[6] The intellectual's effort to free his inner self from the anxieties of social life is nowhere better and more honestly stated than in these writings of Nishida Kitarō.

Through meticulous documentation, Miyajima Hajime's recent work on the formative years of Nishida's philosophy shows that its basic leitmotif was Nishida's strenuous attempt to attain an emotional state where one might be free from all the concerns of this life.[7] The shortest path to this state of enlightenment was neither Christianity nor any of the philosophical doctrines introduced to Japan from the West, but the indigenous Zen. In 1905 he wrote in his diary: "Zen is music. Zen is art. Zen is motion. Besides this there is nothing which gives our soul consolation . . . If one's soul can be as pure as that of a child there is no greater happiness in the universe." [8]

Nishida, however, could not long remain satisfied with the philosophically loose manner in which the tenets of Zen had been stated. In 1911 he published his epoch-making *Zen no kenkyū* (Studies in goodness), in which he philosophically articulated the attainment of that spiritual state he had so long been seeking. The book at once became a sensational bestseller. Again and again, Japanese intellectuals today mention this work of Nishida's as one of the books they most cherished in their adolescence. Within a decade of its publication, a copy of the book became an indispensable possession for all the young intellectuals and college students in Japan.[9]

To the experience of the enlightenment in Zen, Nishida gave the name *junsui keiken* (pure experience). This category of pure experience is the essence of existence. "In order to comprehend the essence of existence and the genuine nature of the universe, we have to proceed from knowledge which cannot be questioned, knowledge which is free from all artificial hypothesis . . . Science, for example, is based on hypothetical knowledge, and does not purport to be, or to attain, the profoundest explanation of real existence." [10] "So-called scientific knowledge cannot be the perfect truth," for "perfect truth is individualistic and real." It is in the moment of pure experience "when the essence of existence reveals itself." And as we attain this category, "we feel as if we were enchanted by exquisite music."[11]

Beginning with a search for the attenuation of worldly anxieties through Zen, Nishida arrives at the category of pure experience. As the basis of his epistemology, this is an aesthetic quasi-religious, and intuitive category, which impugns scientific knowledge.[12] In a way, this gives Nishida's philosophy an individualistic quality, but this side of it should not be exaggerated. In him we find the basic assumption of classical idealism that the contradictory elements in man's experience are fundamentally in harmony.[13] The category of pure experience allows the individual to transcend trivial and fragile realities. It is universal and absolute. Worldly anxieties give the individual the drive and the initiative to comprehend pure experience. Yet once this stage is attained, it deprives the individual of his social individuality.

In defining goodness, Nishida writes: "Goodness is what satisfies the internal need of the self. The greatest need of the self is the ability to find the unity of consciousness. The personality of the self demands such unity. For us to satisfy this demand is to actualize the potentiality of the self. And it is the greatest goodness." Nishida then goes on to say that the goodness of the individual is the "basis of the goodness of all." Above all, therefore, for the goodness of all, "we have to aim at the actualization of the individuality."[14] This unquestioned and *a priori* insistence on the identity of the individual and the whole, the subject and the object, reflects Nishida's belief that the tension or dichotomy between the two elements must be transcended.

The process through which Nishida accomplishes this philosophical end is the second leitmotif of his philosophy. The need is no longer to reconcile the Oriental and Occidental cultures but rather to give a clear logical structure to Japanese thinking and culture, which are "often thought of as mystic and illogical."[15] In 1927, in the preface to his *Hataraku mono kara miru mono e* (From a doer to an observer), Nishida wrote:

It goes without saying that there is a great deal to respect and learn from the brilliant development of the Occidental culture which sees existence in form and goodness in formation. On the contrary, beneath the foundation of the Oriental culture . . . there is something that sees the form in the formless and hears the sound of the soundless. Our hearts cannot help longing for such experiences. I intend to give a philosophical basis to such longings.[16]

It is difficult to measure his success. Although Nishida believes that there cannot be two systems of logic, from East and from West, in the end he produces a philosophy of "nothingness" that is opposed to the philosophies of "existence." In this argument he equates Hegel's idealistic dialectic method with Marx's dialectical materialism, for both are concerned with existence and do not see the realm beyond.[17]

In *mu* (nothingness), according to Nishida, all dichotomies are united in the higher unity of consciousness—the category of pure experience. Pure experience precedes the existence of the individual. Hence Nishida's famous and basic statement: "The individual does not precede the experience. Rather it is the experience that defines the individual." Elsewhere, commenting on T. H. Green, whose influence he often revealed, Nishida remarked: "In individualistic idealism there is the tendency to think of experience as determined by the individual. Yet should we consider the individual personality so fundamental? . . . In the moment of the pure experience there is neither the self (subject) nor the others (objects). There is only One experience." [18] Therefore, by the actualization of the self, Nishida means not so much individualized self-perfection as the unfolding of the self into *mu* through the pure experience that gives unity to the individual's consciousness and, at the same time, binds him to the whole. Thus insistence upon individuality, uniqueness, and autonomy within a social situation become meaningless. The idea of juxtaposing oneself to one's society in order to define and manipulate the relationship between the two will yield to the imperative to go beyond this dichotomy.

Some time after he had elaborated his philosophy, Nishida commented on the Hegelian view of the state. Concluding his discussion on the "Problems of Raison d'État," he admits the similarities between his theory of the state and Hegel's. "Yet there are differences between the logics of the two," he continues. "From Hegel's point of view of reason . . . the state cannot free itself from the totalitarian (*zentaishugiteki*) negation of the individual. In terms of the logic of Hegel, after all, it is impossible to think of genuine individual creativity." [19] Written in 1941, this is a remarkable critique of the prevailing political sentiment among the Japanese; but it should not be confused with advocacy of either liberalism or individualism in any Western sense. For what Nishida proposes in its stead is a state of being that transcends any such conflict. He considers both individualism and totalitarianism to be anachronistic.[20] What characterizes the nature of Japanese history, Nishida argues, is that "it was neither the whole opposing the individual nor the individual opposing the whole, but rather that with the Imperial Household as the center, the individual and the whole mutually negate themselves [for the imperial sovereign]." [21] The main theme now forming his philosophy is called "the contradictory sameness of the whole and the individual self." [22] This transcends the ordinary dichotomy of the individual and the whole.

By this rather ambiguous expression, "the contradictory sameness," Nishida meant the unity or harmony available between opposites. Epistemology should have as its basis neither conflict nor elimination, but collaboration. This is not a Hegelian version of the philosophy of the state, for there is no clear vision of the state presiding over men. For the achievement of the higher unity, the imperial sovereignty demands the negation of both the state and the individual. This is the ideal of harmony, not at the expense of either the individual or the whole but through the negation of both. The negation of the self, the self not only of the individual but also of the whole, is in fact its sublimation.

The underlying motif of Nishida's philosophy, however, is his abiding concern to base the emancipation of the self from society upon the category of pure experience. Compared with his voluminous papers on philosophy, Nishida wrote only a few pages on specific political problems. Nowhere does he urge the need for the category to be applied as a social regulative principle. Even if the Platonic Idea was to be carried to society by the philosopher kings, Nishida's concept of enlightenment remained closed to social realities. Indeed, emotionally, Nishida was closer to the liberals than he was to the fanatic nationalists or the Marxian socialists. During the "Minobe incident," his letters indicate his affinity with the liberal group of Japanese constitutional lawyers who had tried to create a constitutional form of government within the framework of the Meiji Constitution of 1889.[23] These lawyers considered the emperor an organ of the state with limited and specific functions, but removed from the arena of actual politics. As an attempt to overcome conflict by absorbing opposites into a whole, this effort was in conformity with Nishida's philosophy. There was, however, a basic difference between the two points of view. While the constitutional lawyers insisted upon making the state the supreme sovereign body and the emperor its organ, they in fact intended to preserve a place for party politics. Nishida, on the other hand, abhorred conflict in any form whatsoever. He had already stated that what characterized Japanese history was the presence of the Imperial Household and that this presence should be able to overcome the realities of political conflict.

This almost careless transmutation of the individual ideal of harmony into the sphere of politics or society is a pronounced characteristic of such cultural historians as Watsuji Tetsurō. In Watsuji's description of ancient Japan, the Imperial Household is presented not as a political but as a sacred entity. As such it never commands. Rather, the people naturally obey its spiritual authority, not in fear of its power but in reverence to its benevolence. "In Him was expressed the wholeness of the people." In retrospect, it is difficult to believe that competent university scholars of this century could preach the idea that the "prehistoric period" of Japan "consciously formed" "the sacred authority of the emperor." "The authority of the emperor led to the unification of the Great Eight Islands, and therefore was the force to produce the national consciousness of the whole people. It was not an outcome of the national unification." [24] The primary sin of a Nishida or a Watsuji was not that their ideal of harmony in the individual might be untenable, but that they confused the realities of politics with personal longings for serenity and harmony.

Nishida's philosophy reveals certain general features of the intellectual concerns of modern Japan, perhaps the most important being the primacy of the individual. At the same time, Nishida's willingness to embrace something that would dissolve emotional tension or "the disunity of consciousness" opens the possibility that the self could eventually be sacrificed for the sake of a better, more harmonious, cosmos. The tendency to shun any conflict is another feature that runs throughout Japanese thought. Even though it may be only implicit, there is a pronounced desire to withdraw from any deep entanglement with the world. We have already seen that one motif of Nishida's thought was the urge to free himself from anxiety (which he had experienced himself during the years when he was not recognized either as a scholar or as a teacher). This book will deal with many intellectuals whose secular ambitions had been similarly frustrated. With no intention of belittling their work, one may still state that many of them took to the world of art and letters as a way of nursing the emotional wounds they had experienced in being removed from the limelight of historical events. The philosophical category of pure experience, with all its logical embellishments, was used to preach social resignation as a means of achieving individual enlightenment. It gave unity and harmony to the individual consciousness and feelings; it was "like music." Yet it was completely free from the Platonic imperative to return to the cave, which was perhaps fortunate. Later, during the thirties, Nishida's students at Kyoto University came to find "the better cosmos" for the individual specifically within the divine nature and mission of the Japanese state. By then, however, their attempt to rationalize and philosophize the myths was overwhelmed by the cruder forms of fanatic nationalism which the populace accepted with such obvious ease.

Nishida's concept of experience is another important aspect of his thought. There is no objectification of the experience of the individual. By negating the opposition between the self and experience, by supposing that experience precedes the individual, the individual becomes incapable of manipulating his experience. When the idea of pure experience is realized within the individual, it encourages a kind of religious submission to reality. This being the ultimate reality, there is no need for the self to remold its social surroundings. One achieves the unity of the individual self and the ultimate reality outside society—the very essence of an asocial philosophy.

Finally, Nishida shares with many of his contemporaries the philosophical attempts not so much to reconcile East and West as to give a comprehensible logical structure to hitherto vague Oriental cultural legacies and to make them universally valid. We shall see in the work of Uchimura Kanzō another effort of the same kind: to make Christianity the universal in which the categories of East and West become altogether irrelevant. Yet, ironically enough, it is to Japan alone that Uchimura assigns the mission of making Christianity genuinely universal and Christian.

II / Uchimura Kanzō:
The Politics of Spiritual Despair

Since the Restoration, Christianity and Marxism have been the two intellectually "popular heterodoxies." Their failure to achieve wide public acceptance is partially due to the process of intellectualization to which both doctrines have been submitted. At the same time, the awe, respect, or suspicion that Christianity and Marxism inspire in the public are the results of the same factor—the social eminence of the intellectuals who have become their disciples. Both Christianity and Marxism show in extreme form the tension between what is and what ought to be. With Christianity, this tension is between the worldly (the state of sin) and the otherworldly (the hope for salvation). With Marxism, on the other hand, apocalyptic anticipation is brought down to the very process of human history. More than any of their indigenous religions, Christianity taught the Japanese the worth of man independent of society, and Marxism taught them more about the nature of their society than did any other social doctrine. Through Marxism the Japanese experienced genuine radicalism—the deterministic content of Marx's dialectical materialism was explained in terms that formed an intensely activist philosophy. Thus, from Christianity and Marxism the Japanese could have learned a great deal about both the practice and the ethical basis of constitutionalism. In retrospect, however, the two doctrines were seldom put into such a framework.

This chapter deals with one of the most prominent Christian leaders of modern Japan, Uchimura Kanzō (1861–1930). Although the uniqueness of his thought far outweighs those attributes he shared with his contemporaries, by portraying this man in relief against the background of his time we may understand the nature of the intellectual anxiety the Japanese experienced as they began to adapt to the changing realities of life in the late nineteenth and early twentieth centuries. All the intellectuals dealt with in this book are the product of such experiences.

For our purposes, it is particularly important to note that in Uchimura's theology the Christian dichotomy between the worldly and the otherworldly expectations find its purest expression. In his later years, Uchimura came to believe in the doctrine of the Second Coming, and since social fatalism is one logical conclusion of such a view, Uchimura's hopes were never finally translated into worldly concerns. Thus he removed man from a creative role in history. His argument, however, does not convey the logical consistency of the theologian. In fact, what characterizes Uchimura's thought is its ambiguity and ambivalence. The Janus-like tension between his commitment to the universal and his manifest sense of nationalism, for example, reflects the complexity of the intellectual experiences of most Japanese after the Restoration.

Uchimura and Nationalism

It is difficult to ascertain the validity of the statement that "every era has its own spirit." In the case of Japan, however, it may be asserted without undue simplification that the predominant if not the sole motivation of the conduct of the Japanese after 1868 was an awakened sense of nationalism. Uchimura, too, was conditioned by this sentiment, which was almost a blind acceptance of the value of Japan as a unified and independent nation.

There were indeed many factors unifying Japan as a society: race, language, cultural heritage, national myths, and the nation's insular position. These, however were not sufficient to create the need for a politically unified and consciously independent nation. This need was stimulated by two new historical facts. One was that Japan had become, at the beginning of the nineteenth century, the last object of European power rivalry in Asia. As early as 1797, discussing the threat of Russia from the north, Ōhara Kokingo wrote: "The foreign threat is not a menace to a single clan, but it is a threat to the entire body of the clans. Therefore, it is necessary for us to try our best to plan the means to defend ourselves together." [1] The other fact was the acute economic need for a unified national market. Until these elements were in evidence, neither the political leaders nor the people consciously recognized the need for a politically united nation-state. It was these two facts which eventually inspired the slogan of the Meiji era, *fukoku kyōhei* (wealthy nation and strong defense). In the period immediately preceding the Restoration, the political factions then contending for hegemony over troubled Japan—under such slogans as *sonnōjōi* (revere the emperor and expel the foreigners), *kōbugattai* (collaboration of the nobility and warriors), and *keibaku kaikoku* (revere the bakufu and open the nation)—has in reality but a single common objective—the political unification of Japan.

Concurrently with the coming of Perry, the han system collapsed and the individual found himself bereft of traditional ties in the old order of social stratification. When an established social order disintegrates and men lose their accustomed places in the hierarchy, individual self-awareness increases. In Fukuzawa Yukichi's *Gakumon no susume* (For the advancement of learning), glorifying the English utilitarian approach, in Nakae Chōmin's work of introducing Japan to the French Enlightenment and Rousseau's writings, in Niijima Jō's educational ideals based on Christianity, even in the writings of Katō Hiroyuki, who introduced German idealism and later synthesized a state-organic theory on the basis of combining this idealism with traditional Chu Hsi Confucianism, there is ample evidence of the extent to which intellectuals of the time were concerned with the problem of the individual and his values.

There were, therefore, two conflicting elements in the intellectual orientation of Japanese nationalism—or of any nationalism, for that matter. One tended toward political unification, the other toward concern with the individual. In this context, nationalism has both a confining and a liberating character. It is liberating insofar as it defies and disregards the divisions by social status within national boundaries, and consequently plays an important role in destroying the mentality behind a hierarchical order. It is confining in that its sense of unity and national independence does not allow alien elements to penetrate its own sphere. Even if the people accept technological knowledge from outside, their interests, aspirations, and burdens are defined in terms of national consciousness.

It is impossible to discuss Uchimura's mental outlook without keeping in mind the ambivalent elements of this nationalist sentiment. In his view of the virtues of the samurai, unique in Japanese history, and in his definition of Japan's mission as a nation, Uchimura is more pronouncedly committed to the confining elements of nationalism. At the same time, his discussion of theology, concerned as it is with the conscience and salvation of each individual, represents nationalism's more liberating aspect. It is interesting to note that the reason why many Japanese became converts to Protestantism lay in their concern for Japan as a nation. "The first reason for which we came to believe in Christianity is that we believed that only Christianity was able to save Japan from various threats both from within and outside Japan. Our involvement with our nation is so deep that we cannot think of our salvation apart from Japan. If our nation is to be cursed, we would rather be cursed with it." [2] According to Uchimura, there are only two subjects worthy of love: one is Jesus and the other is Japan. He writes elsewhere that man's most virtuous concern is patriotism: "My Christianity is patriotic . . . Patriotism means that one believes in the divine mission of the nation and devotes one's entire self in behalf of the mission . . . The Japanese should not be merely satisfied with imitating the West but we shall have to add to what the Europeans have created." [3] This sentiment of personal identification with the ends of the Japanese nation was not confined to Uchimura. Even Christian socialists related their ideals to the needs of Japan rather than to those of the individual.

The liberating element is shown in Uchimura's effort to propagate Christianity among the people as a whole regardless of class divisions. Particularly in his later years, after 1918, through his conscious effort to propagate among all classes of the nation his doctrine of the Second Coming, his concept of Japan became less restrictive. Since Uchimura internalized religion, and also made his doctrine irrelevant to the national boundaries of Japan, the main features of his religious teachings were apolitical. But even in this stage, because of his identification of materialism with the West and especially with the United States, he was not free from the desire to maintain the purity of the Japanese and Japan's divine mission in history. His concern with his nation became inseparable from his concern with the individuals within it: "We cannot say that there is no sign of the fall of Japan. Our recent observations of moral degradations of the people and corruptions of society as a whole are some symptoms . . . that may lead to the withering away of the Japanese nation." [4]

In 1916, however, he wrote: "Now that Christianity is dying in Europe and America because of their materialism, they cannot revive it; God is calling upon Japan to contribute its best to His service." [5] This nationalistic concern with Japan held on tenaciously in Uchimura's thinking throughout his life. Like earlier samurai converts, he felt that since the old, traditional ideologies had lost their vigor, Christianity was the only religion that could give direction to Japan and retain the best elements of Japanese asceticism.

Mysticism: Religious Individualism

Troeltsch defines mysticism as "the insistence upon a direct and present inward religious experience." [6] So, too, Uchimura believes that salvation is possible only through man's personal communication with the divine, through his individual confrontation with God through Jesus.[7] The experiencing of grace, however, does not result from participation in church sacraments or any adherence to a particular creed. As Uchimura writes: "I have not set my name to any set of dogmas formulated by the theologians. If I am a Christian at all, I am a Christian only in my inmost soul." The bestowing of grace is an act of God and not of an individual. God has, beyond time, predestined man either to eternal damnation or to salvation. Grace comes into one's soul as the spirit of God. That is, grace is internalized in the elect, and, as the spirit of God, it will work "as the will power of the individuals from within." Since Uchimura's faith is in the invisible spirit and not in visible institutions, his concept of salvation is individualistic in that it allows nothing to come between God and the individual. "Religion," he says, "is personal. It is not 'we' but 'I' . . . the first person singular" with whom God is concerned. Christianity is the religion of individual inwardness. "God is found only in one's inmost soul . . . Modern Christianity is tasteless and powerless because it is general and social, and not personal and individual." [8]

By regarding the individual as capable of experiencing divine grace without the traditional mediation of the church, sacraments, and the sacerdotal order, Uchimura united the finite and the infinite in the elect. "I let God pray for me. . . . God the Spirit dwelling within me, praying through me the will of God . . . that is my true prayer." [9] Thus the elected one is capable as an individual of knowing the divine will, and God becomes to him an immanent and ever-present reality. "The spirit within me is a present reality and makes the Christian religion to me not merely a thing of past, or of future, but a working power, NOW and HERE." "God IS eternally." [10]

Involved as he is with the infinite, the elected one is independent of and superior to the sinful world. At the same time, only those who have the courage to face God are capable of resisting this world, which turned away from God. Completely isolated from society in their encounter with God, only those who "have the courage to be" [11] can be called true Christians. Such men cannot be afraid. Because of the cleavage between the elect and immoral society, Uchimura's theology came to express a strong opposition to the world, an intense aversion to the actual.

In spite of his rejection of the church as an institution, Uchimura did not reject the idea of a spiritual communion among the elect. "Only when independent people gather is there real unity in Spirit." [12] This group of kindred spirits constitutes an elite in the moral rather than in the practical sense; the Reformation concept of a vocation or calling (*Beruf*) in secular affairs is lacking. Subjective holiness is the proof of divine election, and this holiness manifests itself in the fulfillment of ethical demands.

Uchimura's Concept of Personal Ethics

One current of Uchimura's thought is his doctrine of personal ethics, which indicates the ideal image of his "righteous man." This doctrine may be delineated in terms of two basic components: the samurai code of *bushido* and Christian asceticism. He says: "*Bushido* is the finest product of Japan. But *bushido* by itself cannot save Japan or individuals. Christianity together with *bushido* will be the finest product in the world." [13] Although Uchimura seems to consider *bushido* to be the highest conceivable criterion for human conduct in a heathen world, he never clearly analyzes his concept of its meaning. However, it does appear from his writings that, for him, *bushido* contains three basic elements which are inextricably interwoven to form a standard of human conduct: Buddhism, Shintoism, and Confucianism (especially that of the Chu Hsi school).

Buddhism fostered the warrior's positive attitude toward death. It tried to find the ultimate expression of man in the negation of his very existence. As the Bible of the Japanese warrior class, *Hagakure,* states:

> *Bushidō* is death. There is no particular reason for this, but if a samurai finds himself in the position of being obliged to make a choice between life and death, it is his duty to choose death. Then he will be calm and serene . . . When one denies himself morning and night and remains indifferent to himself, he will find true freedom and perform his duty impeccably.[14]

Yamaga Sokō, a great teacher of the samurai, writes: "It is better to die, if you find something worthy to die for such as loyalty to your lords or filial piety. The wise will not fear death. But the samurai will be ashamed of being alive." [15] This constant awareness of the imminent presence of death inculcated in the samurai class a recognition and appreciation of the existence of values higher than their own individual existence. Death meant sublimation to a higher dimension of value. The samurai's acceptance of death as natural imbued them with a genuine "courage to be," and the fact that they found virtue in death detached them from worldly pleasures and made frugality, modesty, and simplicity the guiding principles in their daily lives.

Shintoism created the attitude of revering Japan as a divine and unique nation, of religious piety toward the "Eight Million Gods" of Japan, and of reverence toward the emperor as a being of divine origin. Therefore, although Uchimura strongly denied the validity of polytheism, his intense ascetic piety and his highly sustained reverence for Japan and the emperor reflect his original training in Shintoism.[16]

The third component of *bushidō,* the Chu Hsi school of Confucianism, is perhaps most important for the formation of Uchimura's ethics; it created the basis of his conception of ideal human relationships. The Chu Hsi school held the optimistic belief that man is by nature good and that this natural virtue lies in man's possession of such innate virtues as loyalty and filial piety, which make it possible for him to serve society with an unquestioning acceptance of a hierarchically ordered authority. The purpose of education or *shūshin* (moral training of individuals), therefore, was to bring these natural virtues to light and thus to produce a well-ordered and peaceful society. As Maruyama cogently points out, such optimism was possible only while the Tokugawa hegemony peacefully maintained the hierarchical order of Japanese society.[17] When the order of the Tokugawa hegemony was disturbed and eventually destroyed by external threats and the emergence of a money economy, optimism died. So, too, in Uchimura, the introduction of the Christian idea of original sin replaced the optimism of the Chu Hsi school. Furthermore, as we shall see, his adherence to the Sermon on the Mount implicitly presupposed a pessimistic view of the common man.

Uchimura describes St. Paul as an ideal samurai:

> Paul, a Jew and a disciple of Jesus the Christ, was a true samurai, the very embodiment of the Spirit of *bushidō*. Said he, "for *it were* better for me to die, than that any man should make my glorying void." He preferred death to dishonour, to dependency, to begging whatever cause. Again he said: "For the love of money is the root of all evil." Commercialism, in his view, was the cause of all evil, individual, social, and national. Then, none was more loyal to his master than Paul was to his, Jesus. Paul was a type of the old samurai, not to be found among modern Christians.

But Uchimura realized that *bushidō* was not sufficient for his prototype of the ideal man. It needed to be supplemented by Christian ethics. "When am I certain that I am a Christian?

. . . When I can do that which Jesus commands me to do." [18] Uchimura's yearning to obey the commands of Jesus grows naturally out of his concept of salvation, which denied the efficacy of the church and other institutions in assuring man of salvation. The elect must be capable of observing the often seemingly unbearable ethical demands of God transmitted through Jesus, in the quest for subjective holiness. Uchimura believed that this could be achieved through the strict observance of the Sermon on the Mount. Interpreting the verses: "And seeing the multitudes, he went up into a mountain: and when he was set, his disciples came unto him. And he opened his mouth, and taught them, saying . . ." Uchimura saw that the Sermon was not given to all men, that it was a grace bestowed only on the elect. It was the "Constitution of the Kingdom of Heaven," not made for the multitude in the present moment. "Give not that which is holy unto the dogs, neither cast ye your pearls before swine." [19]

Uchimura stressed the discrepancy between the demands of the Sermon and those of the secular authorities, which are not God's, since the law of the Kingdom of Heaven has not yet come to the world. In the face of this dualism, the responsibility of the elect is to bring the finite closer to the infinite, to bring man's sinful inclination closer to God's design. This tends to produce what may be called the spiritualization of politics,[20] that is, the judging of poltical and economic questions in terms of one's ideal ethics, here the principles enunciated in the Sermon on the Mount. This painful task of judging the world by the standards of the Kingdom of Heaven is what Uchimura meant when he referred to the elect as "bearing the cross with Jesus." [21] Nevertheless, although the elite must bear heavy burdens and often live in obscurity on earth, they are certain to inherit the Kingdom of Heaven. They alone are morally the bearers of man's history. But the strict observance by the elect of the moral imperatives of the Sermon is an indication that grace may have been bestowed upon them as the gift of God, rather than a means for attaining salvation.

Uchimura regarded the human relations of loyalty and filial piety as subordinate to man's first concern with God. He writes that Christianity includes reverence for one's ancestors and piety toward one's parents.[22] At first, "Let your parents understand your attitude to God. And then obey them. This is the filial piety of a Christian." [23] First comes God's demand for absolute obedience; then follows the establishment of correct human relationships. The prototype of Uchimura's ideal individual, then, although in a sense asocial and apolitical, is at the same time capable of a highly disciplined and ascetic life, and observes the proper relationships based on loyalty and filial piety.

Max Weber divided ethics into two types: *Heldenethik* (hero ethics), and *Durchschnittsethik* (average ethics). He writes that the former alone deserves the name of idealism.[24] By its implicitly pessimistic view of the average man and by its refusal to compromise in the extremely high standards it sets for the elect, Uchimura's ethical code seems to belong to this category of hero ethics. In this respect, Uchimura's ethical code stems from the very qualities of *bushidō* and Christian asceticism. *Bushidō* as an ethical system, although admired by all classes, was never universalized, being exclusive and a prerogative of the warrior class. Also, by internalizing the spirit, Uchimura expected the elect to achieve holiness—to abide by the Sermon on the Mount as the children of God.

The Doctrine of No-Church

Developing the doctrine of salvation through individual experience with God, Uchimura denied the necessity of the church as a mediating institution. "It was neither the Church nor man that kept Christianity alive for nineteen hundred years. It was the Spirit of God working through the elect . . . It is a fellowship of those who stand with Christ that I call the church community. It is a spiritual group, not an institution." Uchimura's negation of the church can be viewed from two aspects other than the theological, however. The doctrine of no-church (*mukyōkaishugi*) was an expression of anti-Westernism and anti-Americanism, of his desire to maintain the independence of the church in Japan. It was also a negation of the then-existing form of the church in Japan, a reflection of his refusal to compromise with worldly institutions. Chronologically, these two positions of Uchimura preceded his theological negation of the church: "The no-church is an antithesis to the church only in the sense that I negate the church as it has existed which served for man's desire and not for God." [25]

This desire for the independence of the Japanese church is not peculiar to Uchimura alone. Particularly, the early Japanese Christians had accepted Christianity specifically with an independent Japan in mind. Therefore, they did not "feel right to receive even a cent from the missionaries in those days. They considered independence and self-help to be their life." [26]

As early as 1881, Uchimura broke away from the American Mission Boards. A group of Japanese led by Uchimura was planning to build a church in Sapporo, Hokkaidō, and for this purpose they received seven hundred yen from the American Methodist Foreign Mission Board. The decision of the group to call the new church Dokuritsu Kyōkai (Independent Church) irritated the board, which immediately wrote to Uchimura accusing the group of forming a church independent of Methodism. Upon the receipt of the letter, Uchimura and his group abandoned the idea of building the church and immediately returned the money. They eventually built a small church on a loan. When all the money was returned, Uchimura wrote in his diary: "[The] Church is independent! Joy inexpressible and indescribable!" [27] Although this shows how tenaciously the early Christians craved independence, at the same time the group's action was quite extraordinary in that, in spite of the desire for independence, only 14.7 percent of the Japanese churches were actually self-supporting in 1882. [28]

Uchimura's conviction that the Japanese churches should be independent of foreign aid never changed, in spite of the increasing rate of dependency of Japanese churches on foreign missions. In his eyes, therefore, as time went on, the Japanese churches appeared not to be really Christian:

> Japanese Christianity is Christianity received by the Japanese directly from God without any intermediary: no more, no less . . . the Spirit of Japan inspired by the Almighty is Japanese Christianity. It is free, independent, original and creative . . . Only Japanese Christianity will save Japan and the Japanese.[29]

> They [the missionaries] cannot understand us, and no wonder that, after spending half their lifetime in this country, they still remain utter strangers to us. The fact that these missionaries despise our language is sure evidence that they have no true love for our souls.[30]

Uchimura's doctrine of no-church, therefore, is to a great extent a reaction against the missionaries' influence in Japan. This was already indicated while he was in the United States, when he came to feel that real Christianity was dying in the West under the weight of its materialism and hedonism.

In the late Meiji era, with all legal restrictions removed and with the mood of Westernization becoming fashionable, Christianity penetrated into many echelons of Japanese society, but especially the upper classes.[31] The government softened its attitude of resentment, and Inoue Kaoru, as Minister of Foreign Affairs, even entertained Christian missionaries and ministers at his official residence. Fukuzawa Yukichi, a Utilitarian and the founder of Keiō University, wrote in 1894 in his newspaper, *Jiji shimpō* (The daily times), that Christianity should be accepted as the national religion, for he felt that, according to the theory of evolution, Christianity alone could be useful in this world. Toyama Shōichi (1848–1900), a professor at Tokyo Imperial University and once a staunch opponent of Christianity, published *Kirisutokyō to shakai-shimpo* (Christianity and social progress), in which he expounded a theory that Christianity had improved music, developed man's sociability, and normalized the relations between men and women.

With the public in such a mood, Christianity grew in numbers between 1880 and 1890. Sumiya observes that the Congregational Church, composed in the main of the Christian leaders from Kumamoto who were politically inclined, was most successful in this period. Between 1886 and 1890, as the number of Congregational churches increased from thirty-one to sixty-one and that of church members from 3,468 to 10,142, Congregationalism became the most important denomination in Japan. In the same period, Christanity as a whole developed at a spectacular rate. In 1885, there were 168 churches and 11,000 members; in the following year these figures increased to 193 and 13,000 respectively. In the next three years (1887–1890), the number of churches almost doubled, increasing to 300, and that of church members rose to 34,000. It was in this period that the Jiyū Minken Undō (Liberal People's Right Movement) came into close contact with Christianity. Some of the outstanding liberal politicians of the time were Christians, including the speaker of the House of Commons during the last decade of the century, Shimada Saburō, and two other members of the House, Kataoka Kenkichi and Nakajima Noboyuki.

This fairly wide acceptance of Christianity was inevitably accompanied by the secularization of Christianity and by the lowering of the puritanical standards of the earlier samurai Christians. Uchimura was extremely dissatisfied with this tendency of the Japanese Christians to compromise with secular trends. He felt that such Christians were not the real children of God, and that the ministers who flattered this world could save neither Japan nor the Japanese. He believed that the Church as it had historically existed was not Christian, for it had turned out to be a social gathering place instead of a holy place.[32] The success of church or of mission school now depended on the diplomatic ability of the ministers rather than on their faith. The

Christians who were baptized by the followers of the missionaries were traitors to Christianity and Japan.

Eschatology: Uchimura's Doctrine of the Second Coming

The central theme of Uchimura's theology after 1918 is the doctrine of the Second Coming of Christ. After the outbreak of World War I, Uchimura became convinced that man could do nothing to improve human society. Uchimura thought that, though man's intention's were often good, such actions as the building of the Hague Peace Palace on the eve of the war gave testimony to human frailty. Before the war, the socialists had stood for peace and for international harmony among the proletariat. But as soon as war broke out, they turned into zealous patriots. Uchimura felt that the war was bringing about the "rebarbarization" and "repaganization" of all civilization and that it also was a proof of the "incapacitated modern Christian Church." [33] This acute disillusionment in man and in the power of the elect led him to an exclusive reliance on eschatological hope in which man's efforts play no part.

Usually students of Uchimura's social and political teachings do not deal with his works written after 1918 or even after 1905, and actually he wrote few articles specifically dealing with current problems. But for our purposes, it is important to analyze his doctrine of the Second Coming as a solution to social and political problems.

In the dualism of his ethics, the separation of the finite and infinite, Uchimura had assumed that the elect could bring the mortal and finite closer to the infinite, that is, to improve society. But when he emerged in 1918 after thirteen years of scholarly seclusion, he no longer felt able to rely on the efforts of the elect for the improvement of the world. In the new dualism, therefore, the elect are reduced to bearers of the cross with Jesus. The observance of the *Heldenethik* by the elect no longer has the effect of improving the world. It can only ensure a feeling of holiness within individuals. Therefore, the only hope left for the bearers of the *Heldenethik* is the intervention of the infinite. Until Christ comes again, the elect are separated from temporal concerns, and all hope of improving society must now await his coming.

> Often idealists now say that nowhere can they find any source of peace. It is because they cannot believe in the Second Coming of Christ . . . the final triumph of God through the elect whom Jesus will employ as he rules this earth.[34]

> How stupid I have been to try to improve and reform this world with my little power. It was not my business. Christ will come to achieve this end. Only with the coming of Christ will peace be forever realized.[35]

Though it was quite accidental that Uchimura came to be acquainted with this strain of Christian thought,[36] his feeling of the certainty of the Second Coming was persistent. Until his death in 1930, he never changed his belief that "this doctrine is the faith of the Bible" and that "the central aim of the life of Jesus was His Second Coming." [37]

Uchimura concretely envisioned the coming of Christ as the realization of the Kingdom of God on earth—it would be like "the society of Comte, which is based on the perfect union of moral men." The moral men, the elect, will be called the children of God and men of flesh will no longer rule. The one to rule the Kingdom is Jesus Christ himself, under whom all have to live abiding by the Sermon on the Mount. The Kingdom also will be the Court of Jesus: "For he shall have judgment without mercy, that hath shewed no mercy; and mercy rejoiceth against judgment." [38]

Uchimura's insistence on the final judgment by Christ is a consequence of his originally juristic conception of God. He is bitter against Japanese society for not accepting his moral standards.

O Jerusalem, Jerusalem, *thou* that killest the prophets, and stonest them which are sent unto thee, how often would I have gathered thy children together, even as a hen gathereth her chickens under *her* wings, and ye would not!

Behold, your house is left unto you desolate.[39]

His frequent reference to this Biblical phrase indicates that, even at this stage, he is very seriously concerned with Japan. The notion of the fall of Japan, a basic theme in his thought, becomes more intensified as its antithesis, the apocalyptic hope in the Second Coming, is heightened. Uchimura, therefore, does not consider the separation of the finite and infinite to be unavoidable, but he believes that it must be remedied.

The idea of a forgiving God of love was alien to the Japanese. Christian love that forgives the utmost human frailty is possible only when there is an equally extreme consciousness of guilt fostered by such legalistic traditions as the Mosaic law and other laws of the Old Testament, and these do not exist in the spiritual heritage of the Japanese. In Uchimura's earlier writings, a righteous God is more emphasized than a God of love. But as Uchimura became more and more disillusioned by the failure of the Japanese to keep pace with his ethics, his desire for atonement to an ever-loving God grew stronger. These two, the juristic God and the desire for forgiveness, are fused to form the Kingdom, which is a court as well as the paradise of the elect. This marvelous universe cannot remain in the hands of Satan forever. It is a temporary phenomenon that the wicked rule. The world will be soon returned to the children of God.[40]

Until the Second Coming, however, so long as the world is ruled by Satan, the elect have to say "nay" uncompromisingly. His stubborn insistence on "nay" made Uchimura apolitical, asocial, and retiring. His solution was of little avail in dealing with the types of problems the Japanese were then experiencing: the postwar inflation, the failure of the Siberian expedition in August 1918, the economic depression of April 1920, and the rice riots and labor unrest throughout the nation.

If man's political concern is to be understood as a "more or less conscious participation of all strata of society in the achievement of some mundane purpose, as contrasted with a fatalistic acceptance of events as they are, or of control from above," [41] the problems the Japanese faced in 1918 were too political for such an apocalyptic solution.

Uchimura's Social Teachings

Uchimura's social thought is limited by the basic contradiction in his ethics: his ideal society is predicated on an ideal moral order. Social reform is dependent on the prior moral reform of man, and moral reform is equated with spiritual membership in the elect. Yet because only a few are chosen, it follows that social reform is in fact impossible. The elect, logically speaking, can only sit back and await the direct intervention of the infinite in this world. Then they would come to hold the reins of human affairs. After 1905 Uchimura did indeed give himself up to this "logic of withdrawal." But the positions he took on the issues of his day reveal much about contemporary Japanese intellectual life.

Pacifism. Just before the beginning of the Sino-Japanese war in 1894, Uchimura wrote a series of articles, some in English, supporting the Japanese cause. He expounded the menace of China, with its *comprador* character, which would serve as a stepping stone for European ambitions in Asia and maliciously threaten the independence of Korea.[42] "China which produced Confucius for the world no longer knows the way of the sage. There is but one way left for a civilized nation to take against this harmful and untrustworthy nation . . . it is the way of iron and blood . . . by iron and blood alone, can we make them know justice." [43] At this stage, he wrote: "to be peace-loving is not a sign of a noble state, for there is ignoble peace. Justice is always worthier than peace." [44] As the war progressed, however, while another supporter of the war, Fukuzawa

Yukichi, wept when he heard the news of the Japanese victories, Uchimura wrote: "The trouble is over; or rather, it is said to be over . . . [but] a righteous war has turned into a piratical war . . . and now a prophet [Uchimura himself] who wrote to justify it is in shame." [45]

Soon after the war, Uchimura became one of the first advocates of pacifism in Japan. He enumerated the following factors as having motivated his pacifism: (1) further study of the Bible; (2) realization that nonresistance is empirically the most effective weapon; (3) careful observation of world history since 1895, which led to the conclusion that the menace of war and the rise of imperialism implied a subjugation of backward nations by the more powerful; (4) the influence of *The Springfield Republican,* a Quaker journal, and that of his Quaker friends in the United States; and (5) the realization that war tends to enrich a few while impoverishing the many.

His pacifism, in spite of the recognition of some of the economic and social effects of war, is almost entirely religious and moral, based on his firm belief in the Beatitude, "Blessed are the peacemakers: for they shall be called the children of God." In 1904 Uchimura is writing quite differently from a decade earlier: "The armed is not a Christian state," for "man's anger is not capable of executing God's righteousness." "We cannot speak of peace apart from Christianity." [46]

In the midst of the mounting chauvinism of the Japanese people on the eve of the Russo-Japanese War, he consoled himself by quoting Carlyle: "Truth always opposes the populace." [47] This quotation indicates Uchimura's feeling of isolation from the people as a whole, which was like that of many other intellectuals. During the Russo-Japanese War he wrote articles on pacifism in *Seisho no kenkyū* (Biblical research). In October 1904 when one of his students was killed, he wrote an article entitled, "The Death of a Pacifist in Battle." His only answer to the man who died, caught in the dilemma between the ideal of pacifism and the reality of patriotism, was that "God waits for thee in Heaven. Thy death, therefore, was not in vain." [48] In

Uchimura's view, it was the burden of the elect that, though not accepted by the world, they were nevertheless fettered by it. One might expect that this basically negative pacifism of Uchimura's would not have a dynamic appeal to the people in general. And in the face of the imminent hostilities with Russia in 1904, the tone of Uchimura's pacifism softened considerably. Feeling that it was a citizen's duty to be patriotic, he actually encouraged his fellow ministers to render some indirect services to the nation, such as visiting the homes of soldiers and arousing patriotism among the people.[49] This, however, was a compromise on the part of Uchimura, for the elect are not expected to yield to this world as long as it is ruled by Satan. They should forever say "nay" to the demands of this world.[50]

A striking feature of Uchimura's pacifism is its prophetic character. As early as in 1904 he observed:

> Those who let their soldiers attack other nations eventually will become the victims of their soldiers. The Japanese are offering the bulk of their wealth to maintain their soldiers whom they commanded to slaughter the Chinese . . . The little that is left of the Constitution and liberty will disappear in the smoke of shells. The nation will become one big imperial military headquarters. The Japanese will be eating gunpowder and harvesting sabers instead of wheat.[51]

Uchimura, however, did not try to bolster his intuitive apprehension over the coming of the militarist era with any political solution. Instead he came to consider war an unavoidable punishment of God. When World War I broke out in 1914, he wrote: "The deceit, hypocrisy, and moral degradation of the Europeans have brought forth this turmoil into the world. This is God's indignation and punishment. This is Noah's flood." [52] Therefore, the final solution for creating a genuine peace could not be human. Divine intervention became indispensable.

The Right Human Relationships. In 1895 Inoue Tetsujirō, professor of philosophy at Tokyo Imperial University, wrote an article entitled "Collision of Religion and Education," published in *Kyōiku jiron* (Journal of education), in which he argued that Christianity was intrinsically incompatible with the intent of the Rescript of 1890 on Education. The rescript was issued to recreate Confucian ethics regulating individual relationships, both vertical and horizontal, and also to inculcate the Japanese with respect for the political authority that emanated from the emperor. The word *shimmin* (subjects of the emperor) was emphasized and the obligations of the *shimmin* to imperial Japan were enumerated to indicate the way to virtue. In reading this document, however, one can hardly dismiss it as merely reactionary moral teaching, for it has some surprisingly enlightened aspects, such as its emphasis on universal education.[53]

Inoue pointed out quite correctly that the Christian concepts of individualism, universal brotherhood beyond national boundaries, and the denial of the divinity of the emperor and of the nation contradicted the spirit of the rescript, and that the introduction of this religion would destroy such traditional virtues of the people as the family system and reverence for elders and the emperor. Inoue concluded his essay by saying that, since even in the West Christianity was declining under the shadow of the domination of science, the acceptance of such a religion would be an anachronism in a scientific age.

A few weeks later, Uchimura wrote an open letter to the *Journal* in which he contested Inoue's argument. Stressing that the teachings of the rescript were desirable for the Japanese, he accuses those in public or responsible positions for having failed to practice what the rescript preaches. "The emperor did not grant us the document to worship it, but to follow and practice it as the basis of the people of the new nation." Uchimura expounds the idea that Christianity does not contradict the newly created ethics. He then goes on to say that the ideas of such philosophers as John Stuart Mill and Herbert Spencer, who were widely read by university students, were destructive to the Japanese nation. He quotes Spencer: "It [the instinct of subordination] has been the parent of countless crimes . . . you equally find the submission to authority decreases as morality and intelligence increase. From ancient warrior-worship down to modern flunkeyism, the sentiment has ever been strongest where human nature has been vilest." Since this is a negation of reverence for authority, "it is the responsibility of university professors that such reading material should not be brought into Japanese higher educational institutions." Uchimura attacks Inoue for his adherence to those philosophers "whose materialism and the spirit of the rescript cannot coexist." [54] In this effective rebuttal, Uchimura shows his natural inclination toward ethics of the old type, which revered secular authority as the basis for social harmony.[55]

Uchimura agrees with Inoue's statement: "The Christians have grown up under the protection of the foreign missionaries. Therefore, they lack the spirit of patriotism." [56] In answering Inoue's argument that Christianity is declining in Europe, Uchimura writes that "although Christianity is on the wane in Europe, so too is European culture." [57] Japan now should take up the burden of Christianity to keep history marching toward its completion. But since Western Christianity is no longer valid in other parts of the world, Japan should adopt Christianity in its genuine biblical form.[58]

It is not, however, fair to conclude simply that in regard to his view of ideal human relationships, Uchimura was a conservative. There is another important element he introduces into his ideal of the perfect man: *dokuritsu-shin* (independent spirit). In 1903, he wrote an article entitled "Christianity as a Solution for the Agrarian Crisis," his answer to the acute agrarian problem arising from the conflict between tenant farmers and the landowning class. "The method of solving this problem," he writes, "is not different from that for any other problem in human society . . . It is neither money nor land, but the creation of men with independent spirit who will deal with each other with respect and consideration." [59] In the article, he criticized rather extensively the traditional family structure of the Japanese peasants as hindering the development of this independent spirit, and in the letter to Inoue he did not fail to point out the folly of formalism in Japanese education, which frustrated "the development of independent ideas." [60]

In discussing the rise of labor disputes, Uchimura wrote that the roots of this social turmoil were attributable to the people's lack of filial piety, which led to the total atrophy of proper respect for men and for authority.[61] He presumed that the ideal man is independent in spirit and that the outcome of this is the observance of the right human relationships which, according to him, were closer to the traditional Confucian ideal than to any other system of ethics.

Antimaterialism: Anticapitalism and Antisocialism. After 1895, with the rapid industrialization of Japan, new social problems became painfully evident. Urbanization, slums growing like mushrooms, labor disputes, the impoverishment of the peasants, the decline in the peasant population, the rapid rise in population, the disintegration of the traditional hierarchical structure of authority, and chronic inflation and depression with consequent unemployment—all were ominous threats of instability for which there were no ready solutions.

About 1890, some mineral poison from the copper-mine region near Ashio polluted the Tone and Torase rivers. Since the rivers run through the Kantō plain, the largest and most fertile agricultural area in mainland Japan, the poisonous water began to ruin the farms. The government, in spite of constant protest from the peasants, took little notice of it. In the spring of 1900, out of desperation, a group of peasants came to Tokyo to appeal directly to the emperor. When this attempt failed, many of the group were arrested on the charge of inciting a public disturbance. In this incident, some Christians as well as socialists played an important role in enlightening the peasants and arousing public opinion against the government's inaction. Even those Christians who had been working very closely with the government, like Honda Yōichi, Matsumura Kaiseki, and Ebina Danjō, now denounced it. The public was particularly infuriated by the rumor that Furukawa Ichibei, the owner of the mine, had bribed officials. The failure to arrive at a satisfactory solution came not only from the combined strength of the government and the landowners, coupled with the relative weakness of the intellectuals, but also from the submissive character of the peasants. Tanaka Seizō, a member of Parliament, who devoted his entire life to the welfare of the three hundred thousand peasants in the prefecture of Tochigi and who planned the direct appeal to the emperor, wrote in his diary:

> Look at the peasants of the locality. Having been accustomed to the benevolent authority of the Tokugawa for over two hundred years, they have come to call virtuous negative humility, meaningless formality, hypocritical loyalty, stingy frugality, and cowardly submission to any authority. They are imbued with an attitude of forbearance in everything. They flatter the officials with a feeling of awe and fear. And they complain of nothing.[62]

Although Tanaka himself was not a Christian, he was deeply moved by the Christians who worked with him throughout the dispute. He further wrote in his diary: "At this moment, there is no other religion to enlighten the people. Christianity is the only religion capable of saving the masses, teaching them independence." [63] A historian of Christianity in Japan writes that this was the last time before the end of World War II that Christians were united in a challenge to temporal authority.[64]

In the spring of 1901 Uchimura wrote a series of articles in *Yorozuchōhō,* reporting his travel through the copper-poison district." In these emotionally charged articles, one look in vain for some suggestion of a concrete solution. At times Uchimura does little more than indulge in a mere literary description of the miseries of the peasants: "Such an incident is unfit for an empire which possesses an army of thirteen divisions and a navy of two hundred and sixty thousand tons." He thinks that this indicates the very illness of Japanese society, "which may eventually decline as a result of its moral deficiency and whose real problems lie not beyond Manchuria but within itself." In this situation, Uchimura deprecates materialism but finds no other solution than to "pray and express sympathy." [65]

In his commentary on the Ten Commandments, he denounced the capitalistic system for committing innumerable homicides. I have already mentioned that Uchimura attributed the cause of labor disputes to the lack of proper human relations.[66] He further comments on the problem:

> I am an amateur on the subject of labor problems which have attracted so much of our attention. But at least one thing is clear. This is the impoverishment of thousands by the capitalists.
>
> It is the profit motive of capitalism which created the war industry, alcoholic beverages, and other degrading products which are either directly or indirectly tending to destroy humanity.[67]

The question that naturally follows from this is whether Uchimura advocated socialism, if he refuted capitalism as an economic system. On *Yorozuchōhō* he had an opportunity to work with some socialists, all of whom left the paper with him on the eve of the Russo-Japanese War to advocate pacifism. A brief sketch of the character of the socialists at the beginning of this century will give some indication of Uchimura's conception of the movement.

Five out of the six who founded the socialist party in May 1901 were Christians. Although they did not advocate a Christian socialist doctrine, they claimed that the doctrine of love in Christianity does not confine itself to individual relations, but must be exercised in social life as the basis of securing man's collective happiness. They believed that economic egalitarianism was the most important single factor for the formation of a just society. The party proclamation reads: "Our theory is radical . . . But the means we will employ are absolutely peaceful. To achieve these desired ends, we will utilize existing political institutions." [68] The early Japanese socialists were idealistic, nonviolent, humanitarian, and often naively optimistic about the future of Japanese society. The strength of the group lies in the fact that they alone had a specific program for replacing the existing order with another set of political and economic principles.

One particular episode furnishes a striking illustration of how little the Japanese were concerned with socialism at this time. When the Socialist Party was formed, the government was unprepared to face the phenomenon of a group of young intellectuals openly and articulately denouncing the government, the emperor, business, and everything else. At any rate, Minister of the Interior Suematsu Kenchō decided to dissolve the party on the day it was formed and to prohibit the circulation of the newspapers that carried the party proclamation. His reason for making this decision was that somebody in the ministry had heard that there was a group called the Social Democratic Party in Prussia and that Bismarck did not like it. It was deduced that the Socialist Party could not be a good thing for Japan either.[69]

In 1903 Uchimura wrote an essay entitled "Christianity and Socialism" in which he refuted socialism for the following reasons: (1) Christianity is primarily concerned with the teaching of individuals, whereas socialism is devoted exclusively to reforming the world and hence cannot be a real solution to the problems confronting modern man; (2) the Bible preaches neither nationalization nor common ownership of property, although it attests that God possesses everything; (3) from this it can be deduced that Christianity has no preference for a particular social, economic, or political system. "Imperialism is fine, if it is fair, merciful, and will respect the rights of other people. Socialism may be good if it is pious, merciful, and will not disgrace the rich for the sake of the poor." [70] In reading this passage, one should not forget that in the same year (1903) Uchimura, advocating pacifism, denounced imperialism as tending to incite hostilities among nations in contention for markets.[71] This apparent contradiction is a symptom of the underlying confusion in Uchimura's theories. In his earlier writings and occasionally in his later works, he maintained that religious ethics and the social and political behavior of man are inseparable. But as his discussion of socialism indicates, he tried during this period to remove the religious content from political affairs, to separate the worldly concerns of individuals and their concern with salvation.

The solution of this apparent contradiction is a simple one. Faced with the problem of finding the cause for the mounting social problems of an industrial society, Uchimura ascribed it not to the social and economic structure of Japanese society as such, but to the recalcitrance of immoral modern man, a disease for which the only remedy was Christianity. As Uchimura saw it, Christianity is concerned only with transforming man, not with improving institutions and organizations.[72]

In 1901 Kuroiwa Ruikō, president of *Yorozuchōhō,* took the initiative of forming an association named Risōdan (Idealists' Association). Its membership encompassed a wide range of opinion, from socialists to Christians to political liberals. In his essay "What Is Risōdan?" Uchimura wrote in 1901: "It is an association organized for the purpose of social reform. It wishes to reform with one particular method—the improvement and reformation of individuals first." [73] This description of the Risōdan would not have been accepted by the socialists, who considered that the social and economic system was the root of all evil. The essay, however, explicitly points out the nature of Uchimura's concern with social problems—that individuals are always the basic units of society: "Reform first has to start with individuals. To make one righteous man means an improvement of the state . . . Good individuals form good families which, in turn, will form a good society." [74] In 1901 Uchimura relied on such human efforts as the Risōdan to enlighten and reform individuals. But a decade later, he had ceased to rely on the human capacity to achieve this end, and instead placed his trust in the will of God. As he recorded in his diary in 1918: "True politics will start only with the Second Coming of Christ." [75]

Uchimura's understanding of wealth and poverty was at best naive. His basic indifference to men's material desires is most vividly shown in reference to poverty: "If you suffer from poverty and want, remember that there are many others who suffer from the same . . . Remember also that there have been many who were wise, virtuous, and worthy but did not enjoy material comfort. Think of Christ who was poor." [76] From this, it is apparent that Uchimura was not concerned with the problem of improving men's economic lot here on earth.

Uchimura's Comments on Politics. Although Uchimura did not formulate a systematic political ideology, he did, at least until 1905, comment on certain problems of government. His interest in the form of government was inevitably limited, however, because of his adherence to the Confucian ethics of Chu Hsi and to Christian individualism, both of which regard forms of government as secondary in importance.

Perhaps the best way to view Uchimura's political ideas is to consider them as symptomatic of his dissatisfaction with the present, a dissatisfaction shared by many intellectuals who either defied, acquiesced in, or became indifferent to the government. In the late nineteenth century Uchimura believed that one of the causes of the social troubles of Meiji Japan was the Sat-Chō oligarchy. "Without replacing the Sat-Chō government," he comments, "no reform will become effective." [77] As a samurai from Jōshū, Uchimura never liked those men from Satsuma or Chōshū who occupied the important positions in government and society during the Meiji era. His criticism of the Sat-Chō government was more emotional than logical, and although in this connection he sometimes expressed surprisingly liberal political ideas, he never expounded them in logical fashion.

Soon after the Sino-Japanese War, which was won under the leadership of the Sat-Chō group, he wrote:

Let us re-examine the history of the Restoration. If Katsu Kaishū had been resistant to the demand of the combined military forces of Satsuma and Chōshū on the eve of the Restoration, the people of these two clans would not have been so despotic as they are now . . . Katsu worked for the interest of the Tokugawa, but did fail to see the future of Japan. He sowed the seed of this present degraded government. The sin of Katsu is not insignificant.[78]

I do not want the Itō [Chōshū] cabinet to be replaced by the Matsukata [Satsuma] cabinet. I want to establish a constitutional government according to the will of the people by annihilating the clan-clique politics.[79]

The time for a revolution is being accelerated by the Sat-Chō oligarchs. Stand up, men of Sabaku [bakufu retainers], to cleanse the epitaph "insurgent" stamped on you![80]

Here we see that his idea of constitutional government was merely an expression of his political dissatisfaction rather than a craving for a new form of government. It has been observed that liberalism was frequently taken up by former warriors as an outlet for their frustrated ambitions, for those who were not of the two major clans could seldom hope for any advancement in government circles.

Uchimura's political ideas were liberal not because of his intrinsic trust in constitutional democracy, but because only liberal ideas constituted an effective challenge to the existing system of government. However, in his essay "The Reforms I Desire," which he wrote in 1898 it is interesting to see how deeply he was influenced by liberal doctrines. Here Uchimura made some concrete proposals for government action: (1) expansion of educational institutions, (2) reduction of armed forces, (3) abolition of class differentiation with the aim of promoting political equality, (4) abolition of decorations except in the armed services, (5) popular franchise, (6) popular election of prefectural governors and local officials, and (7) admission of commoners to membership in the House of Lords. None of these proposals was original with Uchimura, and because of his basic indifference to social institutions, he did not seriously develop or advocate any of them. Although Uchimura was perhaps unaware of it, the liberating elements of his theology and his concern for Japan were quite consistent with those political ideas that are individualistic and advocate the abolition of class distinctions.[81]

There are many ways to escape from this tension between the ideal and the actual: one is to rely on the future; another is to eulogize the past. Hedonism suggests still another solution, whereas its antithesis, asceticism, furnishes yet one more possible answer. In an effort to relieve the conflict, Uchimura relied on both his chiliastic hopes and his eulogizing of Japan's past history. In his social teachings, the tendency to eulogize Japan is especially pronounced. Uchimura was emotionally antimodern, even resentful of the present.

Antimodernism. About 1890 a new reaction against Westernization appeared, which took the form of extreme praise of the virtues of the Japan of the past. This antimodernist movement was at once sophisticated and vigorous: sophisticated in that it had been disciplined by the experience of Western rationalism; vigorous in that it had the implicit and explicit support of the government and also, later, that of the peasants and the military.

Not unlike the Fukko-ha (traditionalists) in failing to recognize "individualism" as the key element in the modernization of the West, Uchimura identified "modernization" with materialism and industrialization and their concomitant social evils.[82] It is understandable that he took such a view, for, empirically speaking, industrialization is probably the only common factor in the process of modernization of societies. And if one is disillusioned by the social problems thereby created, he is apt to think of his social ideal in terms of the "good old days," provided he is not preoccupied with the goal of national power. Through his antimodernism Uchimura expresses his intense aversion to Japan's chief preoccupation, *fukoku-kyōhei:*

> Can present-day civilization compensate for the loss of the independence of our souls through modernization . . . ? Are the steam engine, radio, champagne, torpedoes, and guns . . . better than peace . . . love and satisfaction? Does civilization mean to spend six billion dollars to maintain the standing army of two and a half million soldiers in Europe and to produce anarchists and to increase nervous disorder? [83]

Along with such people as Taoka Reiun, to whom the nineteenth-century world was the stage on which "the strong prey upon the weak, and the stronger nations satisfy their insatiable appetite at the expense of the weaker," [84] Uchimura blamed modernization for the ugly power struggles and moral degradation so typical of the nineteenth and twentieth cenuries. "I do not deny the claim that the Sat-Chō oligarchy contributed greatly to material progress. But it has failed to infuse morality into the people." [85]

As early as 1896, Uchimura wrote " [Today, is it] Gold, Silver, Man's Will or God's Grace [that we seek]? I think the sixteenth century was a grander one than the nineteenth." [86] Five years later he wrote in his diary: "I often think that I would have been, indeed, much happier than if I had been born in the Teiō-Teiei periods [1222–1233]. Then I would have been a member of the Kamakura warrior caste, and would have acted, to the best of my ability, as a samurai." [87] Uchimura's escape from the present is definitely directed toward a particular past: to the virtues of the samurai class. "There is no longer left a samurai Christian," he remarked in 1920, referring to the Christians of the post-Restoration era.[88]

In 1924 he wrote in his diary: "I am an old Japanese and an old Christian. Without the traditional Japanese ethics, an Old

Christian faith unspoiled by the turmoil of the machine age, I could not appreciate the meaning of life." [89] When the government tried to revitalize the study of Confucianism, Uchimura was sympathetic: "I rejoice at the news that the government has a plan to restore Chinese studies in school. It is not the time to argue over the difference between the ideas of the West and the East. What we should do now is to destroy *kindai-jin* [modern man] and *kindai-shisō* [modern ideas]. To achieve this end, the restoration of Confucianism and Chinese studies is useful." [90]

Of Uchimura's antimodernism, Ienaga writes: "Uchimura was one of those people who were too conscientious to praise the modern civilization unconditionally. And at the same time his attachment to the past is too strong to visualize a concrete future." [91] Shirakawa Jirō summarized this state of mixed feelings that was shared by many Meiji intellectuals: "He is too loyal to the nation-state and the emperor to be an internationalist republican and socialist, and yet too democratic to belong to the aristocracy, too aristocratic to be a plebian, too passionate to retire from the world altogether, too involved with this world to dissimulate it." [92] It was for this reason that he praised certain agrarian states in Europe. He considered agriculture to be an ideal profession in that it complemented religion. The destruction by industrialization of the social and spiritual harmony of earlier times had produced the present moral degradation of the individual, which was at the root of all social evils.[93]

This contrast between Japan's ideal past and the degraded present created in Uchimura a state of emotional tension. He sought the ultimate solution in the doctrine of the Second Coming, but this chiliasm could have but a limited audience in the twentieth century.

Uchimura was not alone in his aversion to the Meiji era. In January 1909, Nagai Kafū, one of the outstanding writers of modern Japan, published *Furansu monogatari* (Tales from France) in which, "through a successful recreation of the old Japanese esthetic sense," he deprecated the machine age as depriving man of his best qualities.[94] Nagai thought it vain for a writer to discuss modern political and social issues unless he had the courage to resist such acts of government repression against individual freedom as the execution of the anarchists in January 1911. His works were on the whole concerned with the vestiges of Edo culture in Tokyo in which he found an escape from the "suffocating oppressiveness" of Japan.[95] However, this hardly amounted to any solution of the problems of society.

Uchimura's concern with *bushidō*, as well as Nagai's idealization of one aspect of Edo culture, is typical of the mentality of many Japanese intellectuals of the time. In one way or another, they failed to face the challenges of the new society. Neither Uchimura nor Nagai criticized Japan as a nation. They both believed that it was only such alien elements as industrialization and capitalism that had destroyed the beauty and ethical superiority of the Japanese nation.

Emotional attachment to the past is natural to any group of people who share the same heritage. But when the eulogizing of the past becomes an exclusive and overriding preoccupation, it tends to blind people to the reality and to the future. Uchimura, in his efforts to envision the future of Japan, was extremely vague as far as specific details were concerned.

Although Uchimura denied the value of the present and was prone to dwell on the past, his theory of history actually was evolutionary. In 1900, he wrote a series of essays under the title *Kōkokushidan* (Historical study of the birth of nations). In the introduction he writes: "The march of mankind will not end in ruin but in a complete growth. Although some nations may decay, humanity as a whole will march day and night towards perfection. Individuals wither, but the world of mankind goes on forever. The individuals exist for nations and nations for mankind as a whole." [96] In this march of mankind, Uchimura thinks each nation has a specific and divinely ordained mission. This resembles the theory of Hegel that "each particular national genius is to be treated only as one individual in the process of universal history." [97] Similarly, Schleiermacher thought that in history "God assigns to each nationality its definite task." In the case of Japan the definite task was to act as the intermediary between East and West and to fuse the two into a dialectically higher unity. But to perform this difficult task, Uchimura felt that the Japanese first had to work for the moral rearmament of modern man.

While searching for the historical mission of the Japanese nation, Uchimura came to feel that between the potentiality of Japan and its actual present there was a wide discrepancy which he, like Hegel, interpreted as a "cause of pessimism and futility and the ground for new hope and activity." Uchimura's writings before 1905 were an appeal "to the communal will of the nation which is based on the self-help of its individual members." [98]

A nation ceases to perform its function and begins to decline precisely at the moment when its people fail to comprehend their historical mission. Uchimura's favorite expression, *Bōkoku* (the fall of a nation), is a direct derivative of this notion of history. He therefore defines patriotism as the conscious comprehension of the national mission. In this context, "it is a great mistake to assert that Christianity has no patriotism and that only the love of humanity is truly Christian." To understand the mission of one's nation means to understand the will of God in history. "All the prophets in the Old Testament and great historical figures like Luther, Dante, Cromwell, Milton, Washington, and Lincoln were patriots, knowing the missions of their countries." [99] Hence patriotism is a Christian virtue.

Unlike the latter writings of Hegel, which considered the Prussian state as the actualization of the Spirit in its march through history, Uchimura's writing became more and more pessimistic in his concern with the actualities of Japan. With Hegel, Uchimura believed that "secular life is the positive and definite embodiment of the spirit . . . manifesting itself in outward existence." [100] The moral degradation of Japanese secular life was symptomatic of the underlying illness of the nation. Uchimura consistently maintained that, if a nation ceased to perform its mission, it would lose its claim to existence in history.[101] He felt that it would be a great tragedy if Japan remained indifferent to her special mission, which was perhaps nothing less than the consummation of the historical process. In this sense, he actively tried to arouse patriotism in the Japanese.

In essence, Uchimura sees in history not the will of man but the will of God. When he preached the doctrine of the Second Coming, he assumed that only the elect were real patriots, in that they alone understood the historical mission of Japan. To await the intervention of the infinite meant that there was no longer in history a place for the individual to play a positive role. So the real patriot had to await this intervention of the divine in human affairs.

Finally, Uchimura arrives at the logical conclusion of his theological premises. It is revelation, not reason, that determines the meaning of man's existence in past, present, and future. Reason, meaning the tool by which man consciously manipulates his surroundings, becomes irrelevant. Uchimura overcame the original dichotomy between the otherworldly expectation of salvation and the demands of this life by rejecting the social worth of man. The dignity of man still exists, but only within the framework of God's creation and its purpose: man is the end of God's design, which is the ultimate deliverance of humanity from this world. Society is no more than a meaningless conglomeration of trivialities that reveal man's finiteness and sinfulness. Even the elect are eternally suspended in the limbo that divides the world and the apocalyptic state of salvation.

This uncertainty reminds us of the world of the early Church Fathers and Augustine. To Uchimura the Thomistic attempt to reconcile reason and revelation was irrelevant, as was the Hegelian translation of revelation into the reason of history. The more he felt anxiety about the plight of man and society, the more intense did his chiliastic hopes become. Here the early Christian tension is recreated in all its stark force. History no longer provides the individual with the comfort that he can by his own volition form his world. He is caught by the moment of helpless anxiety and apocalyptic hope.

III / The Anarchists:
The Negation of Politics

The otherworldliness of the doctrine of the Second Coming led many a Christian intellectual into completely nonpolitical attitudes. In Uchimura's view, as we have seen, all human expectations have to await divine intervention, and man can play no part in their realization. Thus, insofar as man's ultimate happiness is concerned, politics become altogether irrelevant.

The anarchists also belived that this world was the source of all human suffering and anxiety. Unlike Uchimura, however, they envisioned themselves as able to actualize the ideal society where there would be no need for coercion or political power. Although political action had a definite place for the anarchists, in the long run it would work toward its own extinction. Both Uchimura and the anarchists saw the existing world as irrelevant, insofar as the ultimate emancipation of man is concerned. The anarchists' vision was a kind of political alternative which had as its final objective a society where politics would play no role. Politics must be used merely as a transitory instrument for the encouragement of violence and the destruction of the old society.

The Antiparliamentary Mentality

In January 1911, Kōtoku Shūsui and eleven other anarchists were executed, in one of the most harrowing episodes of modern Japanese history. The sense of helplessness with which liberal intellectuals witnessed the trial and execution is vividly portrayed in Nagai Kafū's "Hanabi" (Fireworks).[1] From then on, such intellectuals as Nagai consciously turned from social reality to the world of art. The refined eroticism of Nagai's art and his recreation of Edo culture, apart from their artistic excellence, bear witness to the intellectual tyranny of the government. The magnificent reign of the Meiji emperor was coming to an end. The Kōtoku incident symbolized the atrophy of the popular consensus that had prevailed in Meiji Japan. In the decade that followed, although the political left became untenable as a real alternative, socialism received considerable attention on the intellectual level.

The government was cruelly harsh toward the activist, the anarchosyndicalists, who tried to keep radicalism alive during this trying decade. As an excuse for his evasive retreat into the academic world, a Marxist could invoke history, saying that it had not yet prepared Japanese society to call for his services. A moderate socialist could find his vocation in legitimate labor movements and in social work. But the anarchists had neither the historical expectation to justify their silence nor the patience to work within the realm of the law. Such was the group that dominated the leftist movement until the great earthquake of 1923.

During and after World War I, the intellectual mood of Japanese society became noticeably more tolerant. Moreover, the conspicuous failure of the Japanese economy to adjust to the wave of postwar recessions induced intellectuals of all schools to entertain every conceivable explanation of the shortcomings of capitalism. Insofar as the government was concerned, a line was drawn between socialism and anarchism. In the spring of 1919 a member of the Diet expressed the view prevailing within ruling circles, in a statement addressed to the Minister of the Interior.[2]

> National socialism is not at all dangerous. In fact, it ought to be encouraged. The pure socialism of Marxist theoreticians, although it ought not to be encouraged, threatens our society as little as the hallucination of utopian communism. Undoubtedly, the most frightening of all are the revolutionary trade unionists—syndicalists and anarchists—who preach the elimination of all forms of political authority and praise the ideal of complete individual freedom.

For the radicals, it seemed that the worst, "the winter time of the socialist movement," was over.[3] In January 1919, Kawakami Hajime, then professor of economics at Kyoto University, started publishing *Shakai mondai kenkyū* (Journal of social problems). In April, the Marxists Sakai Toshihiko and Yamakawa Hitoshi started another journal, *Shakaishugi kenkyū* (Studies in socialism), which dealt exclusively with socialist thought. During the same year a series of magazines and newspapers appeared under such suggestive titles as *Warera* (We), *Demokurashī* (Democracy), *Kaizō* (Reform), *Kaihō* (Liberation), *Rōdō bungaku* (Workers' literature), *Shinshakai* (The new society), and *Kokka shakaishugi* (National socialism).[4] The intellectuals who were frightened in 1911 and remained silent during the following decade now found themselves increasingly allied with bolder and more vocal allies of a younger generation. Theoretically, the younger intellectuals had only vague and hybrid visions of the ideal society. But they all believed in the illness of capitalist Japan and felt it their obligation to recreate Japanese society. Many a graduate of Tokyo University, for example, now chose to enter the labor movement or settlement work, educating the working-class people and publishing radical journals.[5]

All these developments were just as disturbing to the intellectual guardians of the established order as they were to the state. Mori Ōgai (1862–1922) who, together with Natsume Sōseki (1867–1916), presided over the leading Meiji literary circles, showed concern and anxiety over the emergence of these radical ideas, and devoted the last few years of his life to a study of socialism. It was far less politically amateurish than one might expect from a literary man.[6] Some of his letters indicate that he attempted to combat the movement on the left by influencing the prominent military and political figure, Yamagata Aritomo. Mori suggested that if the government would take the initiative in erasing the ills of modern Japanese society and fulfilling some of the legitimate objectives of the socialists, it could head off trouble. He went so far as to name his proposal "national socialism" or "state collectivism."[7] Yamagata himself groped for a way to put this conviction into practice. After all, in the absence of laissez faire as a political dogma, the government could well address itself to larger tasks without hesitation or moral qualms.

Thus it was not the specific ideals proposed by the radicals that Mori or Yamagata feared, but rather the means by which they would carry out their ends—the use of violence. Had these radical ideas been confined to the outer fringes of Japanese society, as they had been before World War I, the government would have been faced with the alternatives of eliminating them or incorporating them into the national framework through such means as Mori's national socialism. But now the governing circles were compelled to recognize that radical ideas had begun to take hold within their own institutions, the universities.

In 1919 the faculty of economics became independent of the faculty of law at Tokyo University. During that winter, it published the first issue of a journal entitled *Keizaigaku kenkyū* (Economic studies). In it was printed an article by Morito Tatsuo, an assistant professor at the university, which was nothing more than an introductory comment on the ideas of the

Russian anarchist Kropotkin, who had described the "best society" as that which enables man to "develop and possess free personality." Morito argued that economic and political freedom, the two prerequisites for such a society, would remain unattainable so long as society defended private property and encouraged the sentiment of nationalism. Only an anarchistic and communistic society would allow the free personality to develop. Although he explicitly urged that violence be avoided in the effort to realize the ideal, at the same time he insisted that such an ideal was both reasonable and historically appropriate. The government, taking particular note of this assertion, found Morito's article repugnant and menacing. Kropotkin's name was associated with the memory of Kōtoku, the executed anarchist, who had earlier introduced the Russian's ideas of anarchism.[8]

On January 10, 1920, the day before Morito was due to leave for a European tour on a government grant, the university forced him to resign. Simultaneously, the government brought suit against Morito and Ōuchi Hyōe, editor of the journal, charging them with "disturbing the imperial constitutional order." Ironically, in the same issue of the journal, Kushida Tamizō, a Marxist lecturer, translated part of the *Communist Manifesto* with annotation—this two years after the Bolshevik Revolution—but the translation was completely overlooked.

Despite the fact that their defense counsel included some of the most illustrious liberal intellectuals of Taishō Japan, the two defendants were convicted.[9] But the first verdict indicted Morito's article more for its use of "unnecessarily provocative words" and "emotional expressions" designed to incite the emotions than for its threat to the "existence of the imperial state" —and it was on the latter count that the government particularly wanted Morito and Ōuchi to be convicted. Dissatisfied with this first verdict and obstinately determined to secure a full conviction, the government prosecution appealed. The final pronouncement was that, even though Morito disavowed the use of violence, his dissertation was repugnant to the "fundamental Japanese constitutional order: the right of private property and the principle of imperial sovereignty." [10]

Morito and Ōuchi had on their side the sympathy of interested college students, intellectuals, and the major newspapers. Yet we should remember that as professors at a national university, they were government officials and as such were particularly vulnerable to government censure. But the real threat to the government lay elsewhere. The enthusiasm of the young intellectuals was no longer confined to mere discussion. It was reflected in the mushrooming of organizations in universities devoted to studying and putting into practice various radical social innovations. Labor-union movements also gained momentum. The intellectuals' prewar nonchalance was replaced by a mood of optimistic concern with the future of Japanese society.

The government's anxiety over the particular threat posed by the anarchists was by no means without reasonable foundation. Not unlike their counterparts in Europe at that time, the anarchists differed from other groups in flatly refusing to place any trust in a parliamentary mode of government. As early as the Second Congress of the Japanese Socialist Party in 1908, the classic socialist and anarchist controversy over parliamentary methods was a burning issue.[11] The first clause of the party charter, which had read, "The objective of this party is to advocate socialism within the limits of law," was modified to assert, "The objective . . . is to execute socialist ideas." To this more radicalized version of the socialist policy platform, Tazoe Tetsuji (1873–1908) tried to add another clause calling for concerted action to attain the universal enfranchisement of the working class: "Universal suffrage is a powerful means to awaken the political consciousness of the people as well as to inspire unity among them." [12] The attempt was nullified by the anarchist Kōtoku Shūsui, who warned in an impassioned speech of the danger of national socialism and persuaded the audience, composed primarily of intellectuals, of the "incompetence of parliamentarianism" and of the danger that it would dampen the worker's desire for "direct action." [13] Even those who had some sympathy for parliamentarianism were in no way certain of their feelings. As Kagawa Toyohiko (1888–1960), the renowned Christian socialist and social worker, put it: "We are as yet *too immature* to abandon the parliamentary system." [14] Whatever Kagawa meant by the expression "too immature," this half-hearted commitment to parliamentarianism could hardly withstand the anarchists' impatience. A decade later, when the question of universal suffrage was placed on the political agenda of the progressive and liberal elements within the political parties, the socialist and anarchist groups remained indifferent and never once became allied to this popular movement. [15]

The reasons why the radical leftists persistently refused to accept and abide by the rules of parliamentary government, and why they gave no effective assistance to a movement for universal enfranchisement during the early decades of the twentieth century, have to do with the origins and functions of the Japanese parliamentary system, and with the doctrines of the anarchists who theoretically led the leftist movement until 1923. During the Meiji period, parliamentarianism seemed an alien political institution devoid of the sanction of tradition. In terms of the Meiji Imperial Constitution the role of parliament was that of a subordinate political organ. Moreover, corruption was endemic and the parliament repeatedly succumbed to ignominious compromises with oligarchic cabinets.

The anarchist doctrines themselves were hardly more congenial. Parliaments, the anarchists insisted, could not serve the interests of the working class. Believing in the higher efficiency of direct action, they were in a state of perpetual irritation at the slow and inefficient procedures of parliamentary government. This view, with its heavy reliance on action, was deeply imbedded in the indigenous political ethics of Japan. The ultranationalists, as the self-acclaimed orthodox heirs of the samurai class, exhibited the same kind of impatience. [16] During the Tokugawa period, as the samurai class had come to acquire bureaucratic experience, the ethical standards of this class lost

their old pristine simplicity and became intricate and ambiguous.[17] But even though adjustments had to be made to
peacetime conditions, there was one basic samurai attitude that
did not change: the readiness to resort to violence. Nor did they
repudiate the cult of death. Assassination was an accepted political instrument during the decades around the time of the
Restoration: in the absence of formalized channels of communication, personality played an increasingly greater role. "Direct action" often meant simply assassination, for it was not
only effective but also socially acceptable. How often have we
heard Japanese political figures of both the left and the right
speak of their "spiritual readiness to accept death." [18] This attitude, indeed, became a prerequisite if one was to become a
politician of any significance. A general mood of impatience, an
inclination to act, to resort to violence rather than debate and
compromise: this tendency characterized the antiparliamentary
mentality of radicals, anarchists, and ultranationalists alike.
For all these factions, their immediate willingness to invoke violence, whether it entailed assassination or seizure of control,
always beclouded the vision of the specific future for which they
were striving.[19]

The anarchists also criticized the system of representative
government for its tendency to depersonalize politics.[20] The
idea of having a candidate chosen by a few hundreds or thou-
sands of disparate people was, they believed, preposterous. To
advocate universal suffrage under the guise of the people's
sovereignty, an anarchist would argue, was to propose that the
people annihilate their initiative and creativity. "The idea of
enfranchisement is political suicide," wrote one anarchist.[21]
Not unlike Rousseau, they demanded that impersonal political
authority be replaced by a community of individuals, which
could dispense with such a distortion of politics. Because of its
distance from the electorate, parliamentary government could
never give the individual a sense of personal participation and
emotional affinity with the authority that governed him. For

similar reasons the ultranationalists advocated the "personal reign of the emperor directly over his children" and the idea of the "people's direct assistance of his reign." To them, parliamentarianism was an artificial barrier erected between people and emperor. By eliminating this artificial institution, the two extreme brands of radicals believed that Japanese society could attain a perfect harmony—a harmony that the nationalists saw in a fancied past and the anarchists vaguely envisioned in a distant future.

Preoccupied with the dual vision of total destruction and total harmony, the anarchists had no sense of legitimate individual or group interests, either economic or social. In this respect they differed from both Marxists and ultranationalists. The traditional raison d'être of parliamentary institutions became of no theoretical significance to the anarchists. The Marxists at least had a conception of the interests of the proletariat. The unfolding of the historical process was directed toward a particular goal, and within that process some Marxists argued for the preservation of parliament. The ultranationalists and rightists, on the other hand, insisted on the supremacy of national interests, to which they would sacrifice all other conflicting interests as trivial. In either case, whether the person in question was a Marxist or an ultranationalist—Kita Ikki or Kawakami Hajime, Gondō Seikei or Yamakawa Hitoshi—there was a genuine attempt to articulate interests that demanded political solution. The anarchists, however, saw no more than a jumble of conflicting interests, none of which had a justifiable claim. Indeed, they spoke of a new Fourth Estate. Yet was not their concern more with the working class's destructive potentiality than with its specific interests? Ōsugi Sakae (1885–1923), the most prominent theoretician and leader of the movement after 1911, could feel "neither sympathy nor pity for the miserable life of a worker," [22] but he was aware of the worker's power to destroy.[23] Inasmuch as parliamentary government was to a large extent preoccupied with the representation and reconciliation of conflicting interests, it was inevitable that the anarchists, in rejecting all such conceptions, would either reject or remain indifferent to parliamentary government as well.

Ōsugi Sakae

Guided by their impatience with indirect action, their distrust of parliamentary government, and their sense of alienation from the regular processes of politics, the anarchosyndicalists emerged from the subdued silence that followed the episode of January 1911 into strident militancy. Whereas Marxists and socialists were forced into a decade of hibernation, the anarchosyndicalists managed to develop contacts with labor unions and to publish their journals in the face of the government suppression.[24] Not only were they theoretically unable to justify their silence, but they also possessed a charismatic leader in the person of Ōsugi Sakae, an articulate and voluminous writer-translator and a proven activist who had only accidentally escaped death in 1911.

Ōsugi's writings were far more attractively acute and precise in describing the demise of society than in depicting the means by which social rejuvenation was to be realized. In the final analysis, his speculations reflect an apolitical longing for "individuality." [25] In this sense, the quality of Ōsugi's social defiance was more romantic and aesthetic than political. Insofar as he was political, it was only to the extent that he recognized in the working class that potentiality for violence which might be directed against the present order. His preoccupation with the immediate vision of upheaval blurred both his sense of strategy and his image of the phoenix that was to arise. Until the end of his life, it was no clear political belief in improving man's lot, but rather a fascination with the destruction of the existing order, that motivated his actions and gave an underlying unity to his idea of "individualistic anarchism."

Whatever Ōsugi meant by the expression "individualistic anarchism," [26] which recurs throughout his writing, he shared with his contemporaries a common preoccupation: concern with the nature of the individual. Yet he was one of the first to voice an accusation against intellectuals who showed insufficient social concern as they probed for a definition of the individual. It was not obsession with the individual that was wrong, Ōsugi believed, but the particular type of asocial individualism that plagued the Japanese intellectuals.[27] He wrote of the early 1910's:

> In those days, the literary and intellectual circles were saturated with the ideas of individualism. Self-perfection, the fulfillment of the life of the self, the isolation of the self from its social surroundings, the conscious escape from the social reality that interferes with the purity of the self, quiet and introspective meditation—these were the reality and practice of the "individualists."

Ōsugi dubbed this tendency among the contemporary intellectuals as "prison philosophy," and criticized the social indifference of those intellectuals whose preoccupation with the search for individuality hovered about the abstracted and isolated self. Ōsugi also speaks of the dignity of the individual and his creativity and of the man unfettered by the incubus of social conventions. In this sense, despite his acute observation and criticism of the asocial nature of individualism as evidenced by his contemporaries, Ōsugi's anarchism in its final stages was to fulfill a vision that he shared with them.[28]

Arishima Takeo was another intellectual who felt that, in the quest for total liberation of the self from conventions and social obligations, the social dimension of existence ought not to be disregarded.[29] In his *Aru onna* (A certain woman), Yōko is led to self-destruction as she frees herself from the codes of society and family: freedom and license are confused. The knowledge of this dilemma led Arishima to recognize that somehow society and the free self should be reconciled, that the former should be recreated by the latter's volition. In the end, however, Arishima evaded the responsibility for creating the ideal and left it to the "Fourth Estate," the proletariat. Ōsugi, too, felt that it was the working class that was predestined to carry out the burden of regenerating the present, and that the creativity of the individual proletariat was the saving element in history. But one peruses the pages of his writings in vain for any clear description of the social content of the proletariat's individual "creativity." In fact, the very expression came to have an ironic quality. Starting out as a conscious and judicious critic of the asocial intellectuals' quest for individualism, Ōsugi came to solve the problem by negating society rather than by reconciling it to the individual, the answer implicit in Arishima's novel.

Since the creative action of man has no chartered course to follow, what Ōsugi favored most was "man's blind action—the explosion of human spirit." [30] To him, "life is an eternal struggle of the individual with nature, with society and with other individuals." "Fight!" said he, "for struggle is the flower of life that alone bears fruit." Ōsugi challenged traditional religions and art for having taught "resignation from life and acquiescence in the power of nature." [31] Only in the conscious destruction of such past cultural residues can man find his creativity. Ōsugi believed that this task—the creativity of destruction, as it were—should be shouldered by the working class. Peculiarly, he deprived the intellectuals of their raison d'être: while criticizing the nonchalant intellectuals of the prewar period, he assigned no specific role to the socially conscious intellectuals as a group.

To Ōsugi, it was one thing for the intellectual to have come to understand the ills of modern capitalist society too late to rescue Japan—but quite another thing for him to make an inherently spurious alliance with the rising proletariat.[32] As Schumpeter did years later, Ōsugi noted that the intellectuals were invading the politics of the working class.[33] He included in his indictment of the intellectuals not only those who were indifferent but also, most vehemently and suspiciously, those who longed to find a place within the proletariat. In a social democrat like Yamakawa Kikue, he detected an air of arrogance. Similarly, the adoration for the worker affected by such labor leaders as Suzuki Bunji seemed to Osugi no more than a form of condescension. He was irritated by the Tolstoyan pacifism of Yoshino Sakuzō and the humanistic sentiment of those who proposed the ideal of harmony between labor and management, for these attitudes stifled the destructive potentiality of the working class.[34]

"Workers fight for their own nourishment, and destroy their obstacles," Ōsugi observed.[35] He was wary of the opportunism of the intellectuals: "The workers themselves should know when they are cheated" by the revolutionaries.[36] Skeptical of the intellectuals' leadership in the labor movement, he flatly rejected the overtures that the Japanese Communist Party made to him.[37] The party had to acknowledge the powerful influence wielded by Ōsugi within the labor unions in Taishō Japan. (Katayama Sen, for example, while directing the Japanese Communists from Moscow, highly valued Ōsugi's intellectual and organizational competence.[38]) Some have suggested that it was Ōsugi's feelings of nationalism that dictated his stern refusal to abide by the party directives or to collaborate with the Marxists. More probably, however, the wariness came not so much from Ōsugi's nationalism as from the attitude of suspicion with which he observed the radical intellectuals flooding the labor movement in the years following World War I —the ones who a few years earlier had invoked history to justify their silence as well as their refusal to collaborate with the anarchists.[39]

In some respects, Ōsugi's view of the intellectual is close to Hegel's. Intellect can tell us only what has taken place; reality is revealed to us only when it has completed its course.[40] But then Ōsugi, unlike Hegel, proceeds to argue for the destruction of reality altogether. In the destruction, however, it is not intellect but passion that ought to direct man's action. This is a negation of the Marxist stand that insists on the intellectual's seeing the concrete need of a historical moment to act. Intellectually as well as politically, therefore, Ōsugi could not have collaborated with the Marxists.

Furthermore, in his insistence on the destructive potential of individual passion, Ōsugi refuted the deterministic implications of socialist thinking. On the one hand, he asserted that "freedom and creation do not exist either outside of ourselves or beyond the present. They are within us, within the present." But on the other hand he also believed that "the present society is the world of necessity rather than that of freedom." [41] To free himself from these mutually exclusive assumptions, Ōsugi proposed to annihilate the present order (necessity) through the use of violence (freedom) and to create *ex nihilo* an ideal order altogether devoid of political authority. Originally, Ōsugi thought that his hope depended only upon himself: "Being aware of my own ability and authority, I believe that the hope [for the future] depends on a very small minority." He even stated his despair over the "stupidity of the proletariat." [42] This elitism gradually gave way to an egalitarian sentiment: "I believe in the great individual artistic and social creativity of the working-class people." [43] After 1920, he tried repeatedly "to foster within himself the feeling of a common worker." [44] No longer was it a band of chosen few who could create the ideal society. Ōsugi deserted the intellectuals in order to realize his vision of the anarchist future; he replaced Marxist determinism by confidence in "the blind action of the working man."

Occasionally, indeed, Ōsugi made references to historical materialism and did not conceal his admiration for Marx's insight into modern capitalist society. His articles often abound with references to Marx. In the final analysis, however, Ōsugi admired the working class for its power to destroy, not because he saw it as a creative instrument of history fulfilling a mission rationally explained in terms of economic determinism. As Berdyaev notes, "economic determinism humiliates man, only faith in human activity raises him—faith in an activity which can accomplish a marvelous regeneration of society" [45]—and

Ōsugi shared this opinion. Therefore, his real heroes were Stirner, Sorel, and Bergson, "who beyond the predictable world of science found the world of freedom, creation, and passion." [46] The "philosophy of life" of Bergson, the "myth of violence" of Sorel, and the "individualistic anarchism" of Stirner form the tripartite basis for Ōsugi's political thought. Through them, the traditional concept of direct action is channeled to the destruction of the present: harmony, form and order no longer give Ōsugi any sense of beauty. It was the very process of discord that Ōsugi found most beautiful. He located the root of creation in the desire for destruction, and in his writings the terms "creativity" and "destruction" become uncomfortably synonymous. [47]

Preoccupied with destruction, seeing no concrete alternative in reality, Ōsugi saw in history only cause for despair. A Marxist is a faithful disciple of history, but to Ōsugi, an anarchist, history becomes an irrelevant genre. Just as the concrete future is an alien category to him, he sees the concrete past only as that which fetters the individual. Thus he observes that "the past is dead." "Death cannot be married to life. Already most of bygone art is dead." Ōsugi goes on to say that "the art forms of the past cannot offer us anything of value. Nay, in fact, they plague our life. As life is renewed, art too will be rejuvenated." [48] Although these remarks are taken from his writings on art, they parallel his indifferent attitude to the past and its legacies. If history meant anything to him, it was simply the irrational and meaningless accumulation of regrettable and painful experiences.

Ōsugi's thought on art and letters suggests that he was more Sorelian than Sorel himself. This partially explains why Ōsugi failed to evaluate and take into account the meaning of history for the planning of his ideal society. Sorel, brought up as an engineer-scientist, had been aware of the scope and limits of scientific thinking, and his escape from science was "a search for reality." He was "curiously distrustful of precision" and wanted to be "satisfied with provisional approximations." [49] Acknowledging the role that irrational sentiment and myths play in life, and having suffered from the intellectual tyranny of positivism, which refused to recognize the strength of the individual will, Sorel came to believe that science alone could not approximate the reality of life or inspire man to act.[50] Thus Sorel's thought represented an attempt to see what was real and possible, whereas Ōsugi's was a romantic flight from reality. Ōsugi was not a scientist, nor had he ever had a serious encounter with scientific thinking. His love of inarticulateness reflects his ignorance of science rather than his awareness of its limitations. "I am fond of humanism and democracy when they are defined vaguely by literary figures. I however despise scholars and tremble at the thought of them: I intensely dislike socialism [clearly stated] and at times even anarchism."

Both Sorel and Ōsugi undoubtedly were interested in the philosophy of action, and both were distrustful of the monastic impeccability of precision. Nevertheless, the basic difference between the two led them to different mental attitudes. An attempt at approximating reality is by definition an attempt at seeing the given, the present, whereas inarticulate impulse, preoccupied with the vision of the demise of the present, refuses to see the present. Blind faith in what follows the present inspires the use of violence as an end in itself. Sorel's quest for moral rejuvenation through *ricorso* finds its emotional equivalent in Ōsugi's distaste for both dilettantism and convention. Yet in his outright defiance of established social morality, Ōsugi is actually closer to those of his Japanese contemporaries who were naturalists and hedonists in art and ultranationalists in politics, closer than he is to the European Sorel. For Ōsugi as well as his contemporaries, the blind break from social conventions involved no serious moral crisis and was a substitute for the more difficult task of constructing a new moral order for a new society. He was engaged in the breakdown of the form but not in its reconstruction.

If Ōsugi was interested in defying the established moral order, he was just as interested in breaking down the traditional forms of art. For him the ideal vision of man is "the new person who has most effectively shaken off the past." [51] Then, indeed, the conscious alienation from history, from the past, is a virtue. As the necessary prelude to the attainment of the ideal, one first has to eliminate what has already been created and, for the time being, this act of destruction becomes the essence of creativity. Ōsugi denies the two primary categories of aesthetics which Kant believed to give necessary order to imagination: "purposiveness without purpose" and "lawfulness without law." In Ōsugi purposelessness expresses art's purpose—destruction—and lawlessness expresses its form.

Not all artists, of course, wished to break down the established forms of communication. Nagai or Tanizaki Junichiro found the sickness of their society congenial to their art; while the art of Akutagawa, although hopelessly morbid and lawless in content, still retained to a remarkable degree the traditional forms. But Ōsugi's view of art was shared by a group of his younger contemporaries, the "anarchist-artists" of the period between 1910 and 1930.[52] Their work was more conspicuous for its destruction of tradition than for its achievements: they tried not only to depart from tradition but also to break down the forms of communication that transmit tradition's legacies. Futurism, dadaism, and cubism attracted the attention of these young poets, sculptors, painters, and dramatists. "We have moved into the unlimited realm of free intuition," wrote Kambara Tai in an article on Italian futurism, published in 1922 in *Shisō* (Thought), the most eminent of the intellectual journals.[53] The infatuation with "purposeless violence" and the cult of intuition were the implicit assumptions of futurist poetry. Maruyama Motoyoshi, influenced by German expressionism, tried to translate this mood into the world of the theater. In refusing to have any recourse to tradition and the existing forms of art, all these artists were making deformation into a new art form and, indeed, adding a new dimension to aesthetic communication. The end result, however, was the intensification of the social alienation of these intellectuals rather than any prolific outburst of creativity.

Katō Kazuo, one of their few patron critics, voiced the con-

cern Ōsugi had already expressed: "We are not living in isolation. We are sharing our life together with humanity." [54] But
Katō's warning against the isolation of the intellectuals was not
heeded, for the public, except for an exotic few, could not
understand either them or their art. The anarchist-artist waged
a relentless assault upon the established order; but his dissatisfaction with society found no concrete course of redemption,
and destruction became an end in itself. In this he was a faithful follower of F. T. Marinetti, whose *Manifesto of Futurism*
(1909) stated these major principles: "Courage, audacity, rebellion, are to be the essential elements of our poetry. Literature
hitherto has exalted pensive immobility, rapture, and sleep: we
shall exalt aggressive movement, hectic sleeplessness, the quick-
steps, the somersault, the slap, the blow." [55] If the influence of
futurism in Italy was felt in "the simulation of a baleful nationalism," [56] the Japanese futurists did their somersault in a
political vacuum. Their anarchistic nihilism had no serious social consequences except that of isolating the artist from his surroundings. And his fate paralleled the fate of the political
anarchist.

Ōsugi once asserted that "art has its birthplace where and
when life fails to satisfy us. There we cry out for something desirable by appealing to art . . . Art, therefore, is a confession
of our social impotence." He then went on to say that he
"would not at all regret it, if we could satisfy our life by sacrific-
ing art." [57] If violence, destruction, and chaos are the necessary
prelude to the ideal society, in Ōsugi's thought both politics and
art are working toward their own negation. Politics employs
violence to eliminate authority and power in society. Once they
are eliminated, life is rejuvenated. With this rejuvenation of
life, art as well as politics loses its initial motivation and its
function, since one no longer craves the ideal.

A few days after the great earthquake of 1923, Ōsugi, his
mistress, and his nephew were arrested and strangled to death
by an army officer. The Ministry of the Army at once made an
official apology for the officer's act: "His motivation . . . was

the fear lest Ōsugi and the others, capitalizing on the chaos, should commit unjust acts against the state. It seems that he wanted to eliminate the poisonous elements from the state." [58] Soon afterward, ten anarchosyndicalist labor leaders were massacred in the courtyard of a police station in Tokyo under the same pretext. After the death of Ōsugi, there were two abortive assassination attempts on the lives of political and military figures. The government efficiently suppressed the now disorganized remnants of the anarchosyndicalists. After 1923 it was the Marxian socialists who came to predominate in the radical left.

To an anarchist like Ōsugi, political action is a "conscious encounter with death and violence as the measure of his freedom." [59] But violence without a concrete end is political irresponsibility, "the breaking of the butter plate." [60]

The experience and ideas of Ōsugi, however, were not without effect. His courage to rise above the given social order, his unceasing effort to enlighten the public, his role in revealing the sins of industrial society, and above all his warning against the indifference and the acquiescence of the intellectuals in society and nature are still relevant today. The real legacy, however, is a negative one: how often have radicals denied their own usefulness to society through their refusal to abide by the rules of politics? Violence and destruction can never be the end of politics. They are a symptom of its failure.

IV / Japanese Naturalism:
The Limitations of Experience

Naturalism as a literary movement came into its intellectual prime in Europe during the last decades of the nineteenth century, in close alliance with the general popularity of what was held to be scientific thinking. Although the naturalist writings of such authors as Zola, Flaubert, and the Goncourts ranged wide, they had in common a "scientific" approach. Human experience, they thought, could only be conceived as part of the social process, and they shared the belief of their positivist contemporaries that this social process could be subjected to the method of analysis already long applied to natural phenomena. As Roger Martin du Gard put it, perhaps more radically than was usually taken for granted: "I believe in universal determinism; that we are conditioned by circumstances in all respects . . . Good and evil are mere arbitrary distinctions . . . though all the phenomena of life have not yet been analyzed, they will be . . . one day." [1]

Though firm in their belief in science, the naturalists were wary of making dogmatic moral assertions. They were confident of their method and yet denied themselves the dangerous privilege of making presumptuous moral judgments. But on occasion they could forgo all restraint and pose as judges and accusers. Determinism and moral resignation did not deter Zola from becoming involved in the Dreyfus affair. Arnold Hauser plausibly suggests that Zola's naturalism disposed him to identify himself with the fortunes of the lower classes during the Third Republic. Zola was "by no means hopeless about the future," although his "attitude to the present [was] thoroughly pessimistic." [2] By his own declaration he was "a determinist, but not a fatalist." He "is perfectly conscious of the fact that men are dependent on the material conditions of their life in their whole behavior, but he does not believe that these conditions are unalterable." [3] Zola felt that the great task of the intellectual was to "transform and improve the external conditions of human life" by means of the social sciences. Speaking of positivism, Karl Mannheim has observed that "it was precisely . . . its faith in progress and its naive realism which enabled positivism to make so many significant contributions." [4]

Why did Zola's naturalism lead him not to fatalism but to moral activism, not to acquiescence but to participation? Hauser contends that Zola reversed an earlier tendency to consider science the handmaiden of art and instead subjected art to scientific manipulation. This explanation, however, does not extricate Zola from the logical dilemma of how to turn scientific determinism into a doctrine of progress. In fact, it only adds to the difficulty. For how can science give man a deliberate and creative role in society when, by definition, this role would be prescribed by laws of nature in terms of which man was himself determined?

Any satisfactory answer to this question must lie in the very nature of scientific activity. For ordinary purposes, scientific thinking may be defined simply as the conscious and systematic investigation of phenomena revealed in the human environment and in man himself. "Such investigation," A. R. Hall writes, "always assumes that there is in nature a regular consistency, so that events are not merely vagarious, and therefore an order or pattern also, to which events conform, capable of being apprehended by the human mind." [5] This pattern of investigation assumes not only that nature has a set of laws to which phenomena conform, but also that the principle for the reconstruction of nature may be found within man himself.

Kant tried to generalize this principle from his observations of the French Revolution. "The Revolution had attempted to define the principles for the reconstruction of society as these are found in the rational nature of the individual." Kant "undertook to find in the mind of the individual the principles for the organization of nature itself." [6] The wish or the mental disposition to manipulate nature according to the rational designs of man had its material counterpart or expression in the Industrial Revolution and even, perhaps, in the idea of a modern nation-state. It was, in other words, already a reality when European writers came to consider it.

What the naturalist writers did, therefore, when they applied scientific thinking to their artistic work, was to raise the individual ability for organizing nature to the level of reconstructing society. It was this transposition that made it possible for them to avoid fatalism. For even if he lived in a natural and social environment that was scientifically determined, man could still be expected to predict and control the organization of his social environment. It was open to him to suggest what ought to be done to his society. In fact, the naturalists' belief in the scientific character of society made it possible for them to rise above seemingly nonpredictable realities. In this important sense, naturalism presupposes a particular view of man's relation to nature and society. There is a significant difference between considering nature as essentially rational and considering it as the product of accident. Without its original theological underpinnings, the first view led to the development of the modern natural sciences and also made it possible to resist the temptation of fatalistic acquiescence. Unaccountable tyrannies did not need to be endured, if they were not in accord with the scheme of the universe. The second view, that nature is the product of accident, more easily breeds an attitude of acquiescence, since there is never any need to ask whether there is a larger scheme beyond the arbitrary realities of immediate experience.

As a literary device used to represent experience, realism, of which naturalism is a form, can take either of these two views. More often than not, European naturalism narrowed down its view of nature to the belief that, even with all their ambiguities, nature and its phenomena could still be subjected to scrutiny by human reason and would eventually yield up their laws to our cognizance. The Japanese naturalists (who themselves asserted their debt to their European predecessors) continually confused the two views, and this confusion played no small role in promoting the attitude of inner disquiet and outer acquiescence uniformly revealed in their work and social behavior. Nor is Japanese naturalism wholly atypical of the general experience of intellectuals elsewhere. To understand them does not only account for this particular group of Taishō intellectuals, but at the same time also tells us a great deal about the difficulties encountered by many an intellectual as he tries to express his sense of emancipation and to insist on his own individuality.

Shimazaki and Tayama: From Society to Libido

Throughout the last decades of the nineteenth century, the names of the European naturalists, particularly Zola's, frequently appear in Japanese literary commentaries. Yet it was not until the end of the Russo-Japanese War that the public turned its attention to a work with a consciously naturalist bent. In March 1906 Shimazaki Tōson, who had already established himself as a romantic poet, published *Hakai* (Apostasy). The novel had an electrifying impact within literary circles, where criticisms ranged from uninhibited praise to total rejection. Natsume Sōseki, for example, felt that *Hakai* was the only genuine novel written during the Meiji era.[7]

Hakai deals with a sensitive young social outcast (*eta*) who, at the command of his father, tries to hide his social origins in order to win an acceptance and success hitherto denied his caste. The suffering of the protagonist from social prejudice provides a haunting theme in the novel on two levels, one describing the particular case of an *eta* and the other casting an autobiographical shadow. Shimazaki himself was not an *eta*. In the sufferings endured by his protagonist, however, the author sees a reflection of his own conflict with society. Shimamura Hōgetsu, the most acute of the naturalist critics, noted that the Japanese literary world had finally found "an equivalent expression of the works of the European naturalists." [8] Some critics felt, however, that the theme was too particularized to inspire sympathy.[9] "It is a fact that this social prejudice still exists in Japan. Yet this has been recognized as such, and since the Restoration . . . we have intellectually at least freed ourselves from this prejudice . . . Since this subject is localized and narrow, I cannot feel strong sympathy." [10] According to a more recent critic, "today no one questions that among our naturalist writings *Hakai* was [socially] most significant." [11] *Hakai* had no didactic pretensions. But with its manifest anger at a serious social problem, it may have set a precedent for subsequent naturalist works. It clearly followed the path blazed by Zola and his European contemporaries.

There is no longer any serious doubt as to the literary merits of Shimazaki's first novel. The issue of its social relevance, however, remains unsettled. Ino Kenji remarked that *Hakai's* theme should have prepared the intellectuals to cope with larger social issues.[12] Kamei Katsuichirō, on the other hand, felt that the work was of a more general scope, not limited to a social problem.[13] From the author's own retrospective commentaries and from certain lines within the novel, it is indeed clear that *Hakai* was by no means exclusively concerned with the problem of social prejudice.[14] Shimazaki writes: "I was deeply attracted by the sorrow and suffering of an enlightened youth who was born among those ignorant people." [15] Throughout the novel, derogatory clichés are readily and carelessly used to describe the *eta*.[16] It is, therefore, more plausible to see in it an expression of the general conflict between the old order and the new one, rather than a more specific social critique.

Regardless of Shimazaki's original intentions in writing

Hakai, the social theme the work suggested was soon lost in the writings of the other naturalists. As *Hakai* approaches its end, the protagonist, having come to know a young *eta* who was fighting for the emancipation of the entire caste, decides to reveal his social origin. He prostrates himself before the villagers. The manner in which he relates his origins shows a concern for honesty which is greater than personal pride or courage. And it is this confession of honesty, rather than a concern for social justice, that gives sustained unity to the works of the Japanese naturalists.[17]

Eighteen months after the publication of *Hakai,* Tayama Katai presented the public with another epoch-making naturalist novel, *Futon* (Quilt). Shimamura, who had earlier hailed Shimazaki's work, wrote of *Futon:* "This is the confession of a naked man, of the man of flesh . . . The work unrelentingly represents one side of naturalism that depicts exclusively the ugly or the morbid in life." [18] The hero, a thirty-six-year-old writer, falls in love with a young country girl who aspires to be a writer under his guidance. Paralyzed by his attachment to his wife and family, he does not tell her of his feelings and finally lets her leave him. The story ends on a scene with the writer sobbing as he holds the girl's quilt.[19] This novel, any reader today would feel, is no more than a crude, if candid, confession of middle-aged erotic fantasy.[20] At the time it created a stir, however, because of its irreverent attitude toward social institutions and its uninhibited personal honesty. Tayama's insensitive treatment of the writer's wife, whose emotional reactions he altogether disregards, is typical not only of the naturalists but of many other writers. Preoccupied with the emancipation of the self, the naturalists often deteriorate into insufferable egoists, identifying all others with society as incubus.

The best example of this egoism is Shimazaki's confessional novel *Shinsei* (Regeneration), in which he tells of his incestuous relationship with his niece. The temptation he felt toward her, his feeling of guilt and remorse, and above all his fear of social sanctions are the themes of the novel. The novel is an approximation to the actual experiences of Shimazaki himself. When the hero's niece becomes pregnant, he flees to Paris, leaving her behind to take care of his children. Finally, to avoid a public scandal, he sends her away to Formosa, where one of his brothers is working. This is in fact what Shimazaki himself did. In a sense, the ultimate cruelty he commits against his niece is his publication of the scandal. His fear of society and his willingness to sacrifice the niece are only thinly veiled by this presentation in the form of fiction. The naturalists often prided themselves on their passionate attachment to a "fatal woman." In their pursuit of this image they lost all sense of social norms. Yet the dread of sanctions persistently lurks behind the writings not only of Shimazaki but of the Japanese naturalists in general. They are proud of their candid confessions but not of their deviations, apostates of tradition rather than confirmed rebels. In their attempt to express emancipation from all forms of social obligation, they leave society itself alone.[21]

Iwanaga Yutaka has made a detailed study of Tayama's novels, comparing the facts that Tayama portrayed and his fictionalization of them. In the *Execution of a Soldier* a deserter commits arson out of a pyromania that is linked to his desire for a woman. In the *Death of Shigeemon* the hero is lynched and drowned by the villagers of his locality for criminal acts that Tayama invests with sexual perversions not reported of the real incident upon which the story is based. Tayama's literary inventions follow a definite pattern: uncontrollable sexual desires arise in the mind of the hero, and the abnormality of his acts leads to his castigation by society. "What is common to the heroes of the representative novels of Tayama is an agony born of bewitching lust. And the circumstances under which such agony is experienced are always abnormal." Because society is associated with normality, however, the tragic endings cannot inspire any criticism of intolerant society or any sense of sympathy for the hero as its victim. Instead, the reader is asked to appreciate the extent to which the hero is driven to ruin by his own uncontrollable passion. "If we study these stories closely, the undisguised expression of uncontrolled passion is iconoclastic only within the subjective self of the author. Once it is directed against society, the act becomes a crime." [22]

This pattern of Tayama's fictionalization is particularly suggestive, if we study the method of writing Tayama himself sought to follow. In 1908, soon after he published his *Futon,* he wrote:

> I tried to write by relying exclusively on objective materials without infusing any subjective view. The primary objective of writing is to write without adding an author's own views, without going inside the material or into the mind of the personality, to write only according to what I heard, saw and touched . . . *without making any interpretation, explanation or analysis.* [23]

Tayama called this method *heimen byōsha* (flat description). How, then, can we account for the omissions and fictionalizations he does in fact make? Though perhaps meaningless for literary criticism, this question is important in the context of intellectual analysis. On the one hand, Tayama takes the attitude that human action is determined by environment and, on the other, he believes that only the method of flat description can approximate such realities. Thus, through fictionalization, the deterministic factor in human action is internalized into the drives of lust and passion. Leaving the intricacies of environment untouched or unanalyzed—presumably on grounds of stylistic principle—Tayama described his hero's catastrophe in terms of what might be called libertine determinism.

So when writers like Shimazaki and Tayama defied the established social conventions, they did so in a peculiar way. The Japanese naturalists had their own understanding of the idea of environmentalism that was developed in the West during the nineteenth century. Without the crucial assumption of a scientific ability to manipulate nature through reason or knowledge, naturalism in Japan led to fatalism. The naturalists' defiance was based on the particular self rather than on the self that could be universalized. As such it had no chance to initiate any significant social movement. It biologized emancipation instead of socializing it in generalized terms. The longing of the Japanese naturalists to be liberated from the yoke of society soon ended in a painful but acquiescent whimper. Their accusation was directed not against the public injustice that *Hakai* had originally seemed to challenge, but against the instinctual drives of the private self.

Critiques

For all their limitations, however, the naturalists deserve credit for having dealt with problems that intellectuals had previously left unquestioned. It demanded courage to inquire with harsh honesty into carnal desire and to impugn as unreasonable and inhuman the accepted social norms and conventions. Contemporary critics consoled the naturalists with the reminder that "not only in literature but in politics or in religion as well, the pioneers of an ideal always suffer from the persecution of the ignorant majority . . . When they cry aloud they are always alone in their world . . . If they compromise with the prevailing mood, they will cease to be pioneers." [24] The naturalists were courageous, but with a kind of courage that never disturbed the social order. They attempted to emancipate the individual from the undesirable features of society by releasing him from all ties to morality and society. As a result, the emancipated individual they idealized was unable to come to terms with either his society or his own inner impulses.[25]

In 1909 Mori Ōgai published *Vita sexualis,* an autobiography of his sex life which parodies the naturalist's preoccupation with sexual impulses. Far from providing an account of his enslavement to physical passion, Mori recalls episode after episode of evidence for the claim that he never had difficulty in "taming the sleeping tiger." [26] In all innocence he asserts that he "has never been moved by a sexual impulse so strongly as to become deliberately aggressive." [27] The fact that Mori was a doctor and the surgeon general of the Japanese Imperial Army makes his satire especially acute, in view of the scientific pretensions of the naturalists. Mori is contemptuous of the quasi-scientific pose of the Japanese naturalists. He is also aware that the naturalists' search for liberation from irrational social taboos ends in the discovery that passion confines the individual to his own irrationality. What Mori objects to is the claim Zola makes on literature that it ought to become a handmaiden of science. "It is not reasonable of Zola to think that the result of analysis and dissection in and of itself forms a novel. Indeed, the result of experiment is a fact . . . a writer should not be satisfied with it." [28] Mori's training in medical science led him to minimize the scientific factor in literature. He tried to locate the meaning of literature elsewhere than in science. Yet when such criticisms of naturalism in general are applied to Japanese naturalism in particular, their incongruity is apparent. Unlike some European naturalists, the Japanese naturalists did indeed leave facts unanalyzed and undissected.

Mori's literary theory was critical not only of naturalism's scientific approach but also of its self-conscious departure from the past. In this respect Mori was a representative thinker of the more articulate conservative groups in modern Japan. While studying in Berlin he came to believe: "Civilization rests on history. To realize a well-thought-out ideal is an impossibility. One should never forget that ethics and customs which have been verified over many centuries must have a good core; otherwise they would not have endured so long." [29] This approach to history, reminiscent of the German romantics, expresses Mori's distaste for the depreciation of decency and for the downgrading of the social worth of the individual.

The naturalists might be criticized on moral grounds and their claim to science be regarded with contempt, but there were some who took seriously the theoretical issues they raised. Among these issues was the controversy over free will and scien-

tific method. As early as 1910 this question provoked a debate
that revealed a high degree of theoretical concern with the
problem. Ishikawa Takuboku (1886–1912), a young poet and
critic, wrote an article entitled "Jidai heisoku no genjō" (On
contemporary frustration) in response to a short article by the
literary critic, Uozumi Setsurō (1883–1910), "Jikoshuchō no
shisō toshite no shizenshugi" (Naturalism as the idea of individualism). Uozumi had argued that naturalism is the historical
alliance of two mutually exclusive intellectual elements, the
determinism of science and the ideal of individual freedom,
against a common enemy, authority. In place of the authority of
the church, in Japan it was the authority of the family and state
which had interfered with the development of the individual.
"For the young man preoccupied with the desire to fulfill himself, the heaviest burden is these two authorities." For this reason, Uozumi saw hope for individualism in the naturalists'
habit of acting and writing out of defiance.[30]

Ishikawa replied that, although an insistence on individualism has often been considered one of the attributes of scientism,
the theoretical gap between scientific determinism and free will
has never been bridged. He argued, furthermore, that in real
terms naturalism in Japan had never genuinely defied authority, thus contradicting the suggestion of hope in Uozumi's essay.
According to Ishikawa, "man remains forever within the antinomy of fatalism and free will." [31] As to the future, he predicted
that the tendency of naturalism to negate free will would predominate.

Both Uozumi and Ishikawa felt that by definition science
negates the freedom of will. Hence they accepted the idea that
individualistic philosophy and faith in science are mutually
exclusive. The main difference between the two was that,
though Uozumi argued that their alliance in naturalism was
inspired by a realization of the common enemy, Ishikawa went
on to contend that man is fated to suffer from the antinomy
and predicted the eventual victory of the "negation of the free
self." In order to explain the phenomenon of fatalism in Japa-

nese naturalist literature, they both exaggerated one feature of scientific thinking, determinism. Fatalism, they insisted, was inherent in any scientific analysis. They believed that the literary method of the Japanese naturalists was to a great extent scientific and that precisely this method was to blame for the fact that the naturalists took the path of resignation and acquiescence.

The End of the Rebellion

Whatever the theoretical reasons for the naturalists' failure to convey their sense of emancipation beyond the bounds of literature, there is no better evidence than the history of this movement for the conclusion that radical Japanese intellectuals were unable to fulfill the expectation hinted at in *Hakai,* the first naturalist work. It was not long before the naturalists gave up their hostility toward society. Once they came to be accepted by society, they soon abdicated their leadership in the emancipation movement to the younger socialist authors. Within the limited range of literature, they were unable to articulate their demands in broader terms. They were thrown back upon the literary analysis of the self, and the full-scale emancipation ended in the genre of *shishōsetsu* (I-novel).

Recalling the defiant mood of the naturalists' début and the fact that they were at first considered rebels and outcasts, it is surprising to see how rapidly they assumed the leadership of the literary world in the next decade.[32] In November 1920 a large party was held in Tokyo to celebrate the fiftieth birthdays of the two eminent naturalist authors, Tayama Katai and Tokuda Shūsei. The approximately three hundred people present by invitation included not only eminent intellectuals of Taishō Japan, but also leading political and financial figures. To mark the occasion, there was published an anthology of short stories dedicated to Tayama and Tokuda, with its thirty-three contributors representing the best of all Japanese literary groups.[33] Shimazaki, who was a year younger than Tayama and Tokuda, wrote a preface that concluded on a note of reminiscence mixed with anxiety: "As I think of the years we have walked together, I would rather remain silent. I would like this silence to speak my feelings. The path facing us is going to be arduous. The same heart that commemorates your birthdays calls to our awareness the difficult years awaiting us." [34]

Having already lived through one of the most turbulent social metamorphoses in history, the intellectuals were soon to experience what would be, for them, still more trying years. But if Shimazaki was perfectly candid in confessing his sense of anxiety about the years to come, he was remarkably quick to dismiss politics as a remedy for his discomfort. "Neither the voice of social reform nor the cry for democracy [referring to Yoshino Sakuzō, et al.] has anything in itself that would move us." [35] In January 1925, he wrote in *Asahi:* "The Great Earthquake came. As was expected the wave of reaction came . . . If narrow-minded conservatism is being born today, who is to blame? It is the difficulty of our generation. As I enter the new year, I ponder this problem." [36] Who is to blame? One encounters this evasive manner of raising questions over and over again in the writings of the naturalists. Often anguished, yet diffident and uncertain about practical possibilities, they remained outsiders.

Meanwhile an important change was taking place. If literature and politics had been separated until the early 1920s, the emergence of socialism, particularly Marxism-Leninism, now brought them close together.[37] By the late twenties, socialist authors and critics had become the presiding judges of Japanese literature. Just as they let the tyranny of the government go unchallenged during the Kōtoku incident in 1911, the Japanese naturalists remained generally silent as the socialists imposed their political standards on literature.

During this decade, Shimazaki turned to history and also wrote a series of autobiographical novels. In the well-known novel *Yoake mae* (Before the dawn), he directed his concern to the larger issue of Japanese history after the Restoration. He was in the process of completing *Tōhō no mon* (The gate of the east) when he died in 1943. In this unfinished masterpiece, Shimazaki deals with the life of Okakura Tenshin (1862–1913), who was the pioneer in introducing Oriental art to the Western world.[38] Okakura's intimate knowledge of Western aesthetics enabled him to communicate the values of Oriental art in terms comprehensible to Westerners. His principled attempt to preserve and transmit the purity of Eastern art must have provided a sober example to those intellectuals of Meiji and Taishō Japan who hovered between an inescapable commitment to tradition and a primary concern with individual emancipation, which they identified with experiences not indigenous to Japan. Shimazaki, for one, absorbed European intellectual legacies with zeal. He was too closely tied to pre-Meiji Japan to be altogether indifferent to his own inheritance, and yet was too sophisticated to be swayed by the fanaticism of naive nationalism. Okakura, because he had a genuine knowledge of both East and West and still maintained his attachment to the preservation of Oriental art, must have been an attractive figure to Shimazaki, providing him with a solution sorely needed at a time when xenophobia reigned. But Shimazaki was no longer a rebel fighting against society, for he had come to identify his society with its aesthetic tradition.

This first tentative commitment led to more thoroughgoing, more political accommodations. Shimazaki was one of the leading Japanese writers to participate in the first conference of the Congress of Great Asian Writers, held in 1943. At the end of the first day, he was asked to lead the audience in chanting "Long live the Emperor!" "I have never known such a childlike purity," commented one literary critic present. "What moved me was his [subdued] gesture," compared with those who preceded him on the rostrum. Probably it was the first time he had ever had to play such a role. "His certain air of hesitancy toward the resplendence of the occasion made one anxious. But it was not called for . . . He shyly raised his hands and almost without any intonation rapidly cried out, 'Long live the

Emperor!' " In contrast to the "obsequious" or "fanatic" behavior and bravado of other participants, there was even "a painful beauty" in Shimazaki's reserved and unpretentious gesture.[39] But this attitude of reserve was all too typical, and was by then a specialty of the naturalists. These perpetually reluctant participants always managed to trail behind history as it unfolded. Although their sensitivity was hurt by the militarist era's crude attitude toward the feelings of individuals, they were too diffident to criticize. For the naturalists, the passive "I" stood alone in the midst of a burdensome life, in the midst of a hostile world. Such a sterile and marginal existence was no small decline for the naturalists, who had earlier heralded the emancipation of the individual. In the end, they no longer exercised their original leadership in any but the limited sphere of introspective self-analysis in confessional forms. The emancipation of the individual had proved to be a difficult, self-defeating venture.

Social Roots: From Concern to Alienation

If such was the fate of Shimazaki and his literary associates, how can we account for it? There are two connected explanations, sociological and intellectual. In sociological terms, the Japanese naturalists shared impressive similarities in their personal histories, which in many ways account for the role they played in modern Japan. In terms of the structure of their thought, their presumably scientific literary method reveals certain confusions that prevented them from rising above their own immediate experiences, and this in the end led them to fatalism.

In point of age they were all contemporaries. Tayama Katai, Tokuda Shūsei, Kunikida Doppo, and Shimamura Hōgetsu, representative naturalist authors and critics, were all born in 1871, four years after the Restoration. Shimazaki Tōson was born a year later. Iwano Hōmei was born in 1873. They grew up during the time of Japan's emergence as a modern nation-state.[40]

Another feature they shared was family background. Tayama was the second son of a samurai. In the semiautobiographical *Toki wa sugiyuku* (The time passes) Tayama writes of a declining family of former samurai. "After all, everything [that is wrong now] started from the Restoration. If only we had no Restoration." The Restoration broke down their earlier social roles, their ties and security. Shimazaki was born in a family that for many generations had been powerful in the locality. In the novel *Yoake mae,* which was written over a period of six years from January 1929 to October 1934, he deals with the life of his father, describing in microscopic fashion how the radical social and economic changes of Meiji Japan disrupted a hitherto serene rustic family. Aoyama Hanzō, presumably his father, experiences a series of failures. He is unable to obtain a position in the new government in Tokyo. The new railroad deprives his family of its traditional social role of controlling the Kiso route that led to Tokyo. While all the feudal social institutions disintegrate, the intricate personal ties remain, with a tenacity that brings tragic results in the arranged marriage of his daughter. Imbued with the Kokugaku (National School) teachings of Kamono Mabuchi, Motoori Norinaga, and Hirata Atsutane, Aoyama Hanzō expected great things from the new government, which had restored the august imperial sovereignty so passionately advocated by the Kokugaku school. Soon, however, the protagonist comes to view the politics of the new regime with suspicion. Meiji Japan becomes an inscrutable puzzle. His expectation was betrayed not because his previous ideals were contradicted, but because they transcended his imagination. The loss of the sense of touch with reality eventually drives him to insanity.[41]

Shimamura Hōgetsu was the first son of a declining family that had managed an iron mine.[42] He spent his childhood in dire poverty and was prevented even from attending grammar school, although he was later adopted by a local attorney who put him through school. Kunikida and Tokuda, too, had samurai backgrounds and unpleasant childhoods, as a result of their families' inability to steer their way through the changes taking place around them. None of these naturalist intellectuals attended Tokyo Imperial University or other national universities. Tokuda briefly attended Kanazawa Higher School. Shimazaki was a graduate of a missionary school, Meiji Gakuin, which Iwano Hōmei also briefly attended. Shimamura Hōgetsu and Kunikida Doppo studied at Waseda University. All these men spent their adolescent years in the hopeful atmosphere of Meiji Japan. Yet they did not walk in the limelight. As far as the ruling elite was concerned, these intellectuals were outsiders from the outset.

Yet the naturalists at first were not uninterested in politics or socially active careers. On the contrary, they were infatuated with the common preoccupation of this new nation. Kunikida Doppo came to Tokyo in 1887 and entered Waseda University in the department of English. Soon afterward he changed his field and registered in the department of politics. Retrospectively, he writes of his days at the university: "I even thought that it was a shameful profession" for a man to be a writer.[43] Although as a young man Kunikida was contemptuous of literature and had a passion for politics, he had no success in the latter. His diary constantly shows his frustration. "I feel that I cannot even touch this panorama of history, nay, even that I stand outside of history." "Time passes, all these great events pass by me. I stand quietly aside." The sense of alienation from history does not discourage him for long. With a jubilant sense of optimism, he yearns to be active. "I am universal. I am an ideal. I long to participate in politics with the universal ideal." He makes it plain that his desire to go into politics is not motivated by simple ambition. "My job is to reform. I will make the Japanese people stand on truth and ideals. I will make the future of this nation lead the progress of mankind." Before long, however, Kunikida came to choose writing as a profession. Just as he had moralized politics, he gave a moralistic reason for his change of ambition: "For me it was a meaningful evening last night. I definitely decided to be a writer . . . It is not that I dislike politics. But if I were to choose politics, I might love power for its own sake, and even might not be able to avoid dancing in quest for vain glory." [44]

Shimamura Hōgetsu, it has been recently discovered, was for a year registered at the department of law at Waseda University.[45] Eventually he was graduated from the faculty of English literature. While Kawazoe's contention may be correct that Shimamura registered in the department of law to please his foster father, it is still unclear whether or not he was temporarily interested in becoming a politician. Before he came to Tokyo, he had been employed as a clerk in a district court. As for Ishikawa Takuboku, the only genuine social rebel among the naturalists, he had planned to enter the Naval Academy but failed to pass its entrance examination.

In *Sakura no mino jukusuru toki* (The season when cherries ripen), Shimazaki speaks of the memory of his childhood, when he too was infatuated with the political mood of his time:

> "I was a kind of kid who could give political speeches at the age of fourteen." Aoki [Kitamura Tōkoku] started talking half in self-derision.
>
> While listening to Aoki speak of this, Sutekichi [Shimazaki] started remembering his boyhood. Once around Sutekichi was a group of young men fevered by politics. He remembered that his uncle was an enthusiastic member of the Progressive Party . . . Gradually, he started reading some of those political magazines and pamphlets. [Warned of the danger of such literature], Sutekichi continued to read them in secret . . . While studying at Takanawa [the location of Meiji gakuin, which Shimazaki attended], Sutekichi would dream of leading a political life.[46]

Kitamura Tōkoku (1868–1894), who had the greatest single influence upon Shimazaki's intellectual development, experienced the bitterness of politics early in life. Implicated in the plot of the Osaka incident of 1885, he eventually withdrew from involvement in political activities. Both the cruelty of government suppression and the terrorist tactics used by his political associates frightened him. Having failed in politics, he transferred his concern to literature and Christianity, through which he hoped to solve the dilemma of emancipation from society by finding in *sōsekai* (the world of thought) the ultimate humanity.

In *jissekai* (the world of reality), Kitamura asserted, the individual is simply helpless. He saw literature as the only means by which the individual could attain the world of thought. This flight of Kitamura's into fragile idealism was his reaction to a real experience in politics.[47] The naturalists who followed him, however, seem to accept his solution without having had any such experience. Kitamura's break with the world was far more radical than the naturalists' break, precisely because the latter never experienced the same kind of disillusionment. Thus, even after Kunikida decided to be a writer, his attitude toward authority remained ambivalent. "This morning I saw the emperor off to the new conquest. The greatness of the sovereign!"[48] Tayama is another typical naturalist who, in spite of his own claims, remained fearful of authority and society.

The naturalists' diffidence and fear of society caused them to internalize their concerns. The individual self became the central focus of their inquiry. Before these writers established themselves as self-acclaimed naturalists, many went through the literary phase now commonly called "romantic."[49] The poetry Shimazaki wrote during the last decade of the nineteenth century freely expresses his innermost feelings. Love is glorified in forms unknown before, as is confidence in oneself. The sense of loneliness is another theme that runs throughout this phase of Shimazaki's literary work. The people around him refuse to understand the sense of liberation he tries to communicate to them. From a hostile world and from a sense of loneliness,

Shimazaki often made pilgrimages to nature, which always provided him consolation.

In Japan, of course, such a view of nature was by no means held solely by the naturalists. Traditionally, the Japanese have regarded nature as a place of retreat. It mercifully embraces man embittered by human ties, provides no cumbersome norms, is not a depository of moral laws and discipline. To invoke nature, therefore, is an apolitical act, implying voluntary alienation from society. Kunikida wrote: "This I who covets such an experience [the grandeur of public life] is also envious of life in nature. I possess a strangely split mind." [50] Typically, Kunikida splits apart nature and society. One of his best-known works, *Musashino* (The Musashino Plain), is a collection of early short stories and essays celebrating nature. Along with his master, Wordsworth, Kunikida believes that human goodness is easily dissipated in a distracting city life. Man forgets his own simplicity and honesty as he moves into the bustling industrial world. But nature remains ready to receive him when he wishes to return. None of the naturalists could feel comfortable in urban life. As the sons of the warrior retainers of pre-Meiji Japan, they had in common a powerful agrarian past. In this past are rooted their love of nature as well as their constant chafing at industrial society.

One particular form their efforts at reorientation took was an interest in Christianity. Kitamura Tōkoku, Kunikida Doppo, and Shimazaki Tōson were all baptized. For a long time Masamune Hakuchō was interested in Uchimura Kanzō. [51] While studying in England, Shimamura Hōgetsu seldom missed church on Sundays. [52] It would perhaps be more precise to say that they flirted with Christianity, since none of them retained the new faith for long. Yet at first they believed that Christianity was enlightened and would emancipate man from superstitions and antiquated native religions. [53]

One of Shimazaki's first poems resembles in structure and rhetoric a hymn translated by Uemura Masahisa. In Shimazaki's poem, "prayer" becomes "dreams," "blessing" turns into "amorous love," and "God" becomes "the Beloved." [54] The critic Kamei Katsuichirō calls it a paganization of Christianity— or it may be seen as an attempt to "naturalize" Christianity, stemming from a dislike of Christianity's discipline and asceticism. If there were many samurai intellectuals attracted to the puritanical side of Christianity, finding in it the fulfillment of the warrior code or Confucianism, for the naturalists Christianity's ascetic content was one reason for their eventual desertion of it. Shimazaki writes in *Sakura no mino jukusuru toki:* "Why does the poetry of Byron, which seems to disgrace all human decency, charm me so? Whence its charm? Even though the Christian ministers frown upon it, how could one say that his poetry is not beautiful?" [55]

It was Masamune Hakuchō, more than any other naturalist, who probed into the nature of Christianity. In the end, in undisguised hostility, he accused Christians of having refused to see what is beautiful in Byron or Goethe.[56] Kamei Katsuichirō notes in his biography of Shimazaki Tōson that during one of his interviews with him, Shimazaki silently frowned when Uchimura's name was mentioned.[57] Kamei also records that Rousseau's *Confessions* as well as Renan's *Life of Christ* were two of Shimazaki's favorite books during the last decades of the nineteenth century. Indeed, it must have been difficult for these intellectuals to reconcile their interest in Christianity with other trends in European thought.[58]

Despite their confused and even contradictory readings, there is an underlying unity in the naturalists' intellectual interests: their preoccupation with the emancipation of the individual self. After all, Christianity taught the individual to free himself from familiar ties and it taught him his individual worth. Their avid appetite for the new, unsystematic thought—though it was from Rousseau to Christianity or from Byron to Zola— had the self at its center.

All these shared characteristics, however, do not fully explain why the Japanese naturalists in the end confined their attempt at emancipation exclusively to the world of art, or why they believed that to portray life as it is constitutes art par excellence. Art, they believed, never rises above life itself. It is just this identification of art with life that differentiates them from the hedonists, who saw only what is beautiful and pleasant in life. Art for art's sake meant little to the naturalists unless it meant art as a faithful servant of one's own experience.

Art and Reality: The Nature of Experience

While trying to escape from the authorities of the state, traditional conventions, and family, the naturalists uwittingly came to acquiesce in the authority of experience. The naturalist method is thus the primary cause for their final failure to put their notions of emancipation beyond the confines of the self.

Carl Becker has pointed out that "the modern climate of opinion is factual." He goes on to say that, viewed scientifically, a fact "appears as something to be accepted, something to be manipulated and mastered, something to adjust ourselves to with the least possible stress." [59] What Becker calls the modern climate of opinion found an easy inroad into the Japanese mind. Devoid of the Christian experience, Japanese intellectual tradition had its own factual stress, putting the highest evaluation upon experience as perceived in life and nature. But in Japan there was no pattern of thought in which every fact could be fitted into a set of neat categories. The Creator's omnipotent will never set history in order. Lacking an Aquinas, the Japanese seldom raised questions to contradict experience. If they successfully avoided absurdities, they nevertheless lacked a system of thought in which to reorganize and control factual experiences. True, there was the Chu Hsi school, with its well-ordered cosmology. Nevertheless, it is difficult to find in this official ideology of the Tokugawa period a dominating idea of an inscrutable will that orders the universe and history according to some rational pattern. It is easy to overdraw the contrast between East and West. Here it may simply be noted that, in the Japanese naturalists' writings, we find a confusion between the traditional thought pattern—emphasizing empirical and quasi-scientific facts—and the scientific thinking of nineteenth-century Europe.

As early as the 1880's the Japanese literati had turned their attention to the European naturalists.[60] Mori Ōgai was one of the first to call attention to Zola's name.[61] In May 1891 Shimazaki wrote an article discussing Zola,[62] while in the same month Tayama noted that he visited Ozaki Kōyō and discussed Zola.[63] By 1901 Shimazaki had definitely come to believe that the European scientific method was the best literary guide. "The literary vogue of nineteenth-century Europe," he wrote, "has passed over romanticism and the Pre-Raphaelites. From now on, I believe, it is going to be the method elaborated by Zola, Dostoevsky and Turgenev, of observing life on the basis of science." He continued: "We should leave behind the sweetness of life shown by the romantics and the hedonists. We should make a renewed attempt to dissect human nature scientifically with the knowledge of Darwin's *Origin of Species* or Lombroso's study of criminal psychology." [64] Shimazaki's friend noted in his memoir: "His admiration for science was extreme. He finished *The Origin of Species* in one week. Perhaps imitating Zola, he himself started visiting the villages of the *eta*. As he drank tea with them, he would listen to them talk. I was later told that among the people of Komoro [where Shimazaki lived] there was even the rumor that Shimazaki himself was an *eta*." [65]

Nor was Shimazaki an exceptional case. In correspondence with Tayama, he wrote: "I am genuinely stunned by your enthusiastic study and research. I understand that you have read a great deal of Ibsen. I would love to hear your opinion of him." In the same letter: "Having studied and mastered naturalism, are you going on to a new phase?" "As far as I am concerned I still feel that everything is new. It is like taking a maiden voyage." [66]

In addition to the naturalists' enthusiasm for natural science and the scientific method, they were interested in and influenced by another literary method. During the summer of 1894 Shimazaki read Rousseau's *Confessions*. Of this experience he later records: "Vaguely, I began to understand the manner of modern man's thinking through this book. I was taught to observe nature directly." It was about this time that he announced: "What could a hazy harmony give us? We, the youth, ought to consider more seriously what is growing in us." [67] Shimazaki's renunciation of the search for harmony or peace was undoubtedly motivated by his reading of Rousseau. Candid confession based on the observation of one's own experience was considered the primary objective of literature. Dissection through scientific method was replaced in the end by desire for the approximation of experience: confession. This was taken to be the essence of naturalism.

The Japanese naturalists did not rely exclusively on European commentaries on the naturalist method of writing; they themselves also tried to articulate the meaning of naturalism. In a short essay entitled "Mirukoto to kakukoto" (To observe and to write), Shimazaki says: "If you observe, you can write. If you free yourself from any preconception and observe, you always find something new." "There are no two things which are the same in the universe." [68] In another essay, he considers excellent literature to be "the product of observing an object as it is." "There are not many moments in life wherein we live, love, and die, when we can observe *it as it is*." [69] Elsewhere he writes: "I decided to take up the *shasei* (sketch) method. I feel that after I practiced this *shasei* method I came nearer to great nature." [70] When Shimazaki was writing *Ie* (The family) he worked on it inside the house, moving around to the places where the episodes took place. Thus he re-experienced the facts.[71] Before writing *Haru* (The spring), he traveled extensively to collect sketches for his new novel. "For the proposed *Haru* I am in the process of collecting sketches. Tomorrow morning I will go through Mishima to Numazu on foot with straw sandals. I plan to spend four days. Now dusk is gathering on the lake." [72] In this letter, which Shimazaki wrote to a friend, we see the confusion of the Japanese tradition of realism and what was considered to be the scientific method of writing. Shimazaki's excellent treatises on such classical poets as Saigyō and Saikaku reveal the author's respect for the masters' faithful sketching of their experiences in society and nature.

Even Tayama, with his ordinarily crude prose, wrote voluminous travelogues and profuse scenic descriptions which are often surprisingly beautiful. He, too, throughout his life loved to travel in order to collect materials for his writing.[73]

Shasei, as Shimazaki defined it, then, was close to what Tayama called flat description. Shimamura's literary imperative, *zettai mushinen* (the absolute absence of one's own thought), was another way of putting the same attitude toward writing.[74] Masamune, too, had his own thoughts on the subject: "It is foolish to question something like the basic meaning of life. To live each moment, that is all. Anything else would be a hallucination." [75] To write faithfully life's experience as it is lived each moment becomes to Masamune the ultimate concern and the final criterion of literature. All this led to the naturalist literary dictum of *mushisō mukaiketsu* (no ideal and no solution).[76] Paralyzed by and preoccupied with the particular and the immediate, the Japanese naturalist could neither transcend nor escape his experiences.

This gradual shift from the scientific method to the traditional method of *shasei* was explained by Shimazaki himself.

> It was not only the strength of literature alone that produced the works of Balzac. Behind him was the background of the power of French science that had produced the bacteriology of Pasteur or the astronomy and the mathematics of Poincaré. Many Japanese authors are in their nature essentially impressionists. Herein lies both the strength and the shortcomings of us Japanese.[77]

What was considered iconoclastic in the writings of the naturalists ended as no more than a revelation of the tormented self.

Making no attempt to go beyond immediate sense experiences, they ceased to have any social relevance. Commenting on Shimazaki's *Shinsei,* Masamune wrote: "Although his confession has the religious mood [of piety], all in all, it is based on his fear of social sanction." "He is afraid of being derided by society, and being alienated from man." "In him society has become a God." [78]

The gesture of evaluating and toying with one's own experience never goes beyond itself. Society, indeed, does not have to concern itself with such activities. In commenting on his own method of writing, one of the younger writers in the *shi-shōsetsu* genre noted that to describe one's own experience without any subjective analysis or dissection is "the basis, essence and truth of prose literature." [79] The writer aptly equates this method with that of composing haiku, from which the literary ideal of *shasei* emerged. The younger generation did not have the pretensions of the earlier naturalists. Unable to escape from this impressionist quality, they confused it with the scientific thinking of the nineteenth century.

Out of this confused scientism the naturalists drew a peculiar image of man. Once the authority of experience is accepted, man becomes a subject of his own emotion and his own environment, unable to control his own fate. Life is identified with art.

Self-burlesque or candor becomes identical with art. But man cannot build castles out of art. Hedonists like Tanizaki and Nagai felt at home in the world of refined eroticism, or in the subtle human relationships of the pre-Meiji era. Akutagawa's morbid protagonists had their own raison d'être outside society. In general, however, man as envisioned by the naturalists hovers in the limbo between the socially legitimate and the alienated, fearful of the latter and uncomfortable with the former. This limbo is socially insignificant, for it never offers any serious challenge to the established order. Naturalist realism deprives man of the tension between the real and the ideal, for only man's immediate situation as he experiences it has the reality of existence. Neither the concept of man as "infinite in faculty and reason" nor as "the paragon of animals" threatens this naturalist image. Realism, mistakenly construed as the naturalist method, becomes a synonym for fatalism. Man is perpetually pained and defeated; and the description of such realities is the only genuine purpose of art.

There was, to be sure, nothing illogical about this method of writing in and of itself or about the image of man it portrayed. Yet placed in a social context, the real man for the naturalists is a creature compelled to acquiesce in his fate, unable to affect it. More than any other intellectual group in their time, the naturalists suffered from the stifling of individual initiative and aspiration. Their social background and experiences enabled them to expose with eloquence the dehumanizing pressure of social and family ties which characterized old Japan's transition into the Meiji era. But that was all.

Except for the socialist authors, the writers who rose to artistic eminence after World War I on the whole accepted social isolation, not with anguished silence but with varying degrees of acquiescence, and were ready to accept the improved social status and financial security prepared for them by their predecessors. Satō Haruo (1892–1964), the son of a middle-class country doctor, is a good example. Asked about his future when he was fourteen, Satō recalls answering without any hesitation, "I will be a writer." [80] The title of Satō's first novel, *Denen no yūutsu* (The pastoral melancholy), written in 1917, is a suggestive one. It explicitly describes, with its subtitle "Withering Roses," an intellectual's ambiguous relationship to society. The protagonist escapes to the countryside from Tokyo, for "the profile of the countryside has been the object of his adoration." The city has irritated his nerves and senses. "For a while after he moved into the country house, the feeling of violent irritation seemed to have passed away." Yet, too soon, "every time the dusk approached, the conventional regret that 'today again I my time fruitlessly spent' came to haunt him." "Lifeless boredom" visits him every day with regularity.[81] Finally, he comes to realize that "in the country or in the city there is no paradise." In the life of the countryside, to which he escaped with the hope of finding peace, he is driven to boredom.

In January 1922, the continuation of Satō's first novel was published, under the title *Tokai no yūutsu* (The urban melancholy). The hero has now returned to the city, and the focus of the narrative shifts from nature to human involvements. The protagonist's relationship with his wife is now strained by jealousy, doubt, and hatred, all intensified by the interference of the wife's mother. His friendship with intellectuals suggests a dilettantism that verges on despair. Gradually, he is destroyed by the city. He is incapable of making any decision in the face of actual problems. The city, too, has rejected him. In each case he remains on the periphery of society.

The plots of these two novels could be contrasted with the life histories of the naturalists. Satō's naturalist predecessors had originally rejected their agrarian background and had come to the city in search of emancipation. When they were disillusioned, they would often take flight into nature for consolation. Just as they felt an affinity with nature, their sense of attachment to pre-Meiji Japan often supplied them with a source of artistic inspiration. During the years of Satō's frustrated attempt to find a resting place, Shimazaki was about to launch into the historical novel *Yoake mae,* with the conviction that "for better or for worse we should know more about the generation of our parents." [82] Tayama Katai was writing historical novels based on painstaking research and extensive travel. Tokuda Shūsei was living with the residue of Edo culture, now corrupted by modernization. A man like Satō Haruo, however, found no place to go. Although it began as a search for the dignity of the individual, the literary mode of naturalism ended in a total loss of direction, for it never provided a definition of its goal. John Dewey's romantic eulogy of the countryside as the seedbed of democracy would have been out of place in Japan. Shimazaki's return to the past was not an attempt to find a solution, but an effort to understand the frustrations he experienced. Satō was bereft of all such ties.

The urban-pastoral melancholy was one illness that the naturalists bequeathed to their successors. Suspended in social limbo, these intellectuals could neither fully accept their surroundings nor successfully flee them. The melancholy realities were there to stay.

V / The Shirakaba-ha: The Tyranny of Art

When a group of young aristocratic intellectuals started a small literary journal, *Shirakaba*, in April 1910, few recognized the significance it would have for modern Japanese history.[1] Thirteen years later, soon after the earthquake of 1923, the journal was discontinued. By then, the Shirakaba-ha (White Birch School) intellectuals had established themselves as one of the leading literary and intellectual groups of Japan and no longer needed a journal of their own.[2] Whereas the naturalists were not altogether happy in their social isolation, the Shirakaba-ha intellectuals were proud of theirs. In view of their contempt for all but the "genius," it is strange that, whenever Taishō democracy is discussed, this group is considered to have contributed a great deal to the ideological side of that constitutional experiment.[3] They indeed believed in the goodness of man. They thought that man could be educated and could improve himself and that the improvement of society would follow from this. In addition, they lacked that intense inferiority complex which so many intellectuals like Natsume felt in relation to the West— an emotion that could easily turn into hostility.[4] With equal open-mindedness they appreciated the cultures of both worlds: their intellectual tolerance and aversion to fanaticism and dogmatism were conspicuous virtues. But despite these intellectual and emotional assets, the Shirakaba-ha intellectuals could never effectively voice their dissent as they faced the rise of xenophobic nationalism and militarism. Nor had they the will to create a society in which their "ideal man" could survive.[5] For the most part they remained aloof from the social turmoils of the decades that followed.

My primary concern here is to attempt to explain why the group that seems to have been the best qualified of all the Taishō intellectuals to work for liberal principles never undertook the social role that they alone could have assumed. This concern is particularly relevant today, for the attitude of the Shirakaba-ha soon became the standard for those who moved from the major universities into the upper echelons of Japanese society. During the 1920s Marxism attracted many rebellious or academic intellectuals. Even so, the genteel, cultured outlook of the Shirakaba-ha endeared itself to those intellectuals, bureaucrats, and professionals who were educated to be the elite of society. So a proper appreciation of the Shirakaba-ha may help us to understand how well-educated Japanese thought and behaved.[6]

In many ways the Shirakaba-ha intellectuals remind one of the Enlightenment philosophers. Yet in their concern for the individual, their humanitarian sentiments, their iconoclastic reevaluation of the Japanese past, and their optimistic view of human nature, the Shirakaba-ha intellectuals never exhibited the militancy of the Enlightenment philosophers. Indeed, in Europe by the end of the nineteenth century, such an optimistic view of man had already long since become antiquated. There the romantics relentlessly challenged the rational view of man, while the positivists deprived man of any certified *a priori* moral nature. These intellectual experiences of nineteenth-century Europe made it difficult for the Shirakaba-ha intellectuals, or any intellectuals for that matter, to entertain an optimistic view of man and history with the enthusiasm of the Enlightenment. But there is far more decisive contrast between the Shirakaba-ha intellectuals and the Enlightenment philosophers. Viewed in the simplest terms, the Enlightenment was a war waged against the intellectual and social tyranny of the Church. The rational autonomy of the individual had to be asserted with conviction against the Christian view of man as a creature awaiting divine intervention for salvation. Individual "reason" stood against all the established social and intellectual conventions, with the French Revolution symbolizing the bitterness of the opposition between the old and the new.

The Shirakaba-ha's relation to the past was far more ambiguous. In the first place, as I have already noted, the changes after the Restoration were initiated by the old order. The significance of this distinction cannot be exaggerated. The Shirakaba-ha never had to go so far as their European predecessors did to assert human goodness and rationality. The old order had never rejected such views. Nor could the new intellectuals fully disassociate themselves from tradition—it would have been embarrassing, to say the least, for any intellectual group in Japan wholly to reject the political order established after 1868, for invariably they were the products of this same order. The Shirakaba-ha in particular were the product of the *success* of the "revolutionary restoration," and this was their prime weakness. In proposing ideals that were in accord with constitutionalism, they could not take a militant attitude. They were themselves aristocrats, the children of the architects of the existing order. The very success of the Meiji Restoration was demonstrated by their emergence, but it was a success with inherent limitations. The new intellectuals could not stand apart, could not stand against, and therefore could not move forward. They were compelled instead to find in art the purest expression of their ideals, to impose an aesthetic framework upon the highly combustible issues of politics.

Aristocratic Origins: Family and Generation

The Shirakaba-ha intellectuals are a group more because of their common social background than because of the intellectual and emotional attitudes they shared. They also stand out as a group because of their opposition to the gloomy world of the naturalists that dominated the intellectual scene in the transitional period from the Meiji to the Taishō era. But, of course, their literary styles and world views were diverse; it is obviously inappropriate to place a hedonist like Satomi Ton in the same intellectual category with a moralist like Mushakōji Saneatsu.[7] Nor was their opposition to the naturalists articulate, and Satomi today recollects his contempt for the lower-middle-class intellectuals.[8] The bright note struck by the works of Mushakōji is wholly different from the gloomy tones of the naturalists.[9] Yet the Arishima brothers were friends of Shimazaki, and the writings of Shiga Naoya often strikingly resemble much of the naturalist literature.[10] Nevertheless, the similarities in the Shirakaba-ha intellectuals' social background in large part determined the way they responded to their situations.

The oldest member of the group, Arishima Takeo (1878–1923), was thirty-three when *Shirakaba* started in 1910. One of the younger members, Satomi Ton (1888–   ), was twenty-three. The major participants of this journal were born during the 1880s. Arishima Takeo, Arishima Ikuma (1882–   ), Shiga Naoya (1883–   ), Mushakōji Saneatsu (1885–   ), Kojima Kikuo (1887–1950), Nagayo Yoshio (1888–1961), and Yanagi Muneyoshi (1889–1961) all attended the Gakushūin (Peers' School). Shiga, Nagayo, Satomi, Kojima, and Yanagai attended Tokyo Imperial University. Those who later joined the Shirakaba-ha were students from schools of the establishment.[11] Except for Arishima Takeo, who will be treated separately in the next chapter, the Shirakaba-ha intellectuals were born well after the Restoration. By the time they came to receive their higher education, Japan had already emerged as a modern nation-state. The intellectuals of the previous generation, including the naturalists, had witnessed Japan's creation as a nation and often entertained the thought of participating in this creative process. For the younger generation of intellectuals, however, Japan was a "given." It was there to stay and had ceased to provide opportunities either for conscious manipulation or for politically creative criticism. Mushakōji comments on Japan in an astonishingly noncritical manner. "I find no reason why we should be pessimistic about today's Japan. I feel that she is the most interesting country . . . a young nation . . . an awakening nation . . . a country without authority." [12] This intrinsically optimistic view of Japan and its future was altogether alien to the sentiment of either a naturalist or a Natsume. Of course it is perfectly understandable that the intellectuals who had experienced the two major victories in their childhood could not be pessimistic about "today's Japan." Still, it is difficult to understand how Japan could be called "a country without authority."

The lack of realism in such a remark should be understood in terms of the Shirakaba-ha intellectuals' relation to the ruling elite of Japanese society. All of them were intimately tied to the governing circles, not only through schooling but also by family connections. Mushakōji was related to Prince Saionji Kimmochi. The Nagayos were for many generations prominent in the medical profession, and by marriage were related to Matsukata Masayoshi, the architect of the modern Japanese economy. One of Nagayo's brothers became president of Tokyo Imperial University. Among the Shirakaba-ha we find two distinct types of background, one represented by Mushakōji and the other by Arishima. The former was a descendant of the traditional aristocracy (*kuge*), which in the preceding centuries lived in Kyoto. The latter was the son of a samurai who successfully survived and participated in the changes of the Restoration. In both cases they were well entrenched in the ruling elite. Among the contemporaries of the Shirakaba-ha intellectuals who went into active political life, Count Arima Yoriyasu (1885–1957) and Prince Konoe Fumimaro (1891–1945) stand out. The Shirakaba-ha people and these two were classmates at the Peers' School, and the biographies of Arima and Konoe reveal that their intellectual experiences resemble those of the Shirakaba-ha. They were intellectuals in their own right.

Arima taught agricultural economics at Tokyo Imperial University in the Department of Agriculture. Before he was forced to enter the House of Peers upon the death of his father, he had been active in the labor movement and social work. In his autobiography he speaks of his encounter with Kawakami Hajime's *Bimbō monogatari* (A story of poverty), Kagawa Toyohiko's *Shisen o koete* (Beyond death), and Tolstoy's *What Is To Be Done?* (As the conscience of the rich, as it were, Tolstoy was an intellectual of whom the Shirakaba-ha was much enamoured.) Kawakami for many years taught at Kyoto Imperial University and later became a prominent Marxist. Kagawa was a celebrated Christian social worker. All three shared a kind of anarchistic vision which respected the spiritual worth of man and abhorred violence.[13]

Prince Konoe was influenced by the same ideas. He entered the Tokyo First Higher Middle School and later the faculty of philosophy at Kyoto Imperial University, where he came into contact with Nishida Kitarō and Kawakami Hajime. Through his reading of the anarchist Max Stirner, Konoe came to embrace the socialist ideals of Oscar Wilde. In 1914 while at Kyoto he published in a journal a translation of Wilde's *The Soul of Man under Socialism*. In this work Wilde contended that the ultimate purpose of life is not labor but educated and enlightened comfort and leisure. Toward this end, he argued, a new form of individualism ought to be able to manipulate science and socialism. Prince Konoe committed suicide right after the end of World War II when the occupation forces designated him a Class-A war criminal. It is recorded that the last book he read before his death was Wilde's autobiographical record of prison life, *De Profundis*.[14]

Certain anarchistic visions were attractive to many Shirakaba-ha intellectuals. Two days after Kōtoku and others were sentenced, Shiga noted in his diary: "It is a rare historical event in Japan. In some sense I am myself an anarchist . . . although I do not think well of present-day socialism." He is, however, quick to add his distaste for violence. If Shiga was ill-disposed to the anarchosyndicalists' use of violence, he saw no evil in it or at least tried to be indifferent to the violence with which the government responded to the incident. "I have no spirit to read through the articles covering the event. I have for the time being no such curiosity." [15] Shiga never articulated his emotional affinity with anarchism, for his primary concern throughout his life was himself. The egocentricity of his art left no room for such political speculation.

There were some members of the group who went further in expressing their sympathy for radical political doctrines. When Morito and Ōuchi were being tried for having published the article on Kropotkin, Arishima Takeo invited them to a restaurant and gave them encouragement. Ōuchi writes in his memoirs: "Among those who supported us there were many whom we had not known. The most prominent of them all was Arishima . . . I went to see him with Mr. Morito. It turned out that Arishima knew a great deal about Kropotkin. [Arishima had met Kropotkin in London.] . . . He said he studied Kropotkin when he was young. He had brought along with him a couple of books by Kropotkin, and said that he had read them. He said that the books never advocated violent revolution." [16] Arishima later gave away to his tenants the land he had inherited from his father.[17] Mushakōji of his own volition went so far as to start a movement, New Village, in Kyūshū.[18] The principles of the village were those of the nineteenth-century utopian socialists: all property was to be shared, and daily life was based on self-help and friendship. Although the venture was abortive, Mushakōji never lost his sanguine outlook on man and society.

In one degree or another, therefore, the Shirakaba-ha intellectuals were not fully satisfied with the state of Japanese society. But the active life never appealed to any of them. If the naturalists had a grudge against Japan for rejecting their desire to participate, the Shirakaba-ha intellectuals never had any intention of participating in political life. This sentiment is dramatically expressed in Mushakōji's statement that he "never wanted to be a Mr. Itō or a Mr. Yamagata." [19] Mushakōji's attempt at creating an ideal village was from the beginning unconnected to the realities of society. As a contemporary socialist critic commented: "The oasis in a desert has no ability . . . to grow grass in the desert." [20] It was more an aesthetic infatuation with anarchism than a political movement. The very combination of the Shirakaba-ha's aristocratic background and nonpolitical anarchistic sentiment made it possible for them to claim that Japan was "a country without authority," for they never felt its tyranny and did not consider politics a meaningful alternative.

In essence, then, the Japanese aristocracy resembles neither the Russian aristocracy of the nineteenth century nor the Burkean ideal of natural aristocracy. Lacking the European aristocrats' centuries of experience in wielding social and political power, they might well have developed the narrow outlook of any *nouveau riche* group. Remarkably, however, they were open and tolerant. One reason for their intellectual and emotional resilience is that, unlike the European aristocracy, they were not confronted by any serious challenge from egalitarian ideology. In the absence of radical egalitarianism, they had no need to resort to the Burkean defense of the aristocracy's role. For the same reason, perhaps, many lacked a sense of *noblesse oblige*.

One might employ the sociological categories of ascription and achievement-orientations to explain the difference between the Burkean and the Japanese idea of aristocracy. The successful modernization of Japan was carried out by declassing the feudal social hierarchy and by effectively mobilizing human resources. The ancient aristocrats of Kyoto were preserved by the new elite, who desired to share social distinction with the old ruling class under the imperial sovereignty; the old symbols were consciously utilized and exploited by the engineers of the new nation. The pre-Meiji aristocracy could survive the radical transformation through their ties to the new elite; this was a fusion of ascription and achievement-orientations. So the Meiji aristocracy could dispense with a de Maistre or a de Bonald, for the Restoration never destroyed the old institutions of aristocracy.

This combination of the old and the new gives an interesting character to the modern aristocratic intellectuals in Japan. The primary role of the Kyoto aristocracy had been cultural and nonpolitical; its main preoccupation was the preservation of traditional cultural legacies. The new elite, on the other hand, was extremely active, open to the new, willing to absorb everything that attracted its attention. Because of their mental attitude, which combined a refined aestheticism with the intellectual tolerance of a confidently active group, the Shirakaba-ha intellectuals came to be widely accepted by the nonaristocratic elite of Japan.

But it was not only the intellectuals of the establishment who appreciated the Shirakaba-ha. Kobayashi Takiji (1903–1933), the most radical of the proletarian authors of the 1920s, paid respect of an unusual magnitude to Shiga, saying that his prose embodied the best expression and usage of language. In return, Shiga warmly received the revolutionary. Kobayashi was murdered by the police in February 1933, and—in what has come to be regarded as a singular episode in Japanese intellectual history—his funeral altar was adorned by a bouquet from Shiga. Considering the circumstances, it was a courageous gesture for this established writer to make.[21]

Compared with the naturalists, the Shirakaba-ha intellectuals were not afraid of society and its sanctions. Of a younger generation, they were emotionally less committed to the traditional social values and therefore more critical of the irrational aspects of Japanese society. When General Nogi Maresuke committed suicide with his wife soon after the death of the Meiji emperor, as an expression of loyalty to him, Shiga wrote in his diary: "When Eiko [his wife] told me that Nogi-san had committed suicide, I felt that he was a fool in the way I think of a maid who has committed some act of folly out of thoughtlessness." [22] Mushakōji more explicitly stated his contempt for the anachronism of the act. "General Nogi's death can be adored only by those with unhealthy reason. . . . Unfortunately, there is nothing in the death of Nogi which appeals to humanity, whereas the death of Van Gogh is a loss to humanity." [23] But Nogi's death shocked the intellectuals of the older generation. Even during the prime years of the Meiji emperor, Natsume wrote: "Japan was going to decline." [24] Mori reacted to Nogi's death with an intense burst of creativity, and wrote thereafter a series of historical novels based on the theme of loyalty.[25] To Natsume or Mori, Nogi's suicide, with its manifold paradoxes, conveyed a true sense of reality. It impelled them to address themselves to the problem of the tension between old and new. Natsume, convinced that man's egoism could never allow him to be reconciled to society, was certain of his inability to find a satisfactory solution, and Uchimura was also certain that no remedy for the spiritual plight of man could be found within Japanese society. Nagai took a conscious flight from modern Japan. The realist Mori was weary of the emergence of "undesirable isms."

Such anxieties were absent in the Shirakaba-ha intellectuals. They felt that it was possible for them now to be "universal." [26] They were the first nonnationalist intellectuals unfettered by the incubus of the past. Why then did they never oppose the oncoming of undesirable political realities? Why did they fail to weave their sense of personal emancipation into the texture of daily social life? With their ideals and their courage, it seems perfectly plausible to argue that they could have raised their voices against the militarism, xenophobia, and ultranationalism of the late 1920s and the 1930s.

The Politics of Aesthetics

This stunning inability of the Shirakaba-ha to translate their ideals into social action can be explained partly by their theory of aesthetics, which they applied in all situations.

It has often been pointed out that a linguistic analysis of

Shiga's works at once reveals a certain peculiarity. The pattern of his cognition is persistently emotive and egocentric. The recurrence of such expressions as "satisfying," "pleasant," "annoying," "anxious," "painful," "insecure," "unbearable," "concerned," and a series of their synonyms and antonyms indicates on the one hand the absence of a critical attitude toward or objectivization of his own feelings and thoughts and, on the other hand, the excessively, indeed exquisitely, emotive orientation in his thinking.[27]

Social problems, whenever they catch Shiga's fancy, are at once personalized. He either likes or dislikes them. When he finds himself in a position to make a judgment, he will favor what is pleasing to him rather than try to detach himself from the situation and analyze it critically. In all this, Shiga is a practicing Epicurean and utilitarian who makes no pretense at quantifying his feelings of pleasure and pain. His commentaries on social and political issues, although often acute, were always subjective: that is to say, they measured sociopolitical experiences only against their author's own sensitivity. His emotive reactions to situations are tantamount to judgments, and intellectually such judgments lack the essential ingredients of social persuasiveness—an articulated and objective set of standards.

With the Shirakaba-ha intellectuals the category of feeling assumes a critical function. In modern Europe the category of feeling, intuition, and emotion was salvaged only after a thorough experiencing of—and, some feel, the tyranny of—reason. As a means for reaching a better understanding of human experience, reliance was placed upon intuition after a shift had taken place in the intellectual predominance of positivism and after allowance had been made for "preconsciousness" and the "fringe of consciousness." [28] Reason, murdered off by the romantics, was soon resurrected, to accommodate a much wider range of human experience than it had encompassed in the eighteenth century. In Japan, however, the category of feeling maintained its untouched autonomy and survived industrialization. To the Shirakaba-ha as well as to the naturalists, man's sensitivity is nature's law. Sensitivity should not be sacrificed to reason, for the use of reason often suffocates man's natural inclinations. Shiga writes: "In any event anything that gives the feeling of being unnatural is not beautiful" and "what is most reliable is nature." [29] The identity of what is natural with what is beautiful, and the literary attitude of relying exclusively on one's intuition and emotion in judging what is natural, produced an interesting theory of art which could be broadly applied to social situations.

Watsuji Tetsurō, one of the first literary critics to recognize the excellence of the Shirakaba-ha and to encourage them, wrote a short essay, *"Mono no aware ni tsuite"* (On *mono no aware*), in the fall of 1922.[30] *Mono no aware* is an aesthetic category developed by the Kokugaku scholar, Motoori Norinaga. Although the article deals with the traditional category in its own terms, it sheds considerable light on the aesthetic attitudes of the Shirakaba-ha intellectuals. Watsuji finds that in this category of *mono no aware* there was a pre-Kantian separation of aesthetics from philosophy (reason) and morality (religion). The Kokugaku scholars saw in the aesthetic category the autonomy of feeling, along with the qualities of honesty and sincerity. Motoori's original motive in proposing the theory was to show the indigenous excellence of Japanese culture vis-à-vis Confucianism and Buddhism. Preoccupied with this purpose, Motoori neither expanded nor was clearly aware of the epistemological distinction implied by his aesthetic theory. He in fact differentiated the category of feeling from morality, as well as from philosophy and religious asceticism.[31]

Motoori suggested that feeling alone allows one to penetrate through the particular to the universal. What Motoori saw in *mono no aware* parallels *Anschauung*, in Goethe's use of the term.[32] Both terms are mental tools to comprehend experience, and yet neither is analytical or critical. The connotations of *Anschauung*, as Erich Heller observes in *The Disinherited Mind*, "are visual, and it [*Anschauung*] means the mental process by which we spontaneously grasp, through observation aided by intuition, a thing in its wholeness." [33] Both *mono no aware* and *Anschauung* are, strictly speaking, not so much epistemological categories as emotional attitudes alien to analytical approaches to experience. Precisely because Motoori never succeeded in elaborating the distinction between *mono no aware* and the other human cognitive forms, and because his followers carelessly moved in the ambiguous border areas among them, the confusion had significant consequences.

Without doubt, what Motoori proposes is one form of individualism in that one finds oneself at the center of the universe, the only cognitive being. Yet cognition depends exclusively on one's feeling toward *mono* (a particular object), which is ultimately related to the whole.[34] Feeling is no longer subjected to the social laws of Confucianism, nor does it have to be inferior to philosophy or religion. Feeling abhors asceticism. It does not have to rely on the reason of philosophy to understand the nature of the universe. Feeling, or the category of *mono no aware,* is elevated to be the sole epistemological tool whereby man may understand the pantheistic truth of nature. Motoori's argument that literature should not be didactic, for it is useless as a utilitarian instrument was remarkable, especially since it was advanced during the heyday of Confucian ethics, which taught that art and literature are instruments of morality and politics.

Watsuji correctly observes that total commitment to the theory of *mono no aware* makes one incapable of seeing the normative content of a situation. There is a confusion of *sein* and *sollen*. Watsuji further suggests that the category is a "spiritual *Halbheit,*" "immobilized in social situations." Placed in a social context, one is paralyzed in inactivity. One's aesthetic response to the situation, no matter how exquisitely approximate to its realities, has no intrinsically imperative content. Watsuji shows that the Heian literature best represented by the *Tale of Genji* (which Motoori restored from its previous low position to a proper place as the embodiment of *mono no aware* in Japanese art), "maintains a kind of hedonism perpetually conscious of the suffering world." Yet such an awareness, no matter how serious, is socially irrelevant. It acquiesces. "Within this predestined limitation," Watsuji writes, "the Heian people undoubtedly longed for harmony with nature. With their delicate sensitivity they felt all there was to feel in nature, and loved all there was to love." "It was the seriousness of their longing [for perfected harmony with nature] that prevented the aestheticism from deteriorating into rebelliousness and cynicism." In this verbal labyrinth Watsuji points out that *mono no aware,* though logical in and of itself, cannot be a social theory. Feeling is situationally determined.[35]

This description of *mono no aware* applies to the epistemological position of the Shirakaba-ha intellectuals. Their behavior was to a great extent determined by their emotive reaction to situations. Thus their "aesthetic ethics" conformed to what Max Weber calls *Gesinnungsethik.* One concerns himself more with whether his motive is honest and sincere than with the social and political consequences of the act. Social necessity is never taken into consideration, and the freedom of the individual to act is divorced from social relevance. Thus the tolerance shown by these intellectuals, as in Shiga's gesture of sending a bouquet for Kobayashi Takiji's bier, is not a politically oriented tolerance but, instead, a tolerant respect for the motives of opponents. Such tolerance is ultimately fragile, for it was not born of the fierce struggles among genuinely diverse ideas or of the struggle against dogmas. Although the action itself is often relevant to politics, the motive behind it is apolitical.[36]

Indifferent to the consequences of actions, the Shirakaba-ha intellectuals turned away from the ugly parts of society whenever possible. Mushakōji states: "I do not want to get the sense of life from art, but I would like to get the sense of art from life." [37] This is the exact reversal of the naturalists' goal. Mushakōji's view of the purpose of art is underlined by Shiga's statement that "it is even physically harmful to look at the ugliness and stupidity of life." They wished to shy away from realities; and they could afford to keep away from what was not pleasant. Elsewhere Shiga commented that he would choose to sit on the shady side of a train to avoid seeing the floating dust under the sunlight.[38] He recalls that he disliked the gloominess of the themes of Tokuda Shūsei's literature.[39] If nature is considered ultimately good and beautiful, as both Shiga and Mushakōji persistently maintained, what is natural is good. What then is the entity that judges what is natural and what is not? It is the individual standing alone in the midst of the world.

Glorifying man as he is, the Shirakaba-ha discarded the notion that society is of higher value than the individuals comprising it. Mushakōji in 1917 wrote: "I am the only man given to me by nature. Unless I have a desire to fulfill this life of mine, how could I care for the lives of others?" [40] This declaration, refreshing and new to the Japanese, is underlined by an ultimate egoism: "Since I can neither love nor care for the lives of others, nor influence their fate, it is a blessing that I can remain indifferent to the affairs of other people." [41]

Such was the theoretical background of the escapist mentality, aesthetically active and socially ignorant, of the Shirakaba-ha intellectuals.

The Benevolence of Nature

The life of Mushakōji reveals that the egoistic sentiments he expressed in 1917 and afterward are in clear contrast to a previous infatuation.[42] Almost all the Shirakaba-ha intellectuals were at one time fascinated by the humanistic and ascetic thought of the aged Tolstoy.[43] As late as in 1917, indeed, when Mushakōji was proclaiming his indifference, Nagayo was publishing in *Shirakaba* such pregnant phrases as: "Humanism aims at justice. Justice seeks for equality and freedom in the genuine sense of the terms. Justice is the judge for humanity." "It is obvious that without justice there could be neither goodness, nor beauty, nor happiness." "How disgraceful it is that one does not get angry as injustices are revealed in their stark nakedness." [44] Of course, for intellectuals not prone to consistency it is perfectly possible to cherish with sincere conviction two mutually exclusive attitudes. The ambivalence, however, needs a clearer explanation.

Like the naturalists of a generation earlier, the Shirakaba-ha intellectuals were interested in Christianity. It is well known that Arishima Takeo for many years was a dedicated Christian and a prominent disciple of Uchimura Kanzō. Shiga also mentions Uchimura as one of the most influential persons in his life, and from 1900 to 1907 he regularly visited the Bible class that Uchimura conducted. [45] Nagayo writes in his brief autobiographical sketch that while he was in the Peers School, Tolstoy and Uchimura were two of the thinkers whom he most admired. [46] Nagayo's first successful novel, *Seidō no Kirisuto* (Bronze Christ), has an interesting religious theme. [47] A non-Christian artist has been commissioned to make a bronze image of Christ to test the hiding Christians. In the end, he is executed along with the Christians because the officials suspect that the artistic excellence of the image he carved reflects his faith. The woman who loved him was not a Christian, but she too is executed because she refuses to step on the image in reverence to its artistic quality. [48]

Except in the case of Arishima Takeo, however, this interest in Christianity was more an infatuation than a commitment, and lasted only briefly in the adolescence of the individuals involved. Even Arishima broke away sometime in 1911. What attracted them to Christianity was its ascetic demands. The problem of sex, for example, troubled them, and often they turned to Christianity for a solution. But the asceticism in Tolstoy and in Christianity which had originally inspired their interest was—as in the case of the naturalists—the precise factor that eventually caused them to turn away.

"Tolstoyism and socialism tried to place on me a burdensome social responsibility," writes Mushakōji. "If I had quietly assumed such a burden . . . I would have been immobilized. So at first I shook off that burdensome responsibility." "Tolstoy taught me the value of reason. From him I learned the authority of my own reason." Mushakōji resents Tolstoy, however, for having denied the other human faculties: "I even felt ashamed of thinking about them." [49] Nagayo lets his protagonist in *Seidō no Kirisuto* comment on Christianity: "This religion seems too punctilious and too cruel. In this world shouldn't there be a freer religion more harmonious to the worldly?" [50] Tolstoy placed Mushakōji in a burdensome predicament: "So long as there is someone unhappy I cannot be happy." Soon, however, he learned from Maeterlinck "the courage to carry on one's own happiness." [51]

The theoretical means by which Mushakōji extricated himself from this predicament was his view of nature, invoked here again by the Shirakaba-ha intellectuals as by the naturalists before them. The magic of nature is that it relieves men from the weariness of social involvements. It is neither a depository of norms nor a challenge, and unquestioningly they embraced it. Commenting on Natsume's *Sorekara* (Thereupon), Mushakōji attributes the misery of the theme to the protagonist's rebellion against nature through the artificial suppression of his natural desires. Mushakōji concludes the comment by saying: "In the end I would like to see whether Sōseki will continue forever to entertain a hopeless feeling towards society, or will find some harmony between what is natural in man and society. I think he will choose the latter. In doing so, then, Sōseki will attempt to attune society to what is natural in man rather than conform man to society." [52]

For Natsume himself, however, such a harmony between natural man and society was a case of hoping against hope. He ultimately finds that what is natural in man is no more than crude egoism. In *Kokoro* (The heart), the egoism of the protagonist, or what is natural in him, drives him to self-destruction. Sōsuke in *Mon* (The gate) fails to find harmony with society, or even to find inner peace through his attempt at Zen. Natsume would have never felt sympathetic to the unexamined optimism with which the Shirakaba-ha regarded man and nature.[53]

Shiga was far more skeptical about man and nature, far less naively optimistic, than Mushakōji was. To him, what is natural never brought unconditional happiness. Nevertheless, the fact remains that his literary method, the particular way in which he appreciated his experiences, was subjective and uncritical. Speaking of the genre of *shishōsetsu* (I-novel) and of Shiga in particular, Howard Hibbett observes that they "somehow avoid a crisis." [54]

The naturalists, embittered by urban life, often turned to nature as a source of consolation. Yet what tormented them was precisely what was natural in them. Every time they behaved in accordance with their natural inclinations, they faced indignant and nonunderstanding surroundings. The Shirakaba-ha, on the other hand, believed that even if this world is not the best of all possible worlds, it still has a genuine potentiality of moving toward the ideal situation of harmony between man and society.[55] Harmony—which Shimazaki had earlier discarded as hallucinatory—was the deep-abiding object of their intellectual and emotional longings. In following our natural inclinations, all the anxieties of our longing—the tension between flesh and soul, desire and discipline, self and society—eventually disappear. Living naturally, we attain harmony both in our soul and in relations to others.

Nagayo writes in his *Takezawa-sensei to yuu hito* (The man called Mr. Takezawa) of the ethics of the ideal man. Takezawa says: "My morality? It is very simple. As Takezawa, I try to be in harmony with my neighbours as serenely and kindly as possible. As a member of humanity, I try to be harmonious with humanity, working as diligently and loyally as possible." [56] The hero of Mushakōji's postwar novel, *Shinri-sensei* (Mr. Truth), also lives in this fashion.[57] Where the naturalists considered man more in terms of his baseness and fear of society, the Shirakaba-ha believed in man's natural goodness based on feeling. What characterizes Mushakōji and Nagayo in their treatment of man is an aesthetic theory of man's equality. Underneath, then, there lies a contempt for the philistine and bourgeois nature of the modern masses, for they have been stripped of their natural goodness.

The Genius and Social Alienation

The Shirakaba-ha intellectuals were often acutely aware that all was not well with their society. Thus they had to believe that man's natural goodness could not find expression through the existing form of society. In their obsession with being faithful to what was natural, however, they ironically enslaved themselves to their own sensitivities. In so doing they lost sight of society.

In addition, their idea of "genius" made it extremely difficult for them to socialize their potentially liberal ideas. As an abstraction, they could love humanity; in fact, the term "humanity" fascinated them all. Yet they found it more and more difficult to love individuals. "Nowadays we don't respect *any Japanese*," Mushakōji stated.[58] Another member, Nagayo, wrote: "An ordinary man ought to consider it his vocation to adjust himself to the established society as well as he can. And the genius should steer society by making society conform unto himself." [59] If a genius is to steer society, his aim is an aesthetic one—to get "the sense of art from life." Peculiarly, then, the average man is deprived of a social role. Mushakōji also added: "At least this much is certain. The majority of the people are inferior to us." [60] Prosiac life could not excite a man like Mushakōji. He was not concerned with what the masses thought of his art. In one aesthetic controversy, Mushakōji contended that "so long as an artist remains honest to his own feeling, there is nothing more to be desired." "It would be of no value to concern oneself with the vulgar sentiment of the masses." [61]

Kierkegaard writes: "It is . . . proud of the nightingale not to care whether anyone listens to it or not." [62] None of the Shirakaba-ha intellectuals felt it necessary to address himself to society. If a prophet has to return to his society, as does Plato's philosopher-king, to convey to the people the words of God or the vision of Idea, a genius has no such obligation. Judith Shklar argues with clarity that in the struggle between the genius and the philistines, the genius is left out of history.[63] The "Japanese genius" was not aware of the social consequences of his alienation. Mushakōji believed that society ought to conform to nature and to him. Until then, however, Mushakōji would be willing to remain outside society. He remained ignorant of anxiety, and was even proud of isolation.

Aesthetic irrationality was the only legitimate intellectual tool for the Shirakaba genius. Unheedful of the faculty of reason, the Shirakaba-ha intellectual only knew of his own feelings. In social situations, he confused what was with what ought to be. He remained situationally determined and often could not act. Hence he could not rise above the given social situation. History refuses to yield a role to the genius.

The Image of the Family

The naturalists considered the institution of the family as one of the cardinal social vices that frustrated their effort to liberate themselves from the past. So did the Shirakaba-ha writers. Yet the latter soon came to reconcile themselves with the institution. They realized that in order to preserve their sensitivities, untouched by the realities around them, it was necessary to establish a milieu in which to nourish their egos. Therefore, even as they originally defied their families, they never expressed the type of despair that such naturalists as Tayama and Shimazaki perpetually revealed. Cynically and bitterly, Shimazaki wrote in his *Ie* (The family): "We took a long time to teach ourselves how to depend on each other." In *Sei* (Life), Tayama described how children are tormented by their sense of guilt toward their parents: "For us children, they did everything they could possibly afford. What have we done for them?" Affection turns into binding demands. As one literary critic has recently and aptly observed, "so-called Japanese individualism was born of the ego of the son tormented within the framework of the family." [64]

It was in the family, nonetheless, that the Shirakaba-ha intellectuals found the harmony they were seeking. In April 1937, three months before the Sino-Japanese incident, the Ministry of Education published the famous *Kokutai no hongi* (The essence of the national polity). This pamphlet defines *ie* as the "place where the vertical and horizontal relationships of parents and children, husband and wife, and brothers and sisters are harmoniously fused. And it is the place where harmony flourishes." [65] The social and emotional unit of *ie,* the prototype of social integration, was ruthlessly exploited as the basic form of loyalty which could be elevated to higher and more abstract levels of human relationship, such as the relation between the individual and the state.

If the family seeks harmony, the naturalists believed, it is a harmony measured in terms of the absence of open conflict rather than in terms of individual happiness. Individual members of the family are expected to make material as well as emotional sacrifices in order to minimize conflict. At first the Shirakaba-ha intellectuals, too, felt that their families often frustrated their aspirations. Their about-face was first prompted their family background.

Shiga writes in one of his reflections: "Whenever I ran out of money, I would go to the secondhand book stores I knew in the Kanda district, and ask the names of the most expensive books they would buy. Then I would go to Maruzen or Nakanishi-ya, buy the new copies of those books and bring them over to the stores for cash. Maruzen or Nakanishi-ya would collect at my house later. So they would let me charge as many books as I wanted." [66] Shiga and other Shirakaba-ha intellectuals were the sons of successful men from established backgrounds. The Arishimas had inherited wealth, some of which Arishima Takeo gave up. In this respect they were distinctly different from the naturalists, whose social position had suffered a sharp decline during the period of post-Meiji transition. Modern Japan rejected Kunikida, who longed to play a social role, whereas Mushakōji could have chosen any profession he wanted. The irony was that, because the new order created by the old forces allowed the Shirakaba-ha intellectuals to live the way they wanted, this in the final analysis made it harder for them to divorce themselves altogether from the institutions of the past, above all from their families. In *Shinri-sensei*, published in 1952, Mushakōji writes: "One day when I asked him what he thought of the Emperor, he said, 'I love him. I adore him. This is my mother's blood in me, although this is not logical or rational.'" [67] The very ambivalence of this statement, as juxtaposed to Mushakōji's earlier remarks, on the death of General Nogi for example, symbolizes the role of the Shirakaba-ha intellectuals: while they were often iconoclastic, it was a purely emotional iconoclasm. Their break with the past, furthermore, was not so clear as they often boasted. Elsewhere Shiga writes: "What is called Confucianism has become a part of us. This forms a moral backbone of my generation." [68] Even though they were extremely susceptible to the new ideas, their behavior was highly proper.

The egoism of the Shirakaba-ha required a sympathetic atmosphere. In *Ōtsu Junkichi*, published in 1912, Shiga described the tension between the father and the son, Junkichi, who decides to marry one of their maids. Yet in a subsequent novel, *Wakai* (Reconciliation), the tension is soon dissolved through the affectionate intervention of the grandmother.[69] This title is extremely suggestive of the preoccupation of the Shirakaba-ha writers. At the end of *Anya kōro* (Through the dark night), Shiga brings the protagonist and his wife together in harmony. Even as the protagonist discovers the secret of his birth—that his grandfather is also his father—and the adultery his wife committed, even in this nadir of suspicion and hate, the story maintains with sure tenacity a hope for final reconciliation.[70]

In *Yasei no yūwaku* (The temptation of the wild), a postwar novel by Nagayo, the author describes a series of autobiographical experiences involving two close friends and their families. The turbulence of the episodes leads to the final scene where the presence of harmony, though unspoken, is unquestionable.[71] From *Ōtsu Junkichi* to *Yasei no yūwaku* there runs the consistent theme of finding harmony within the framework of the family. I should, however, add that in *Ōtsu Junkichi, Wakai,* and *Anya kōro,* the wives tremble with fear of their moody husbands. The naturalists were victims of their families; the Shirakaba-ha writers were the masters of their families.

The Shirakaba-ha's Contribution to Arts and Letters

The seeming paradox that the Shirakaba-ha intellectuals were caught in the middle of the success of the old and the new placed them in a strategically favorable position to appreciate the civilization of the two worlds.

Earlier, Natsume Sōseki had predicted "the general psychic breakdown"[72] to follow the meeting of East and West in Japan. No longer could he abide by the simple faith professed by the early Meiji intellectuals: either embrace totally Western ideas or sustain the old ethics as the basis of a modern society. Beneath Nagai Kafū's nostalgic attachment to Edo lurks his hatred of modern Japan and his love of France. "Art," he believed, "is of value when it is morally unacceptable to society."[73] Earlier Christians, such as Uchimura Kanzō, Ebina Danjō, and Uemura Masahisa tried to find what is universal and genuinely Christian within the indigenous ethics of the Japanese.[74] Uchimura's attachment to the past equals in intensity only his commitment to Christianity—which was, for him, neither Western nor Eastern.

With the Shirakaba-ha intellectuals, however, both cultures were objectified. Culturally, they became the disinherited souls of Japan and the adopted sons of the European world. If the degree of their commitments to these cultures was shallower, the range of their perspective was much wider than it had been for the intellectuals of a generation earlier, Every issue of *Shirakaba* had a few reprints of Western paintings.[75] The list includes such names as Cézanne, Millet, Goya, Van Gogh, and Rodin. In introducing these European artists and their works, *Shirakaba* contributed greatly toward enhancing Japanese art and art criticism. Moreover, it popularized art in sectors of Japanese society which had hitherto been unacquainted with the outside world. Aono Suekichi, a Marxist writer, recalls that "for the poor students from the countryside, the atmosphere of the Shirakaba-ha was something difficult to familiarize themselves with . . . Yet I was grateful for their effort to introduce us to modern European art . . . I can never forget the exciting joy I experienced when I saw an original of Rodin exhibited by the courtesy of the Shirakaba-ba people." [76]

The same was true of literature. It was the Shirakaba-ha who introduced the Japanese to the works of Hugo, Ibsen, Whitman, Dostoevsky, Tolstoy, Maeterlinck, Strindberg, and Romain Rolland. Devoid of either scholastic pendantry or simple Occidentalism, it was a momentous achievement. It is recorded that in one of the prefectures, Nagano, "there was no primary school student who did not hear the names of Tolstoy, Romain Rolland, Maeterlinck, Rodin, Van Gogh, Cézanne, or Beethoven from his teacher." Many schoolteachers were fascinated by *Shirakaba*. No other single group did more to liberalize the originally nationalistic curriculum than the Shirakaba-ha. They said that "art and learning should be taught together to create a whole personality." [77] In conformity with Mushakōji's optimism, "the acts of the individual with a whole personality would eventually contribute to humanity." Their doctrine implied the autonomy of learning and art as against the ultimate purposes of the state. Indeed, as we have seen, the autonomy of art was so emphasized that it obscured other areas of human concern. Nonetheless, the Shirakaba-ha performed a noteworthy service in opening up the previously closed culture of Japan to the outside world.

With their characteristic enthusiasm for what appealed to their aesthetic sensitivities, the Shirakaba-ha gradually returned to a concern with the arts of Japan. In so doing, they raised the people's interest in indigenous Japanese culture to a much higher level of sophistication and universality. Yanagi Muneyoshi, for example, did much valuable work in bringing long-neglected Japanese folk arts to public attention.

In 1919 Watsuji published *Koji junrei* (A pilgrimage to old temples). In simple but cultivated prose, he recounts his experiences in visiting the Buddhist temples in the ancient cities of Kyoto and Nara, and elaborates his thoughts on their architecture, sculptures, and paintings. The book ends with the suggestion that in our "study of our own culture we ought to return to the observation of our own country's nature." [78] Nature is described as the source of inspiration and consolation. Watsuji feels that for the ancient Japanese, nature bred neither moral commands nor violence, and their works of art, he contends, reflect a genuine understanding of the serenity of nature.[79] This adoration of harmony in nature, which the ancient Japanese faithfully emulated in their art, life, and love, replaces the "rebellion" that Watsuji had expressed through his earlier "pilgrimage" to European intellectual history.[80]

A year earlier, in 1918, Watsuji had published *Gūzō saikō* (The idol restored), on the theme that "God has to be resurrected." He writes: "The lives of the great men in the nineteenth century testify [to the need] for the destruction and the resurrection of the idol." To Watsuji, the models to be emulated were Tolstoy, Strindberg, and those decadent poets who eventually became "the faithful servants of God and His righteousness." Watsuji himself, however, confessed that "he applauded the death of God without experiencing His tyranny and authority." [81] From this it is clear that his translation of Nietzsche was merely an intellectual facade.[82] Failing to attain either the emotional nadir or the intellectual heights of Nietzsche and Kierkegaard, he broke away from them in dissatisfaction. His pilgrimage to Europe was motivated more by infatuation than by commitment. He hastily resurrected an idol, nature.

Watsuji writes: "I do not have to repeat that our life and our behavior should not be 'unnatural.' " "We have to follow nature absolutely." By nature, he means "not nature as opposed to either 'spirit' or 'culture,' " but rather as "including all the elements which appeal to our senses and also . . . the 'very life' which lies behind them all." This pantheistic mood recalls the world of Nishida Kitarō, the world of quiescent harmony called *mu*. Watsuji opposes the naturalists and says that "they know nothing but the nature which appeals to commonsensical and crude observations." He does not, however, create a new idol, but finds its prototype in ancient Japanese culture. Therefore, although Watsuji's observation is correct that Tolstoy returned to the religion he seemed to have destroyed in his youth, his resurrection of an idol has an entirely different character. The transition from licentiousness to asceticism as it existed in Tolstoy or Strindberg is replaced by another form of transformation: from *aimless rebellion* to *normless harmony*. Watsuji confuses the two processes. Indeed, he speaks of morality and love, which he equates "with the restoration of the old." "Undoubtedly, in many ways the Renaissance was the movement to destroy idols. Yet, basically, it was literally the restoration of [what was true in] ancient period. By resurrecting the immortal within the ancient world, the new movement gained its energetic power." [83] In the same manner, Watsuji believed in the restoration of ancient ideals for the new Japan. The difference, however, was that in Japan the old was never exposed to a thorough destruction. Not only did it survive, but it supplied the motivations and energy for the changes after the Restoration. The intellectual now returns to his own society, which has remained essentially "natural."

The last few issues of the journal *Shirakaba* were devoted to the Japanese arts: stone gardens, Buddhist paintings, sculpture, and temples, paintings and scrolls.[84] From an esoteric and often exclusive appreciation by a selected few, they were brought to the level of the common people. This gradual return of the Shirakaba-ha-type intellectuals to their own cultural heritage was a common phenomenon among educated Japanese. Although too sophisticated to be fanatical about their own culture, these intellectuals nonetheless found in the old Japan an oasis, their artistic sensitivity could maintain its autonomy unhampered by the trivialities of everyday life.[85] They rediscovered the harmony in their own past, where they believed that what they considered natural was most faithfully emulated.

If the Shirakaba-ha intellectuals were culturally productive, in the social context of Taishō Japan they lived on a sterile promontory. It is not that they maintained silence. Having traveled through Manchuria in 1936, Nagayo recorded a recollection in his travelogue: "The head of this museum is opposed to imperialism. Therefore, he alluded fervently to how the strongest animal during the diluvian epoch came to be extinct . . . With a set of well-developed bicuspids, they destroyed themselves." [86] Never once did he compromise with the thought of war. Instinctively, he abhorred violence, whether committed against a man or a nation.

Satomi Ton, too, admirably remained antagonistic to the Japanese war effort.[87] It is difficult to conceive that Arishima Takeo would have felt sympathetic toward the rising militarists had he still been alive during the 1930s. Nor did Shiga at any point explicitly support the war. Such visions of violence and blood would have "displeased" his feelings. But Mushakōji cheerfully, even with tears of excitement, welcomed the coming of the war. He accused Chiang Kai-shek of having invited the turmoil throughout Asia because of his stupidity, and he wept as he listened to the imperial rescript read in December 1941. With incredible naiveté, he believed the news reports conveyed to the public and uncritically accepted the purposes of the "sacred war." [88]

The fact that the majority of the Shirakaba-ha intellectuals tended toward pacifism, however, should not becloud our retrospective evaluation of the group. Their reactions to the social situation were more impressionistic than analytical, and they were unaware of the social consequences of their epistemology. As such, although their outlook might diverge from the prevailing social trends, they could never raise their voices in effective opposition.

To explain these limitations, such scholars of modern Japanese intellectual history as Kuno Osamu, Fujita Shōzō, and Tsurumi Shunsuke have tried to call the Shirakaba-ha conservative.[89] In support of this view, they enumerate four characteristics—anti-mass elitism, the high cult of aesthetic experience, the consciousness of tradition, and, finally, the low appreciation of scientism in human and social behavior—as the conservative attributes of Japanese intellectuals.[90] On two counts, such a treatment of the Shirakaba-ha is misleading. For one thing, although there is nothing illogical about the definition in and of itself, the Shirakaba-ha intellectuals possess many characteristics they share with so-called liberals. Far from regarding human nature as depraved, no one sustained a more optimistic view of the goodness of man than did Mushakōji. Few intellectuals were as acutely aware of the limitations of the existing forms of society as Arishima Takeo and Mushakōji. They were not simply satisfied with the maintenance of the status quo. Their historical sense was not marred by arrogant fanaticism or ignorant acquiescence, for they were more steeped in nineteenth-century European culture than was any other single intellectual group of Taishō Japan.

In addition to the linguistic misgiving raised by the use of the term "conservatism" in describing the Shirakaba-ha, still another problem lies in the accusation that they lacked respect for the "social sciences." As far as their aesthetic theory was concerned, there was a nearly perfect consistency in what the Shirakaba-ha writers proposed and practiced. From them, the Japanese learned much about the concept that learning should be independent of the utilitarian demands of the state. The approach of Kuno, Fujita, or Tsurumi depreciates this crucial contribution of the Shirakaba-ha intellectuals: that they freed education from state utilitarianism. In the same vein, the

Shirakaba-ha intellectual is charged with being indifferent to what Max Scheler calls *Technischenwissen* and *Herrschaftswissen,* in favor of *Bildungswissen* or *Erlösungswissen.*[91] Here again, such a charge beclouds the indispensability of the non-utilitarian character of learning. All that is left of Kuno's and Tsurumi's indictment is simply that the Shirakaba-ha were ignorant of liberal and constitutional political principles. Although Mushakōji often reminds us of Rousseau in his optimistic moments, Rousseau would surely have found him hopelessly ignorant of what it means for an individual to be a citizen of a political community.

Shall we call ignorance a sin? After all, the Shirakaba-ha intellectuals were the products of Japan after the Meiji Restoration, which knew little about "constitutionalism." If they rebelled against society, the defiance was of an aesthetic nature, stemming from a dislike of philistine concerns with wealth and power (*fukoku-kyōhei*), which often sacrificed the freedom of thought and feelings of the individual. The real nature of the error the Shirakaba-ha committed was, perhaps, that in placing the individual at the center of the universe, they endowed him only with the "faculty to feel." In so doing they made him an aesthetic being unable to rise above the situations in political terms. They created freedom beyond society itself. For us today, their political ignorance should not be an accusation in retrospect, but a lesson by which we may learn the danger of political ignorance. This is the best of the legacies they have bequeathed to us.

VI / Arishima Takeo: Bourgeois Criticism

Arishima Takeo was one of the original members of the staff of the journal *Shirakaba*. He was, however, almost ten years older than such figures of the group as Mushakōji, Shiga, and Nagayo.[1] Not only in age but also in intellectual orientation, Arishima seems to have been closer to the naturalists than to his literary associates. What we now consider the main attributes of the Shirakaba-ha intellectuals—Mushakōji's optimism about human nature, Shiga's egocentric artistic style, or Nagayo's faith in the harmony of human relations—are all equally alien to the world of art created by Arishima.[2] We find in him instead the anxiety of the Japanese naturalists, who, having liberated the individual from the yoke of society, had been unable to provide their "natural man" with a new sense of direction. Arishima could not remain satisfied with the naturalists' moral neutrality, however. His writings display a keen awareness of such problems as man's moral competence, the tyranny of emotion, and the unfettered individualism advanced by the naturalists and the Shirakaba-ha alike.

Precisely because of his awareness of and dissatisfaction with the literary basis of these two schools, Arishima emerged as the most acute critic of both. If Shiga desired to sit on the shady side of a train to avoid seeing the floating dust, and hoped thus to protect himself from exposure to the unpleasantness of real life, Arishima could not help choosing the other side, even though he suffered inordinately from the exposure. If Shiga far excelled him in aesthetic sensitivity, Arishima had an incomparable sensitivity in the moral and social sphere. It was because of this moral concern with what ought to be done in a human situation that he was one of the few to confront the relation between thought and action—a problem altogether neglected by both the Shirakaba-ha and the naturalist writers. No other intellectual at that time in Japan was more troubled by the ineffectual social role played by intellectuals. Neither the arrogant alienation of the Shirakaba-ha group nor the social acquiescence forced upon the naturalists would have suited Arishima, who believed that one's moral position should compel one to act. He was critical of the indecisive sophistication of the intellectuals, whose knowledge of the ambiguities and the fraility of human experience prevented them from playing a role in society.

Arishima longed to play a social role. "In the beginning was the Word. Or was it action? This question I cannot answer," [3] he notes in one of his many inquiries into the dualism of thought and action. By dissolving this dualism through morality, he believed, an intellectual could reconcile himself to society. Arishima, however, was unable either to locate the source of morality in action per se or to find the moral value in thought (in which he usually includes both art and intellect or reason) sui generis.[4] As a result he could find comfort neither in the naturalist defiance of social norms for the sake of defiance nor in Satomi's flight into a life of decadence as the source of artistic reactivity. Nor was Shiga's complacency about his own aesthetic sensibility (which he often confused with moral criteria) any more congenial to the self-critical style of Arishima's writing.

Caught in the middle of such choices, Arishima never could find a solution. For a long time he was a Christian and entertained the Christian ideal of love as the source of morality, but he eventually discovered that to entertain such moral ideals as love and compassion would not necessarily lead one to act. Later in his life he came to accept the Marxist view that the future of art and intellect depended exclusively on the creativity of the proletariat, and in so doing he removed himself from a responsible role in the historical process.[5] This was no solution to the kind of problem Arishima had originally posed for himself, for in the end he invoked historical determinism to evade all those social responsibilities he had originally sought to assume. The pseudo-solution he proposed—the removal of the "bourgeois intellectual" from society—is therefore much less important than his magnificent—albeit unsuccessful—attempt to find a solution.

Japanese Naturalism Examined: Aru Onna

Undoubtedly, Arishima's most representative work is the novel *Aru onna* (A certain woman). The first part was written between January 1911 and February 1913 and published in *Shirakaba,* while the remaining three quarters of the book was written in the span of less than a month in 1919.[6] The purpose of the novel, the author explained, was to describe a woman whose hatred of men for having subjugated her sex drives her to despair but who still cannot free herself from the lustful desire for a mate.[7] In this predicament, the heroine "unfolds tragedies for herself." [8] Elsewhere Arishima wrote in the same year: "Without the courage to observe the ugliness of the human soul, without the courage to see reality nakedly lurking behind the traditional concept of a soul, man has been forced into eternal longing." In the advertisement for the novel he wrote: "Let us face ugliness without fear. Let us see whether there is something behind all [the ugliness of man's life]. If there is nothing, the possibility of life should be denied." [9]

A cursory glance at the novel reveals a striking resemblance between Arishima's literary work and that of the naturalists. In fact, while his fellow writers such as Satomi remained contemptuously aloof from the self-burlesquing style of the lower-middle-class naturalists, Arishima was intimate with some of them. When Kunikida Doppo died in 1908, he recorded his death in his diary, eulogizing him as a truly remarkable writer.[10] Through his brother Ikuma, Arishima became acquainted with the writings of Shimazaki. (The latter warmly describes in his sketches of the Chikuma River the visit he received from Ikuma.[11]) In the spring of 1916, just as he was preparing to complete *Aru onna,* Arishima recorded in his diary: "I have finished reading Ellis's *Studies in the Psychology of Sex.* I learned a great deal and found the work suggestive: the sex psychology of the female, the relationship between hysteria and sexual instinct, etc. If I can use these materials well, I can write an interesting work. I got many useful points for the rewriting [of *Aru onna*]." [12] This concern of Arishima's with psychology reminds one of Shimazaki's interest in Lombroso's studies of criminal psychology. Yet in Arishima one finds no trace of the single-mindedness with which some of the naturalists studied the sciences. He was less concerned with approximating realities than with the various problems that lie behind them. He could not be satisfied with remaining in the moral limbo of *mushisō mukaiketsu* (no idea and no solution) and was anxious and desperate to find something behind the sordid reality of life in order to hold on to what he called the possibility of life.

Aru onna, however, reveals not so much Arishima's ideals as his awareness of the problems the naturalists raised and left unsolved. He knows that there is a paradox in the naturalists' treatment of the individual as an asocial being. The heroine of the novel, Yōko, is liberated from all social conventions. Through her defiance of decency and established social conventions, she longs for independence. Arishima brilliantly portrays the irrational cruelty of those who are the guardians of society. Yet here again one finds "libertine determinism" and the same paradox. Yōko, freeing herself from society and its sanctions, enslaves herself to lust, and finally she is bereft of all human ties. Indeed, not only the woman herself but also the man is victimized: both are tormented by their destructive attachment.[13]

But the novel also reveals the author's sustained interest in restoring the lost dignity of the individual. Yōko gives herself up to a man, even to the extent of abandoning her self-respect, so that others will recognize her existence. She feels triumphant when her man desires her. The mood of unhappy determinism, so apparent in the naturalists' writings, is here alleviated by the fact that Yōko chooses to succumb to her own appetite rather than be forced into it by circumstances. Even as she is subjected to "the demonic temptation of the flesh," she is perpetually faced with the need of finding the sense of her own being. Ironically, she can at times observe, "like a cold critic, her own love and her lover." She loses control over herself only when she chooses to do so and is aware, furthermore, that a woman often helps a man to subjugate herself to him. Believing, however, that "at no time has a man come to the aid of a woman when she expresses a desire for independence," Yōko expresses this desire through the tortured method of enslaving both herself and the man to their lustful drives. And then, "the thought that her life would wither because it was bound to this man made her tremble with despair." The sense of her independence and the sense of her own being come as a result of her ability to carry her man along with her as she enslaves herself to her own lust.[14]

How can one release oneself from such a predicament? Arishima never answers the question either to his own satisfaction or to his audience's. Yet by explicitly asking himself the question, he was able to observe that one cannot achieve a meaningful independence in total disregard for one's relation to society. After all, independence is a social category—as is freedom, in essence. Just as he was himself aware of the inevitability of the social nature of the individual, he felt acutely the sense of loneliness that the intellectual experiences in society.

The Loneliness of the Intellectual

In 1918 Arishima wrote an essay, "Dai naru kenzensei" (Grand healthiness), in which he wrote: "The more an author emphasizes the particular quality of his art, the more he departs from those to whom the artist addresses himself. If he is extreme, it will end in the isolation of his art." [15] The works of such an artist divorce themselves from the common man. Unlike his admiring fellow-intellectual Mushakōji, who cared little if he had an audience, Arishima was afraid of the isolation of art and the artist from the common man. Many naturalists had the same anxiety. Few, however, tried to examine the possibilities of re-entering society. It was because Arishima had experienced helplessness and loneliness that he sought a path to lead to reconciliation with society.

In *Oshiminaku ai wa ubau* (Relentlessly love steals), written in 1920, Arishima formulates his essentially individualistic philosophy. Although perhaps less a philosophy than a collection of reflections upon life, there is nonetheless an underlying theme. Arishima writes: "Although I am the most impotent, I have nothing but myself to rely on." This recalls a letter that Natsume had written to a trusted student more than a decade earlier: "Nothing is less courageous than to trust in something other than oneself. Yet there is no one less reliable than myself. What shall we do?" Natsume concluded the letter by saying: "Have you ever thought of this problem?" It is precisely this problem which Arishima addresses himself to in *Oshiminaku ai wa abau*. Studying the nature of the self, Natsume had concluded that man is shot through with egoism and that he can neither understand nor sympathize with his fellow men. Thus any human involvement contains from the outset the seed of eventual tragedy. Arishima also felt that in the final analysis man is a lonely being:

One traveler is going through an eternal path. There is no one who understands him so well as himself. When the sun shines, his shadow is the only faithful companion. When it is cloudy or dark, he does not even have the companionship of his shadow. Then he has to find the faithful companion only within himself. No matter how frail and ugly, where else could he find something more certain than he? Sometimes I look at myself as such a traveler.

He is quick to add that "I am afraid that I cannot let my reader fully understand what I want to say." "How can I place myself in the right relationship to the people . . . around me?" "Is such a relationship possible?" "If possible how can I find it?" [16]

"In order to communicate to each other," Arishima continues, "we have to rely on words, but what an unreliable means!" Words are "unfaithful servants." "They often betray us. How can we express ourselves by resorting to these words!" [17] Then the deceitfulness of the beloved becomes one of the themes Arishima entertains, with a passion. Shiga, too, often dealt with the theme of unfaithfulness, but with him reconciliation was always waiting in the end; while the understanding was inarticulate, it was at least available. With Arishima, destruction always follows the longing of two souls to communicate. Words cannot be relied on, and where else can one seek a means of communication? He has virtually given up art or letters as a means of establishing human communication.

In addition to the skeptical scrutiny that Arishima imposes on language, there is the factor of "cowardice," the fear to act, which intensifies his sense of loneliness. Honda Shūgo brilliantly shows how persistently this theme runs through Arishima's writings. To lack the courage to act or participate, as Plato knew, was to lack a social virtue. For Arishima courage was the foundation of all morality, insofar as moral life was the result of freely chosen action. He wrote a short story entitled "Okubyō-mono" (The coward), which most sharply presents his concern with the fear to act. As Honda deftly summarizes it:

He is walking through a residential area in Tokyo in the twilight. The children are playing on the street in that state of excitedness which they sometimes show at the end of the day. On one side of the street is a milk cart. A child of about six, left out of the play, leans on the cart and tips it. Surprised by a sudden noise behind him, he looks back. Somehow the gate of the cart becomes loose and the bottles on the shelves are about to tumble down. He sees the child trying momentarily to keep the gate closed with his small hands, but the bottles start coming down to the ground with an astonishing rattle. The other children all at once run to the cart and surround the child who now stands petrified and helpless. The children start chanting: "Somebody did wrong! . . ." "I am the only witness. I am the only one who knows his innocence." So he thinks. The milkman rushes over to the cart, pushing the children aside. He quietly moves away, saying to himself, "Forgive me, please forgive me." He is lost in self-accusation, calls himself "the coward." Preoccupied with inveighing against his own cowardice, he walks past his own house.[18]

Arishima and Shiga are alike in that they both try to run away from challenges. The difference is that Shiga would not have stopped to observe the incident and would not have accused himself of having run away. He would not plead forgiveness, for he believed that it is the artist's prerogative to protect himself from exposure to such experiences. Arishima, on the other hand, not only stays but faces the moral choice, feels the weight of it, and bows off. "Okubyōmono" presents a case where a moral decision clearly must be reached, and yet Arishima is terrified by the attendant difficulties and follows a natural inclination to avoid responsibility. Even if a moral act is clearly called for, it will not necessarily lead one to act. Even as Arishima understands the child's fear, he cannot come to his help. The sense of guilt, the constant reflection upon what he ought to have done, haunts him. In his failure to act in such situations, Arishima thinks, he denies himself the occasion to communicate with his social surroundings.

Instinct and Morality: Love as the Social Principle

"In the life of instinct there is no morality," wrote Arishima. But he also knew that instinct could motivate him to act, for "instinct as the source of action never demands effort in man." "This life is necessarily the life of necessity," he continued. "In necessity there are no two ways. Where there are no two ways there is no choice of good and evil. Hence, the life of instinct transcends morality. Freedom is *sein,* it is not *sollen.* Effort is called for only when there is a choice to make. How could there be effort when there is only freedom, the world of *sein?*" Life, Arishima believed, depends not on instinct alone, but on the world of *sollen* as well. Without it, life ceases to have any meaning for him. To act according to one's natural inclination is amoral. "Even within the pattern of life I now lead, responding unconsciously to the outside world, one may find what one might call moral. Yet in these instances, insofar as I am concerned, they are not moral acts. *To be moral, I have to make an effort.*" [19] Here Arishima is much closer to Natsume than he is to the Shirakaba-ha, for he and Natusme are far more pessimistic about the natural instincts of man.

Starting from this assertion, Arishima proceeds to impugn accepted social morality, which according to him, has been confused with conventions. Any society, he contends, expects morality and knowledge to contribute to its own stability. The life of intellect which breeds knowledge and morality is altogether inadequate. "I feel within my life the power of impulse more intensely than that of intellect," of which thought and morality are the products. He then asks: "Shall I sacrifice the impulse in life to society, for society demands above all peace and stability which one's impulse might disturb." "In accordance with the demand of society, shall I sacrifice the potentiality for progress and creativity?" [20]

Arishima's thoughts on the relation between the individual and society recall the views of Ōsugi, except that the cult of violence is absent. "Before the outside world will work on us, the individual self will act on the world outside of the self. That is, not by outside stimuli but by the inevitable impulse of the self, one starts one's life." Using the English term, he calls such a life "impulsive life." "What inflames this impulse in me, I do not know." Arishima is aware that, if man follows impulse, it is possible to be led into vain self-destruction. From the point of view of intellect, he thinks, such an act can appear as merely a stupid fiasco. Indeed, the life based on such acts is not rational. Yet this life will be satisfying to the self. The dilemma, however, is that "the world of free creativity is . . . the world without purpose." He had already proclaimed that an effortless act, as the life of impulse undoubtedly is, cannot be moral.[21]

Trying to provide an end for the impulsive life, Arishima says that love becomes "the categorical imperative for man." "Love seems to deprive us of everything. Strangely, those who can love are deprived and yet lose nothing." He speaks of Dante and Beatrice: "The loneliness of the one whose love was not rewarded is very different from the loneliness of those who have never loved." Impulse is elevated above all else as the basis upon which man can act. But since the impulsive life, though creative and individualistic, has no purpose, Arishima proposes the idea of love as the ultimate principle. Love takes everything away from the one who loves but gives everything as well. Thus, even if one still is left in loneliness, life has been fulfilled.[22]

From this amalgam Arishima seeks to eradicate the dilemma of choice among thought, action, and morality. The aim of the theory of impulse and love had been to bring society and the individual together. "Now let us think of social life with the principle of love as the point of departure. Social life ought to be the extension of the individual life. It is wrong to consider that individual desire and social need always produce disparity. If it had to be maintained that the gulf between the two were unsurpassable, I would rather destroy social life." Some "may worry that, since the impulsive life is motivated solely by the inner self, it may not be conformable to social life." "If the idea of the impulsive life is correctly understood, however, it will not be open to such a criticism." The correct understanding of the impulsive life means that love is the regulative principle. Society, like individuals, should be regulated by this principle. If society interferes with the individual acting according to this deal, "society ought to be unconditionally altered and adjusted." [23]

In theory, Arishima tries to draw a distinction between impulse and animal-like instinct. Impulse is conscious of itself. Its very consciousness leads man to recognize love as the basis for human action. Through impulse the individual can achieve fulfillment not in the self alone, but also by translating such a principle into the life of society. "Man moves to embrace love. Where his love acts, all that is outside of him becomes a part of himself." "His own development and perfection" become identical with society's.[24]

So finally Arishima has returned to society—with one reservation. Although he believes that "society must be changed," he does not "dare to explain the manner in which a social reform must be carried out in conformity with the argument I have presented." Furthermore, he is still wary of asserting his new social ideals and writes, quoting Nietzsche: "If there should be a case where I might be burnt to death for persisting in my own ideas, I would try to avoid it." He adds, however, that "if I should be burnt for having changed my idea, I would accept the fate willingly, for this would deserve death." If the public will not listen to him, Arishima would willingly remain silent or would acquiesce. He exhibits a kind of masochistic heroism. It is not that he sees no progress in ideas: "We cannot bind ourselves to ready-made ideas. For the development of life results in changes of ideas." [25] He is typically concerned with his own intellectual honesty instead of its effect on society.

It is remarkable that Arishima often speaks enviously of those who persist in their own ideas even to the point of trespassing on the private lives of others. In discussing the socialists,

Arishima compares himself, as one paralyzed into inaction, with those who can act with passion:

> As I tried to be the observer of the world, I could no longer act . . . The emptiness and helplessness which Hamlet must have experienced went through me. Then I understood the minds of those who believe in isms. At times ism disturbs others, but is fatally necessary for them to act.

Arishima, however, finds out that "I have no ism that could be guarded by my own life." [26] This wonderful absence of fanaticism unfortunately paralyzes him. Not only does he hesitate to insist on his ideals, but even apologizes for his "monologue." "All this is a small plea uttered by one who is ignorant of philosophy, sociology, science, and religion." There is in Arishima none of Faust's demonic pretension, and the complete absence of any such profound ambition makes him again hesitate to act even as he discovers the principle of impulsive life based on love—that principle which dissolves the tension between thought and action and should bring about a reconciliation between the lonely intellectual and society.

The "One Manifesto" Controversy and the Self-Execution of a Bourgeois

Although Arishima was not hopeful that others would heed his "plea," he himself tried to act according to his new philosophy. In 1922, the year before he committed suicide, he dramatically surrendered to his tenant farmers the land he had inherited from his father. By that time he had come to be strongly influenced by socialism and to believe in the common ownership of means of production.[27] It was his social conscience that led him to embrace a view of society not very far removed from that of the Marxists. Because he had been versed in Marxism, he was acutely conscious of the limitations of his individual acts.

According to Arishima's own explanation of what prompted him to give up his land, he had come to question the good of private property as early as 1903. "I studied in the United States between 1903 and 1907. I came . . . to be skeptical about private property through reading the works of such thinkers as Kropotkin." Also, he thought that "contrary to the popularly held opinion that property deepens the affection between parents and children," the consideration of private property more often than not makes such a family relationship into an oppressive chain. Soon after he returned to Japan, he suggested to his father that he give up the land. Although he had known that "it would make his father genuinely blessed," he "decided to withdraw the proposal, for it would pain his father meaninglessly." At the time of his father's death in 1916, Arishima was financially independent. He "found his profession in literature, and this prompted his decision . . . to give up all that had interfered with literary activities." [28]

Originally he wanted to call the emancipated property "Communist Farm." But because of various pressures, he had to withdraw this original name in favor of "Community Farm." Elsewhere he ridicules those who subjected him to this pressure, and says that it was like calling the pacifism of Buddhism right but the pacificism of socialism wrong. Afraid for the farm's future once it was left to the care of the tenant farmers, inexperienced in the cooperative form of farm management, he asked a specialist to draw up a plan to run it. He was soon angered that the legal system as it then existed was inadequate for protecting such ventures as his.[29]

Arishima took a pessimistic view of the farm's future. In fact, the final paragraph of this short note sounds distressingly irresponsible: "This farm is a conglomeration of the ignorant ones surrounded by the wolflike capitalists. I shall be satisfied with finding out that no matter how perfect the plan, unless the surroundings were also communistic, the practice of the spirit of communism will collapse under its own weight. I do not think that the outcome of this plan is essential." [30] Coming from one who had claimed that society ought to be changed so that it would adjust to the creative life of man, the note is an astonishing whimper and its tone would have been inconceivable to such a man as Mushakōji.[31] Earlier Arishima had seen the limits of the naturalists' asocial individualism. He reconciled man to society through the idea of love—the force that will unify man and society and enable the individual to act creatively for society's progress. It was not the life of the individual, but the nature of society that was to change. Why, then, do we find such a sense of helplessness in Arishima's decision to release his property? Arishima gives his own answer twice, once in his response to Mushakōji's New Village movement and then in his famous "Sengen hitotsu" (One manifesto).

In these two articles and in the intellectual controversies that followed, we see how far removed these two well-meaning intellectuals were from the actual arena of politics. Above all, however, we see the mentality of the Japanese intellectuals who were soon to witness or to be absorbed into the intellectual tyranny of Marxian socialism during the 1920s.

In the July 1918 issue of *Chūōkōron* (The central review), Arishima wrote an article in the form of a letter to Mushakōji who was just starting the New Village Movement in southern Japan. The farm was to be run on communistic principles and took in only those who manifested a strong interest in the venture. Arishima's article reveals his skepticism about the project. Although he quite correctly predicted its eventual failure, he also felt that such a venture, even if it had to fail, had its own raison d'être in history.

"[In history] when an old form [of life] is to be replaced by a new, man goes through a crisis like the moment of his birth." Whether one likes it or not, in order to maintain "genuinely an active [creative] life, one has to go through this danger in order to open up a new path." Arishima felt that this was such a moment, "the moment of progress." "One hundred years have passed since the time of Owen and St. Simon. Although it is said that only fifty years have passed since we moved from the age of feudalism to that of capitalism, because we accepted the ready-made economic system, only within those fifty years all the ill symptoms of capitalism as well as its goodness have become manifest." The moment is ripe for a radical change.

But both Arishima and Mushakōji were "born into [material] comfort," the very creation of the system now to be discarded. "We often feel pained," continues Arishima, "as we have to subtract from our own work a part of our talent; our material advantage is a handicap." "Even those like ourselves who have profited from the capitalist system feel this way. It is easy to speculate on the feelings of the stepchildren of this system . . . There must be something wrong." [32]

Furthermore, "our parliament does not represent the will of the people, rather it represents the will of wealth." It is not only parliament that Arishima regards with such a sense of hopelessness. On the subject of war and peace, he remarks: "War and peace are manipulated by a small minority group called capitalists." He adds that, even if authority tries to suppress the expression of such a sentiment, eventually the voice of the people "will palpably cry out with a tone a thousand times more powerful than this letter [to Mushakōji]." According to Arishima, the cause of the evil lies in the capitalist system, in which "both capitalists and workers are subject to money." "How could one find the dignity of the individual or genuine freedom?" In posing this question, he proposes not a concrete solution but merely a "heroic gesture," heroic in that he anticipates that actions of protest will inevitably result in defeat.

Arishima imposes a particular role on the artists to make a breakthrough, as it were. "According to my own personal view," he notes in the letter, "the artists are forced to be the reformers rather than the eulogizers [of life]. From the time of slavery to the period of feudalism, religion joined its hand with that of authority and won the hearts of the people. From the feudal period to the age of the capitalist system, science dominated the basis of the trend of thought." As for science, however, "by its own confession, it never had the power to satisfy the whole existence of man. Nineteenth-century culture that tried to conquer nature through the power of science has already exposed its weaknesses as well as its achievement. What can supplement the deficiency of this state is art." It is not that the quality of contemporary art is higher than that of previous centuries, but that we have to rely on the artists "who have the strong feeling for the future." For art alone can provide us with spiritual motives and visions.

If the artists alone can foresee the future, are they to carry out social changes? They must try. But Arishima expresses a despondent view as to its success. "To be honest . . . the capitalist society that surrounds you will desperately fight a cruel fight." Still, he exhorts Mushakōji to courage, for failure can be eventually turned into success. At this historical point, an artist finds himself in a dilemma; he knows the taste of the future but his attempt is destined to fail, for the bourgeois realities still exist. But Arishima feels that this should not discourage the artist from acting, even though he himself articulates the inability of a bourgeois artist to act in a far sharper form than anyone else among his contemporaries. "Although it is ridiculous to promise what I will do in the future, with the arrival of an opportune moment I too plan to carry out a program resembling what you are trying to do now. Then I intend to fail completely." [33] Although this at the time was only a vague promise, Arishima carried it out soon after his father died. He consistently maintained this note of pessimism. "I shall be fully satisfied by merely finding out that even under perfect planning such a project [running a communistic farm] will be impossible to carry out." [34]

This self-crucifixion of Arishima's is not a political act but, as he himself admits, a product of the life of impulse and of an artist's sensitivity. Love, both as the content and the purpose of the life of impulse, seems to tolerate irrationalism, to forgive the failure of one's social act because of one's goodwill, to deprive the individual of his ability to manipulate the given situation, and above all to breed social fatalism.

It should not surprise us at all that to such a mind the Weltanschauung of Marxism has an irresistible charm. Indeed, in Marxism thought and action do form a harmonious whole. The source of the agonizing conflict—among morality, thought, and action—can be removed altogether through the individual's understanding of the need of a particular moment in history—history that moves with irresistible certainty toward the world of total harmony. What surprises us, however, as we peruse Arishima's later writings, is that he uses the Marxist interpretation of history to excuse his social impotence, his feeling of helplessness vis-à-vis Japanese society.

In the January 1922 issue of *Kaizō* (Reform), Arishima published the essay "Sengen hitotsu" (One manifesto). Here he argues that the future of Japan lies with the working class and goes on to criticize those bourgeois intellectuals who are trying to participate in the emergence of the working class. First of all, he observes that "the movement to solve the social problems is gradually handed over to the working class from the control of so-called scholars and thinkers." This, he remarks, is the most remarkable phenomenon of "the fusion of thought and actual life," a fusion that "always brings about in the purest form a unity in human life." The scholars and thinkers thought that they could speak for the workers who, in turn, "during the period of argument" relied on them as their spokesmen. Arishima judges this faith in the intellectuals' ability to improve the plight of the working class as a superstition, "from which now the workers are gradually being liberated." This movement "no sophistry can frustrate." "Neither the authority of the state nor the aura of scholarship . . . any longer can stifle this fact which was predestined to appear." [35]

The workers would have been brought to an awareness of their own power "without either Kropotkin or Marx. Perhaps even they might have better actualized their ability and independence without them." What then is the primary contribution of Marx and Kropotkin? They teach us "resignation." "Where can we find the relationship between *Capital* and the working class? The merit of Marx is most pronounced in the point of forcing those who, like Marx, were the graduates of universities, the very product of capitalism, to close their eyes in resignation. The working-class people are moving toward the direction whither they are to go regardless of the existence of these intellectuals." Those who claim to have the knowledge for liberating the working class are "the bastard children of the workers and the ruling class." The honest and timid Arishima cannot be so hypocritical. "I would never be able to become a member of the working class, nor do I want to be one. Nor can I commit the hypocrisy of either defending, working, or speaking for the working class." "I remain forever a product of the present ruling class." "My primary responsibility is to appeal to those who are not of the working class." "If there should be any one who is not a member of the working class, yet thinks himself able to contribute to the lot of the workers, he would be most presumptuous. The workers would be merely disturbed by the vain efforts of such pretenders." [36]

In the same essay, Arishima quotes his conversation with Kawakami Hajime, then professor of economics at Kyoto Imperial University. Kawakami tells Arishima that "It might be excusable, if some one said, 'Since I cannot do anything, I am dabbling with art and philosophy. Please leave me alone.' Yet I would be contemptuous of those who are proud of being artists or philosophers, for they do not understand in what kind of historical period they now live. If they are immersed in art or philosophy knowingly, they are the impotent, belonging to the past, left out of the present." [37] This comment by Kawakami was undoubtedly directed against the nonchalant and arrogant intellectuals of Taishō Japan. Arishima's rejoinder is that there is no substantial difference between those artists and philosophers whom Kawakami holds in contempt as imbecilic and the socialist scholars who have not tasted the genuine life of the workers. Kawakami's reply that he has "always loved art and would have liked to work in the world of art, but that an inner need forced him to take a different path [to become a student of social problems]," draws a distinction between intellectuals of Arishima's type and Kawakami himself, who was soon to participate in the socialist movement, leaving the university behind.[38]

Reactions to Arishima's testimony to his own social impotence were varied. In the new year's *Jiji shimpō* (The daily news), the author-critic Hirotsu Kazuo wrote a comment on Arishima's article entitled "Arishima Takeo's Punctilious Manner of Thinking." Hirotsu's essential argument was not unlike that of many other literary figures: "Generally speaking, so-called literature ought not to belong exclusively either to the bourgeoisie or to the proletariat." Our minds, according to the author, are capable of penetrating into varied forms of literature regardless of whether they be ancient, modern, Eastern, Western, aristocratic, or common. Man has the ability to understand the literature dealing with the life he cannot experience. Hirotsu concludes that "to introduce the linguistic distinction between the proletariat and the bourgeoisie into the delicate realm of art is too superficial." [39]

Arishima published in *Asahi* an immediate reply to Hirotsu's criticism. He starts out by saying that he did not mention that within art there is an element that transcends both time and classes, "because it was too palpable." Then he proceeds to divide artists into three categories. First there are those artists whose total life is devoted to the pure world of art, regardless of what takes place around them. Arishima mentions Izumi Kyōka as an example of this group. The second group comprises those "who have to establish some rational relationship between their life and the life surrounding them. Otherwise they feel that they cannot create art itself." Third there are those who "try to utilize their art for their life." Arishima naturally classifies himself in the second category of artists, "who suffer from the problem of trying to maintain a proper relationship between art and their own life." For those who belong to the first category, "what I proposed makes no sense . . . [But] I would respect such artists, who could devote themselves purely to artistic creativity." Arishima writes that he cannot be contemptuous of them, for "any period ought to deal with these artists kindly." But he still insists that the art soon to emerge will be created by the thought and activities of the genuine proletariat.[40]

A month after the publication of "One Manifesto," the critic Katagami Noboru wrote an article in response to some of the problems Arishima had raised, entitled "Problems of Class Art." Here Katagami notes that Arishima had revealed in the manifesto (of which he says, "I dislike the ostentation of the title") "a certain honesty, seriousness, and a kind of defensive sensitivity." "Under the present circumstances [the rise of the proletarian movement] his is one attitude." Katagami then argues that the proletariat in Japan has not yet created its own art forms. Taking it for granted, however, that the proletariat will eventually preside over a classless society, he predicts that, with the coming of the new age, art for the first time will transcend all classes. "Proletarian art will destroy the existing forms of art. The destruction, however, will take the form of a new, free, and honest creation. Art is a constant process of creativity. Without creativity, therefore, there should be no regeneration of art, nor will there be the destruction of the old." Katagami concludes that until the final achievement of a proletarian art, the bourgeoisie will have a part to play in the history of art, either in terms of insistence on their own life or in terms of the pain, anxiety, and contradictions born of the conscious negation of their own historical existence.[41] In any case, Katagami has removed the artists from the actual arena of the social process, and while admitting the relationship between social forms and art, he endows the category of creativity with an independent life of its own. Within its own process art will change, remaking the old and the present, creating the new. Yet until a genuine proletarian art is created, the bourgeoisie have their legitimate place in the history of art, even if this place will soon be abolished.

The Marxian socialist Sakai Toshihiko writes in *Zenei* (Vanguard) that Arishima's manifesto is "the desperate flight of a good-natured humanist." Sakai argues that, within the revolutionary movement of the proletariat, there should be no distinction between the intellectuals and the proletariat. The intellectuals, regardless of their class background, should be able to discern the historical need of the moment. They can even provide the ignorant workers with a strategy for actualizing the potentialities of the movement. For this purpose, they have a significant role to play in the unfolding of history. This is a straight Marxist interpretation of the intellectuals' role in such a transitory period as they envisioned the Taishō era to be.

In regard to Arishima's observation that the proletariat was gradually forsaking the leadership hitherto provided by the intellectuals, Sakai thinks there are three ways in which the intellectuals concerned with the plight of the suppressed class would react to "the betrayal of the proletariat." What he does here is to subdivide the second category of intellectuals in Arishima's argument—those whose conscience could not rest until they had defined their relation to art and society. The first group reacts in irritation against the defiant workers, whom they consider ignorant and crude. The adherents of this group would establish their own image of utopia and resign themselves to their own world. Sakai criticizes Mushakōji's New Village movement as one exemplar of this first group. The second group, where Sakai places Yoshino Sakuzō, tries to inculcate middle-class values into the working class. "They preach the mistake of class antagonism, and exhort compromise. While they present themselves as righteous humanists, in fact, they are the defenders of . . . the status quo." [42] The third group recognizes the position of the proletariat but takes no action. It pretends to carry out its assigned responsibilities, but these include no tasks relevant to the workers. While Sakai criticizes all these groups, he says that Arishima is typical of the third one in its reaction to the phenomenon of the proletariat drifting away from the intellectuals' leadership. One pronounced characteristic of Sakai's argument is his detestation of the idea of compromise. Compromise corrupts the potentiality of the working class. Anyone who tries to advocate the idea of harmony between labor and management is considered a "defector." Here again we detect the same anti-parliamentary mentality which prevailed among the anarcho-syndicalists.

This emotional and intellectual certitude, which gives Sakai's article a tone of arrogance, altogether fades away as we proceed to an article by another socialist, Kawakami Hajime, who at that time had not yet committed himself to Marxism. In this essay, "Individualist and Socialist," Kawakami attributes to one's individual temperament the difference between those who commit themselves to an art devoid of social content and those who are devoted to the welfare of society. In this pluralistic attitude of Kawakami's, there is dignity in place of arrogance. He compares Rembrandt and Kropotkin, whom he regards as representing the two types of life commitment, and he eulogizes both. He suggests, however, that although "it is the individual temperament that finally determines one's final commitment, each period has its own need." He sees the Taishō period as a time when consideration for the material welfare of society and of the individual should be given primary consideration.[43] Faithful to what he considered the need of his time, Kawakami left the social comfort of his position to enter the communist movement of the 1920s.[44] It is a tragedy that he came to think he knew the one solution to all the problems of society. Thereafter, once he came to accept the view that all would be well if a certain view of history could be put into practice, he could no longer tolerate diversity. No other human behavior, no other pattern of thought or feeling, could find a justifiable place. Compromise became a sin committed against history and man. Diversity became a sign of illness. There was one vision, one ideal: the monolithic reconciliation of the self to history and society.

Arishima's response to these criticisms (which ranged from the Marxist rejection of his "flight," through the invocation of literary autonomy, to Kawakami's sympathetic observation) was dramatized in his giving up his farm to the tenants. He had already promised in his letter to Mushakōji that sometime soon he would act in a way resembling the latter's venture in his New Village movement. He also wrote that he foresaw "its grand failure." To Arishima, the act was no more than a confession of his own social impotence, a confession made both to his own conscience and to society. The agony he experienced in the knowledge of the futility of his action is apparent in his note, "From a private farm to a Communist Farm." "My act will end in vain. Yet at least it will show that capitalism is so strong as to suggest that, even as I surrender my private farm to the tenants, the latter could not become happy [within capitalism]. I shall be content with the tribulation of proving how stubborn and evil capitalism is." [45] This defeatism of Arishima's was born of his search for a total solution to the evils of society. He found this in Marxism, which, in turn, removed him from the arena of society.

In his attempt to give the individual a part to play in society, Arishima depreciated the role of intellect. He equated intellect and its products, knowledge and morality, with inaction. Thus Arishima implicitly recognized the meaning of irrationality which could compel man to action. He found the unity of thought and action in the Marxist interpretation of history. Marx, however, gave no place to the irrationality of man or to his impulses: the individual was to be motivated to action by a correct understanding of history. To him, Kierkegaardian existentialism within history, another valid derivation of Hegel, was merely an ideology, confusing the direction of man's action. But Arishima, on the one hand accepting the Marxist interpretation of history, on the other advanced a philosophy of life more like that of Kierkegaard or Bergson. He failed to combine the two, however, even though the merging of the two points of view is not at all unique.

Finally, we are left with the feeling that Arishima made a complete circle—a circle that in no place was tangent to the realities of politics. Starting out with the realization of the limitations inherent in the naturalistic emancipation of the individual, he proceeded to search out the means by which the individual could reconcile himself to society. This was found in his idea of love as the end purpose of the impulsive life, the source of the creative action of man. Having once separated the individual from society, Arishima asked himself what ought to be the proper relation between the two. In the first place, he felt that society ought to adjust itself to the true needs of the individual. Second, he believed that the purposes of the individual's life and the life of society should be identical. In suggesting the desirability of remolding society according to the individual's needs, he revealed his total distrust of society in its existing form. The change to be made had no basis within the present world. Arishima altogether alienated himself from the process of historical change. Here again, he was isolated from the movement of society as well as from what he considered to be the genuinely creative element in his society, the working class. He looked down, albeit with a sense of sympathy, on indifferent and arrogant intellectuals, especially those who were working for the proletariat. Thus, in seeking a solution, Arishima returned to the point he had started from. The solution he found only intensified his sense of loneliness and helplessness, which no longer was an inarticulate awareness but an explored certitude.

VII / *Akutagawa Ryūnosuke:*
The Literature of Defeatism

Although Arishima denied himself the right to participate in the formation of a better future society, he thought it inevitable that there would soon be an ideal society where all man's aspirations would be fulfilled. Akutagawa Ryūnosuke (1892–1927) was one of those intellectuals who did not even once entertain such a hope for man and society. He was certain that to hope for freedom and happiness was an illusion, and was brutally realistic about portraying the chaos of life. It was neither freedom nor happiness that Akutagawa tried to find in life and art, but a "place to rest" in the midst of this burdensome life. His aim was, therefore, far more socially modest than those of the naturalists and the Shirakaba-ha, and its failure far more personally tragic.[1]

Natsume Sōseki, Mori Ōgai, and Arishima Takeo had died during the preceding decade. In literary excellence and intellectual scope no one seemed to come forward to replace them. Furthermore, comments such as "the established authors of Taishō Japan have altogether disappeared from the world of literature" were ubiquitous in literary journals.[2] Shiga Naoya fell silent. Tayama Katai turned to writing historical novels of no major significance. Shimazaki Tōson became less prolific. In retrospect, we find that many fine works were written by so-called bourgeois writers during the years close to the death of Akutagawa.[3] What characterized the years following the great earthquake of 1923, however, was the conspicuous emergence of Marxist literature. When Akutagawa committed suicide in 1927, the Marxists argued that the chaotic and nightmarish quality of his literary works expressed the dying gasp of bourgeois art and that his death symbolically became its epitaph. It is not hard to see how the interpretation suggested itself. The appeal and strength of Marxist literature were such that Tanizaki Junichirō, one of the able writers who remained outside the proletarian literary movement, calls it a tyranny.[4]

Perhaps it was a tyranny. For many, however, it was a benevolent one. Arishima flirted with it, although in the end he came to believe that this, too, denied him salvation. To both Arishima and Akutagawa it appeared that the search for individualism as carried out by the naturalists and the Shirakaba-ha intellectuals had made a chaos of the world; the intellectual and artistic attempt to articulate and practice individualism had never alleviated the pain and anxiety of life but had actually intensified them. Neither was yet willing to accept the conclusion (which the Marxists then welcomed) that if there is ever to be another cosmos, individualism in the realm of art and speculation must be sacrificed.

Both were conscious of such a possibility. Arishima's abiding concern with his relation to society led him to probe Marxism. Akutagawa, on the other hand, was at first interested in art itself and its power to save him. When he came to realize that even art could not satisfy him, he turned his attention to religion, particularly to Christianity. His last work was on the life of Christ: "The life of Christ will forever move us." Yet this was not because Christ could save us but because his life represented a grand failure. "The life of Christ is the ladder to ascend from the earth to heaven, which is now mercilessly broken in the middle." Since everything has already been said about the life of Christ, "We still remain standing in the vastness of life. There cannot be anything but sleep [death] that would give us peace." [5] So Akutagawa chose death in the end; others claimed that had he been courageous enough to commit himself to Marxism, he might have been able to escape the "pain of the nonpredictability of life."

Perhaps he might have. Yet one wonders whether Akutagawa was not actually more courageous in refusing to accept the all-embracing consolation of Marxism. From the life of Christ he had learned, not a hope for salvation, but the message that "unless we are satisfied with being animals, we, the sons of man, cannot find a place to rest." [6] "All the naturalists cruelly dissect the reality of life," he said. He, like Arishima, thought that there was something beautiful behind this reality—"something that tries perpetually to transcend itself." [7] Akutagawa's legacy, then, is not so much a finished product as it is the very courage with which he refused to accept the unrelenting conclusion implied by the failure of freedom: that the individual ought to be sacrificed in the interests of a better society.

Commenting on the literature of 1919, Akutagawa writes that the Taishō authors sought three different objectives: truth, beauty, and goodness. Truth was the aim of the naturalists, beauty that of hedonists like Tanizaki and Nagai, and goodness that of the Shirakaba-ha writers. Akutagawa maintained that the younger writers who came after these schools were trying to harmonize the three goals, which had previously been sought separately. This statement, made three years after Akutagawa's first literary success, does express a basic concern of the younger generation of writers.[8] For Akutagawa, however, the harmony of the three objectives was never attainable. His art possesses no symphonic grandeur; nor does it have complex themes. In form it is like a well-composed piece of baroque music. Each word and each line are meticulously calculated and balanced. In craftmanship and sophistication only the best of his predecessors can equal him. As one goes beyond the well-ordered harmony conveyed by his writings, one recognizes the presence of a highly complex mind. Beneath the stylistic harmony, Akutagawa sustains the theme that man can never escape the hopeless chaos of life. What makes him an unforgettable figure in modern Japanese intellectual history is not only his artistic excellence but also, and perhaps primarily, the sensitive commentaries he made on the life and society he could never escape, even through art. To understand Akutagawa's final failure to attain the harmony he sought, we must consider his views on society, on life, and above all on art.

The Lost Freedom

To Akutagawa, society is no more than an arbitrary conglomeration of men and women. The prototype of all human tragedies is found at the moment of birth, when the relationship of the child to his parents is established.[9] Family becomes the source of all pain and unhappiness, not because it is "a traditional yoke" but simply because it is a human relationship. In *Kappa*, a satirical novel in which all but one of the characters are *kappas* (mythical amphibious animal of Japanese legend), Akutagawa ridicules the family as an institution. "According to Tokku [a *kappa* poet], there is nothing more foolish than the ordinary life of a *kappa*." "The institution of the family," continues Tokku, "is most foolish. Parents, children, husbands, wives, brothers, and sisters have as their sole pleasure the pain they give to each other." Akutagawa believed that although society suffocated the individual through its insistence on conformity, the individual could never successfully defy social convention. He lets Mag, a *kappa* philosopher, proclaim that "the wisest life one can lead is to live without breaking the customs of his generation, while thoroughly despising them." [10] Seeing the ineffective outcome of the naturalists' war against social decency, Akutagawa had pointed out trenchantly that Shimazaki was a hypocrite. Frequently the naturalists did not recognize their own fear of society, whereas Akutagawa was fully conscious of his and often cynically acknowledged it.[11]

How does he then explain his antagonism toward society? What makes life painful, according to Akutagawa, is above all its "lawlessness." "Life is more hellish than the genuine Hell." He writes that even the hell of Buddhism or that of Dante has its own laws; punishment and agony are regulated occurrences in accordance with one's sin. "Yet the torment of this life has no such simplicity." "It is difficult for anyone to adjust himself to such an anarchic world." [12]

The unpredictability of life is a common theme in Akutagawa's works. It already appears in his first two short stories, "Hana" (The nose), and "Imogayu" (Yam gruel). (It was these stories which attracted Natsume's attention, and his praise soon pushed Akutagawa to the forefront of Japanese literary circles.) They are both based on the theme that when one's deepest desire is fulfilled, something unexpected happens to destroy one's happiness. In "Hana," the hero's deformed nose is miraculously healed, but then it invites even more scornful comments. In "Imogayu," a lower samurai longed to eat as much yam gruel as he could, but once this desire was fulfilled, he could no longer enjoy the experience.

The same theme recurs in Akutagawa's famous novel *Jigoku hen* (The hell screen), about a proud court artist, Yoshihide, who is commissioned by his lord to paint a screen depicting a scene in hell. It is Yoshihide's morbid request that a woman be burned in a court carriage, which would serve as the model for the central part of the painting. Once the request has been carried out, he finds his only daughter chained in the carriage. He paints the screen and it is a masterpiece, the culmination of all his artistic activities. But what he has created cannot compensate for his loss, and in the end he kills himself. Akutagawa could never find a compromise between the ordinary life of this world and the world of art, so totally and exclusively dedicated to the creation of a masterpiece that the artist will even allow his daughter to be sacrificed in order to achieve this end. The artist's predicament—the tension between his ties to a despised society and his commitment to art which pulls him away from society—closely reflects Akutagawa's observation that real life cannot give us peace. Even in the moment of the fulfillment of

one's most deeply abiding wishes, one experiences an unexpected disillusionment. The unpredictability of life is the inevitable pity of it.[13]

But if Yoshihide was committed to art, as undoubtedly he
was, why did he kill himself? Why did Akutagawa kill him,
especially at the moment of his artistic triumph? Moreover,
Yoshihide could have blamed his lord, for it was the latter's
intention rather than that of the artist himself to sacrifice the
daughter. Nevertheless, Yoshihide hanged himself, for "That
man could not bear to live on without his only daughter." [14]
The protagonist of *Jigoku hen* represents a character frequently
encountered in Akutagawa's work: the man who cannot be
happy, who is eccentric, lonely, proud, and misanthropic, but
who is all too human in emotions to be totally isolated. Art
failed both the protagonist of the *Jigoku hen* and Akutagawa
himself.

While both the naturalists and the Shirakaba-ha tried either
to identify art with life or life with art, Akutagawa consciously
tried to separate them. In a short sketch entitled "Kentai"
(Boredom), he writes:

> He was walking through a pampas grass field with a uni-
> versity student. [He says to the student], "You still must
> have a strong desire to live." "Yes. But you must, too
> . . . " "On the contrary, I don't have it, although I have
> the desire for creativity." This was his genuine feeling. In
> point of fact he had lost his interest in life. [The student
> replies], "The desire for creativity, too, after all, is the will
> to live." He did not answer.[15]

He had felt that life is like "an Olympic game run by the
insane." "Those who find this ridiculous should remove themselves from it. Suicide is one certain method. But if one decides
to remain in the arena, one should fight unafraid of wounds."
Akutagawa wanted to leave the arena. He could not believe
that life and society could be remolded to please him. "No

matter how often we repeat revolutions, man's life must remain depressing." To reduce material poverty does not necessarily lead to peace. To attain peace, we have to curtail our spiritual wants as well. The remedy proposed by the socialist writers could not have satisfied him. "Unless human nature changes, a perfect utopia is not possible. If we changed our human nature, what we had hitherto considered a utopia would cease to be one." Above all, "we never can do what we want to do. We do only what we can do. It is true not only with us individuals but with society. Probably even God could not create the world according to his own desire." [16]

In one of the well-known literary controversies of modern Japan, the "plot controversy," Akutagawa maintained that in literature he was "more interested in something other than the plot or story." [17] This statement was a response to Tanizaki's earlier remark that "he cannot be interested in stories only with truths." [18] To interest Tanizaki, a story had to contain falsification. When Akutagawa insisted that "there is no artistic value in the interesting quality of a plot per se," [19] Tanizaki retorted that by an interesting plot he meant "beauty of structure" or "architectural excellence." [20] For Akutagawa, too, life itself could never have a clear plot or theme.[21] Tanizaki wrote that creating literature involves falsifying life, and Akutagawa could not disagree with this. But Akutagawa would have tried to portray the chaos of life in his art, believeing that this alone would give his art intrinsic value. It is ironic that what gives apparent beauty to Akutagawa's work is exactly the quality of art and literature which Tanizaki insisted on finding in a work of art. There was no doubt, however, in Akutagawa's mind that life, in and of itself, has neither a plot nor a captivating strength.

If Akutagawa wished to leave the insane arena of life, did he believe that he could find rest in the world of art? Could he accomplish his aim by resigning himself to artistic creativity alone? Like Icarus, he felt that he had the gift of flight, and for him art was merely "a pair of artificial wings." Akutagawa wrote in *Aru ahō no isshō* (The life of a fool), "From Anatole France he moved to eighteenth-century philosophers. He avoided Rousseau, perhaps because the side of him which was easily excited so resembled Rousseau. Instead of the passionate Rousseau he chose the coldly intellectual author of *Candide*." "Although life has ceased to be hopeful for him, Voltaire supplied him with a pair of artificial wings." He left behind him "both the pleasures and sorrows of life. He flew straight up . . . dropping ironies and smiles upon the shabby towns. He kept flying [as if he had forgotten] the ancient Greek who fell into the sea when his wings were burned by the sun." [22] Like Shimazaki, Akutagawa was haunted by the thought of the insanity which was in both their families, and he relied on intellect rather than on passion or, as he put it, reason as opposed to emotion.

This is an aesthetic interpretation of reason. Reason for Akutagawa is not Cartesian reason, which has mathematical order and serves as the basis for scientific inquiry; nor is it that reason which serves as the regulating principle of life. Rather it is that which gives aesthetic order to the chaotic life depicted by artists. Life and society remain chaotic, but reason can make them comprehensible. Only the reason of art can approximate and give form to the pulverized fragments of life. Akutagawa's reason beautifies pain without reducing it; it lacks remedial powers.

Akutagawa sees the limitations of reason thus conceived. Although his recourse to Voltaire is serious, he ridicules him as well: "I am at times contemptuous of Voltaire. If we relied exclusively on reason, it would be to add another full damnation to our existence." Akutagawa felt that Voltaire never recognized the other dimensions of man, instinct and emotion. The intrinsic optimism of Voltaire's philosophy distresses him: "Look at the happiness of the author of *Candide*, intoxicated by world-wide praise!" [23] This is no accurate evaluation of Voltaire, but it indicates Akutagawa's image of him. "In the final analysis," writes Akutagawa, "what reason taught me was its own impotence." 24 It remains a pair of artificial wings which assist a temporary flight from "this shabby world." Yet every man, even the artist himself, is forever chained to that world.

If reason is thought to give artistic form to man's experiences, art simultaneously deprives him of his desire to act. In *Bungeitekina, amarini bungeitekina* (Artistic, all too artistic), Akutagawa writes: "The more artistic art becomes, the more it steals from man his passion for action." "Art has a spellbinding charm . . . It has the power to castrate us." "If we come under the influence of art, we cannot possibly become the sons of Mars." In describing art's power to rob man of the capacity for action, however, Akutagawa is not suggesting that it will finally give us release from the trivialities of life. Although art may paralyze us, it will not give us lasting peace. Since this is all that Akutagawa expects from art, since art allows him to enjoy only temporary repose, he naturally feels an underlying hostility toward those who have found peace in the world of art. He writes that "although Heine could never beget the land of calm enlightenment and bowed humbly to Goethe, he confessed his dissatisfaction with the healthy wholeness of Goethe's world." 25 Akutagawa cannot understand how one can find true peace in art. The world of Goethe, which in the words of Nietzsche knows of neither fatigue nor rebels, is alien to him, and he envies it.26 At the same time, however, he is contemptuous of the effort to produce totality from the self; having given up the possibility of order in life, he finds it an infinitely naive and altogether hopeless venture. His experiences had taught him that such an attempt would only be self-deception.

It follows from this that Akutagawa was skeptical toward those who found peace in art, as well as toward those artists, the socialist writers in particular, who looked so enviously at the passion for action. He believed that "the socialist authors chose a wrong weapon." 27 If art castrates man and deprives him of his potency to act, it is a contradiction to expect art to serve as a motive for action. Akutagawa ridicules the socialist authors: "If all novelists have to paint life according to Marx's dialectical materialism, all poets ought to praise nature according to Copernicus's heliocentric theory. But to say that the earth rotates certain degrees, instead of saying 'the sun sets in the west,' is not necessarily more beautiful." [28]

In Akutagawa we see a prime example of that literary phenomenon to which T. S. Eliot has applied the term, "disassociation of sensibility," meaning the separation of intellect and emotion. The naturalists made an attempt, albeit unsuccessful, to subject emotional experiences to intellectual or scientific analysis and, at times, even entertained the hope of remedying the pain they experienced as they tried to express their liberation from social fetters.[29] The Shirakaba-ha writers made no such distinction and naively believed in the final reconcilability of the two. Akutagawa, however, was acutely aware of the disparity between intellect and emotion—hence the Faustian agony of finding himself altogether dissatisfied with learning was very real to him. Afraid of his own emotion, he relied exclusively on the intellect in his literary works. His art has a perfection of form which appears altogether incongruous in conjunction with the lawlessness of his subject matter. While relying on intellect or reason as the only means of giving one's experience artistic form, Akutagawa was desperately conscious of its limitations; he hid his emotions. "We desire to rationalize experience because it is devoid of rationality."

To depict life as it is experienced—the literary ideal of the naturalists—was not Akutagawa's aim. Yet, even though he wrote that "life does not equal even one line of Baudelaire's poetry," he was aware of his inseparable ties to society. In his posthumously published *Anchū montō* (The dialogue in darkness), he wrote: [30]

Voice: You are a poet and an artist. All things are allowed to you.

> Akutagawa: I am a poet and an artist. Yet, at the same time I am a particle in society. It is no wonder that I have to carry the cross.

Then the Voice asks him: "Are you, too, afraid of society?" and Akutagawa answers: "Who does not fear society?" The Voice suggests that he "trample on both good and evil," to which Akutagawa replies: "I am not a superman. We, all of us, are not supermen. Only Zarathustra was a superman." Then the Voice says to Akutagawa (who speaks of suicide as a way to escape life): "Look at Wilde who was in prison for three years. He says that 'to commit suicide without good reason is to yield to society.'" The same Voice tells him: "You have forgotten your ego. Respect your own individuality and despise the masses." "I cannot despise the masses," answers Akutagawa.[31] Elsewhere he had written: "One should not be proud of the discovery of the stupidity of the people. But it is something to be proud of to discover that he is one of them."[32] "Shakespeare, Goethe, or Chikamatsu will eventually fade away. But that which gave them birth, the great masses, will not disappear."[33]

Then the Voice argues that he is only "suffering from the present social institutions." To this Akutagawa hopelessly and consistently replies that, "even if society were to change, my act would certainly make others unhappy." "In order to smile at life, I would need first of all a more balanced personality, secondly, money, and finally sturdier nerves than those I have." "I have no conscience. What I have is only oversensitive nerves." "Life is dark for everybody except for the selected few. 'The selected few' is the synonym for idiots and scoundrels."[34]

There was no longer any intrinsic worth in society. To the young author who confessed that he was haunted by *fin de siècle* devils, the humanistic optimism of Mushakōji and Nagayo was a hopeless cause, as was the Japanese naturalists' romantic longing for individual emancipation. Why then did social isolation disturb him? If life and human ties were as meaningless and false as Akutagawa described them, why was he unable to retire into the world of art? Was it because of his social conscience? This is what the Marxists suggest, although they are quick to add that his was a petty-bourgeois conscience, ignorant of the objective demands of his historical situation. Be that as it may, within Akutagawa's own writings we can find one reason why it was difficult for him to alienate himself successfully from his social surroundings.

Beneath Akutagawa's misanthropic facade, a powerfully humane mind often reveals itself: some of his short stories, including "Otomi no teisō" (The virginity of Otomi), "Mikan" (Oranges), "Oitaru Susanōno Mikoto" (The aged Prince Susanō), and "Nezumi-kozō-Jirokichi," have an unexpectedly human and warm theme. Although they maintain the stylistic perfection that is always characteristic of Akutagawa, these stories present an entirely different view of human experience from that discussed earlier. In "Nezumi-kozō-Jirokichi" Akutagawa expresses a sentimental and even banal admiration for a thief who distributes his loot among the poor. The same thing can be said of "Otomi no teisō." A young maid barely escapes rape through her decision to submit herself to violence in order to save her mistress' cat. For, unexpectedly, the maid's decision to sacrifice herself has inspired a sense of honor in the man. Years later, she finds the man who threatened her, now an eminent political figure of Meiji Japan. But neither hate nor bitterness prevails in the end, and she remembers him even gratefully.[35] In the touching and humorous endings of these stories, we see Akutagawa betray his assumptions about human nature.

He once wrote: "Pride, lust, and suspicion—in these three all sins have their roots, and all virtues, as well." [36] To Akutagawa, even man's virtuous side is rooted in his essentially irrational feelings. In his persistent insistence on this observation, however, Akutagawa is not consistent. In *Samusa* (The chill), one of his autobiographical sketches, the author speaks of the level-crossing keeper who was killed while trying to save a little girl from an oncoming train. Having seen this event, the author tries to erase its impression by telling himself that there is no difference between the death of a virtuous man and that of a criminal. "Yet what he saw left him with a heavy impression which refuses such logic." He fails to reduce the experience to an abstraction, to free himself from sentimentalism. He feels irritated by the indifferent happiness of the people on the station platform. "Especially navy officers speaking loudly gave him a physical displeasure." [37] The incongruity of this scene on the platform with what the author has just experienced symbolizes the inhuman indifference of society. Hence Akutagawa's profound despair over society and life was occasionally alleviated by the discovery that it still has moments that deserve one's affection.

Kappa

From this ambivalent attitude toward society emerged some of the sharpest and most penetrating remarks on contemporary Japan. Since Akutagawa had no concrete plan to propose, he was a flexible and open-minded satirist, and from his work we can learn much about the illness of Japanese society in the 1920s.

Five months before his death Akutagawa published the satire *Kappa.* The author of "Shuju no kotoba" (The words of a dwarf), wherein he writes that "one characteristic of a fool is that he considers everybody else a fool," could write of life without the self-conscious seriousness of the ordinary intellectual.[38] We cannot dismiss his bitterness toward the things he ridiculed. Nor should we take his frivolity as genuine. It was more an intellectual facade than a style natural to his own feelings. Beneath the often hilarious remarks we see the social conscience of an intellectual who declares that he has no conscience, but only sensitivity and nerves.

This novel is told by a patient in a mental asylum who claims that he just returned from the country of the *kappas.* "Quietly, he would tell you this tale." "We are less happy than mankind, for we *kappas* have progressed farther than mankind has." So-called progress has made the *kappas* unhappy, although in this state one is asked before birth whether one wishes to come into the world or not. A *kappa* fetus answers: "No, I don't want to be born. First of all, the mental illness I inherit from my father is too burdensome. In addition, I believe that a *kappa* existence is evil." [39] Even with this choice, however, *kappas* are not necessarily good at managing their affairs.

A war with otters had broken out as the result of an accident in which an otter visiting a *kappa* couple drank a cup of cocoa containing potassium cyanide, which the *kappa's* wife had originally prepared for her husband. Surprised, the man asks, "Did the war start after that?" "Yes, unfortunately, the visiting otter had been decorated by his country and had a medal." A businessman (rather, a business *kappa*) gains his wealth by sending cinders to the soldiers for food. "It would be a scandal in our country," the man remarks. "Here, too, it is a scandal. But so long as I say this, no one makes a scandal out of it. The philosopher Mag says, 'Speak of your own evil, then the evil will disappear . . .' Furthermore, I was burning with patriotism besides my profit motive." [40] Honesty absolves a *kappa* from the sins he commits.

The *kappas* conveniently solve their unemployment problem by eating the unemployed workers. When the visitor honestly questions why the working-class *kappas* do not rebel against such injustice, a *kappa* answers: "It would do no good to make noise, for we have the Workers-Slaughter Act." Another one adds: "That is, the state eliminates the choice whether to starve to death or to commit suicide. We just let them smell poisonous gas. It gives them little pain." The image has a terrifying suggestiveness. "But it is something else that you eat." "Don't be a fool . . . In your country the daughters of the working-class people become prostitutes. It is sentimentalism to feel angered at eating the working-class *kappa's* meat." [41]

The intellectuals of this state also suffer thought control of a special kind. "Since both literature and painting are clear to anyone in their representation, there is no prohibition of publication or exhibition. Instead we prohibit music concerts." "Music is not understandable to a *kappa* without an ear." "Such a censorship is outrageous!" "On the contrary, it is far more advanced than the censorship of any other country. Look at Japan, for example. In fact, about a month ago . . ." The philosopher Mag cannot continue, for an empty bottle thrown at the police in the concert hall where this conversation takes place accidentally drops on his head.[42] Had he continued, *Kappa* might not have been published.

The musician Craback, whose concert was interrupted by the police, belongs to the Super-Kappa Club to which a poet, Tokku, also belongs. "According to Tokku's belief, art receives no one's control. It is art for art's sake. Therefore, an artist should be a super-*kappa* who transcends good and evil. Naturally, this view is not Tokku's alone. It is shared by his fellow club members." This proud poet commits suicide, and no one understands why. His wife says: "I don't understand why. He was writing something. Then he suddenly shot himself." Someone else says: "He was selfish." The doctor announces: "It is all over. He had stomach trouble. This alone tended to make him melancholy." "The family who had to be with such a selfish *kappa* was unfortunate." "He didn't even think of the aftermath." After the Tokku affair, Mag "feebly says, 'in any event, in order to fulfill the life of *kappa* he has to believe in something beside the *kappa* himself.' " [43]

Akutagawa once confessed that he often envied the people of the Middle Ages who could believe in the Church and the unity of life.[44] Without understanding this feeling of Akutagawa's, one cannot fully appreciate his work on the life of Christ, mentioned above. Yet he was at the same time convinced that it was because of man's frailty that he longed to believe in something besides himself. In "Shuju no kotoba" Akutagawa writes that everybody apotheosizes something other than himself, fearing that otherwise he cannot live peacefully. It can be God or woman or society. In the case of Japan, Akutagawa felt, "we have discovered many reasons to kill God. Unfortunately, however, the Japanese do not believe in an omnipotent god 'who deserves to be killed.' " [45] Since the Japanese lacked such a god, what Akutagawa proposed was to pronounce the death of society, which in Japan probably played the same omnipotent role that God played in the West. Society had destroyed the strength of the individual, had stereotyped man, and had erased the beauty of the individual. Man no longer was capable of genuine freedom. "Everybody seeks freedom. This, however, only in appearance. At heart no one looks for it at all. Even those thugs who do not hesitate to murder people claim that they kill in the name of the impeccable state. Genuine freedom refuses to collaborate with or invoke such ideas as God, morality and society." "Freedom is like the air on high mountains. A weak man can bear neither." [46]

Death as an Intellectual Choice

In the early morning of July 24, 1927, Akutagawa committed suicide. The reaction was instantaneous, large, and varied, for Akutagawa had been closely tied to the major literary figures and groups of Taishō Japan. Since 1916, when Natsume Sōseki had called attention to his short stories, he had walked in the limelight.

Arishima's suicide in 1923 had had certain obvious aspects. He died with a married woman. His heroic pronouncement of the demise of the bourgeois writers (in which he included himself) had alienated many, as had the naively self-righteous style of his intellectual concern. Moreover, he was not a Tokyo University graduate. Though he was allied with the Shirakaba-ha, he was never a typical member of the movement, and the range of his acquaintances in the literary field had been much more limited than Akutagawa's.[47] Nevertheless, Akutagawa's death was a lonely one. Other intellectuals among his contemporaries seem to have shared his feeling of acute loneliness. Akutagawa's favorite expression, *"fin de siècle* pain," was an aesthetic expression of the crisis upon which the Shōwa intellectuals variously reflected.

In his last testament, "A Note to an Old Friend," Akutagawa named the reason for his desire to die—death having been his "only preoccupation for the last two years"—as *bonyari shita fuan* (a vague anxiety). "Last night when I talked with a prostitute about her wages, I really felt the misery of human beings who 'live merely to live.' If it is not a happy thing to choose an eternal slumber, it should at least be peaceful." [48] So he chose this most radical form of social alienation. It was a tragedy that Akutagawa could not be satisfied with artistic flight from "social trivialities" and had to resort to a more radical means of attaining peace. But it would be presumptuous for us even to try to understand fully the real reasons for his suicide.

"For someone like myself," one writer commented, "who tries hard to live a life, it is never understandable why one chooses death and carries it out." [49] A newspaper commented that "the sharp sensitivity of a literary man always feels the agony of his time. The death of Kitamura, the death of Arishima, and now the death of Akutagawa. We see the shadows of their times cast on them." [50] Some were not so sympathetic. "I cannot see the artistic or philosophical uniqueness of a suicide." "I think it is a merely physiological phenomenon." [51]

The Marxian socialists tried to place this event within what they considered the proper historical context. "It goes without saying," said one, "the death of one Akutagawa measured by a social scale is merely a phase in the disintegration of the bourgeoisie." Another wrote: "Briefly stated, that which killed Akutagawa was above all his intellectual position." [52] Aono Suekichi, a Marxist critic, wrote: "He cannot help recognizing the new era. He has the simplicity, intellect, and preparedness to observe (the inevitable coming of) the new era with calmness. If I can borrow his own words, he has 'no passion to embrace the new era.' I feel that no one with his background can have such a passion." "Akutagawa, though less positively, had the same feelings as Arishima." [53]

In his short essay, "Akutagawa Ryūnosuke and the New Era," Aono analyzes Akutagawa's works in terms of the conscience of a petty-bourgeois. He particularly felt that in his novel *Genkakusambō* Akutagawa came close to recognizing the necessity for leaving behind society as it then existed in order to accept the new era. In this novel, written during the winter of 1926–27, Akutagawa brought into sharp relief the cruelty of a middle-class family.[54] But it was the novel's ending that attracted Aono's attention. The protagonist has just died amidst his family's concealed indifference, and while coming back from the cremation, his nephew starts reading Liebknecht. Soon after *Genkakusambō* was published, a group of literary critics suggested in *Shinchō* that there had been no particular reason for bringing in Liebknecht at this point. "It could have been Hara Kei, Admiral Togō, or *Kuraku*." [55] In reply, Aono quotes from a letter he had received from Akutagawa, in which the latter wrote: "Some suggested that Liebknecht could be replaced by *Kuraku*. It would not do, however. In the end of the novel, I wanted to make the tragedy of *Genkakusambō* come into contact with the outside world. . . . In addition, I wanted to suggest that in the outside world is the new era." [56] Arguing against those who depreciated the significance of this final scene, Aono writes that "the artistic impeccability of Akutagawa" would not make the scene accidental and without significance. He goes on to say that neither Marx nor Lenin would have fitted the novel. "It has to be Liebknecht." "I believe that the world of *Genkakusambō* was completed and carved in relief by this final scene, which opened the door of the disintegrating world and welcomed the pleasant prospect of 'the new era.' " "The ending made the novel a powerful work of art." [57]

It was in order to sustain another argument that Aono read so much into this final scene. His point was that such bourgeois writers as Akutagawa and Arishima were not altogether devoid of social conscience and were able to articulate the pain of the bourgeois world. They were even at times capable of seeing the correct remedy for the evil they described, although their background would not allow them "to have the passion to embrace the new era."

It was not until the summer of 1929, however, that the finest and most acute epitaph for Akutagawa was written. In the August issue of *Kaizō*, Miyamoto Kenji won first prize in a contest for his essay entitled "Haiboku no bungaku" (The literature of defeatism). After meticulously examining Akutagawa's entire body of literary works and private papers, Miyamoto concludes:

> The final words of Akutagawa expressed a feeling of hopelessness toward man's happiness in social life. Like all other pessimists he felt that he had to find the conclusive comment on *the eternal Weltschmerz* imposed on man. This is not at all a new idea, not a new sentiment. It has its roots in the fatal logic of the petty bourgeoisie *to replace the despair of the self with that of the whole society.* Thus Akutagawa identified the pain born of and defined by his physiology and his social class with the eternal agony of humanity.

Miyamoto deduces as a legacy from Akutagawa's life and art the conclusion that "although there is a period in history when the nihilistic spirit can play a progressive part to a certain extent, today we cannot expect such a part from his literature." "In this sense we have to recognize clearly the class character stamped on his literature." At the same time, Akutagawa's death was a serious warning to indifferent bourgeois intellectuals. Miyamoto quotes Akutagawa: "The coming generations will not so much accuse us of our mistakes as they will understand our passion sympathetically." Akutagawa, Miyamoto believed, hoped that the future would remember him not as a hollow man but as a doomed and fighting intellectual. Contrasting his earlier and later works, Miyamoto observes that Akutagawa became a seeker after realism. This search, however, was doomed to fail, for Akutagawa hesitated to embrace the law of history. To study his art, Miyamoto contends, is to study the process of the formation of the literature of defeat. At best, it was an instructive preparatory exercise. "We have to cross over the literature of defeat and its class-soil." Miyamoto, further- more, notes that the sympathy many socialist intellectuals felt toward Akutagawa at the time of his death proved the presence of a petty-bourgeois attitude in their consciousness, an attitude that ought to be altogether removed in order for them to keep in step with history.

"Like all other lonely petty-bourgeois intellectuals, Akuta- gawa Ryūnosuke also desired to stand beyond good and evil." Akutagawa himself confessed that "the two contrasting things hold the same charm for me. Only by loving goodness can we love evil." "I bless the ugly as well." Miyamoto argues that Akutagawa's effort to go beyond social morality had been a fail- ure. As proof of this, he enumerates the conventional moral themes often found in Akutagawa's stories. He concludes that "Akutagawa could not go beyond the morality of the class of his time." Thus Akutagawa's final failure to stand beyond good and evil was his failure to bring about social change. Instead, he universalized his pain—pain that in fact was particular to his class. As a Marxist critic, Miyamoto shows no sympathy for those intellectuals who refuse to see "truth" in history. To achieve the genuine success of going beyond good and evil, for a Marxist, means "the achievement of a great historical project which cannot be judged according to the established concept of morality born of the soil of a certain social order." Miyamoto writes: "The psychological basis of trying to identify good and evil reflects the hopeless disharmony the petty-bourgeoisie ex- perience vis-à-vis the present society." It is his belief that history marches inevitably toward the revelation of its own truth, a classless society, and that Akutagawa's time was no time for being skeptical about the social ideal and being quiescently pained by one's social surroundings.[58]

Such was the Marxist epitaph written on Akutagawa's death. With all its deterministic assumptions, it contains a greater measure of truth than any other commentary written at the time. However, even if the Marxist argument—the idea that Akutagawa's mistake lay in the universalization he made of his individual (class) agony and the loss of the possibility of replacing the present with a new and more hopeful world, that his art expressed the demise of the bourgeois art—even if this argument has its own logical consistency, it was not able to fulfill any of its own expectations. Presumably rectifying the sin committed by Akutagawa in his ignorance, proletarian art killed itself long before the war came to destroy art altogether. The question of what Akutagawa might better have done is, therefore, irrelevant. What is more important, both for Akutagawa and for others, is to recognize his failure to distinguish between the artistic and the socialized dimension of his existence. Even if one assumes that art and politics are ultimately related and cannot be separated, the total subjugation of art to the demands of politics, which the Marxists required of artists, certainly could not have solved the problems that so pained Akutagawa.

Undoubtedly, Akutagawa's art and thought reflect the absence of an intellectual as well as an emotional consensus within Japanese society during the decade preceding his death. The chaotic state of the intellectual atmosphere during the Taishō period, which the Marxists tried to improve by imposing one world view and which the hedonists tried to disregard by taking flight into the world of pure art, still exists in Japan. What is most impressive in Akutagawa's life and art, as well as in his death, is his refusal to turn to those easy outlets available at the time: the totalitarian solution of Marxism or an irresponsible alienation from society.

Here again is vivid testimony to the Japanese intellectuals' failure to conceive of the emancipation of the individual in social terms. For Akutagawa, the failure of freedom was an established fact: its anarchic consequences, unforeseen by his predecessors, stood out in his consciousness.

VIII / Proletarian Literature: The Tyranny of Politics

The death of Akutagawa in the summer of 1927 intensified the intellectuals' feelings of social impotence and alienation. Many felt that the expression "vague anxiety" in Akutagawa's last testament referred to his belief that he had no place in the coming of the new era. Theoretically, Arishima's *One Manifesto* was a clearer exposition of the same sentiment. Few, however, felt any emotional affinity with that lonely and unique intellectual. The death of Arishima was that of a prophet, whereas Akutagawa's was a reaction to a newly established historical reality. By the mid-1920s, socialist literature, which had experienced a temporary eclipse under the severe government surveillance after the earthquake of 1923, again became popular and powerful. This time, unlike the previous radical literary movements which were based on hybrid socialist theories and vague anarchist sentiments, the socialist writers committed themselves to the aesthetic theory of Marxism, albeit to varying degrees.

The Paradox of Intellectual Impatience

To such authors with literary longevity as Tanizaki Junichirō and Nagai Kafū, Shimazaki Tōson and Tayama Katai,

Akutagawa's death was another milestone in their experience of frustration by the outside world.[1] It was primarily among the self-conscious younger "bourgeois" intellectuals that Akutagawa's suicide justified their sense of urgency to find a place in history. They noted that their predecessors—naturalists, Shirakaba-ha, and hedonists alike—asocialized the individual in their enthusiastic search for individualism. In social terms, their individualism either made a chaos of this world or remained indifferent to it. The younger college graduates, the social elite who would have ordinarily gone into government or business bureaucracies, acutely recognized such shortcomings. They soon came to the view that Marxism could answer all their questions. Above all, in Marxism the role of philosophy changes from that of an Owl of Minerva, merely observing what has become real, to that of an active participant in history, revealing what ought to be done. The individual becomes temporarily anonymous under the commanding need of history. This self-eradication, however, is a temporary phenomenon preceding the culminating point of history where the individual becomes genuinely free. In addition, Marxism guarantees the identity of thought and action, and hence the integrity of the intellectual's social conscience.

The reality of Taishō Japan challenged the intellectuals' social indifference, and it was explosively receptive to Marxism. The chronic depressions conformed to Marxism's predictions. The labor-union movement became conspicuously active under the leadership of various brands of socialists. A series of strikes haunted the government. The rice riots brought down a cabinet. And there was formed for the first time a cabinet in September 1918 headed by a party leader rather than an oligarch. Agrarian discontent was general all over Japan. In order to survive, poverty-stricken families in the rural north sold their daughters into white slavery. All cities presented scenes of decadence. Precisely at the moment when political parties began to play a more important part in Japanese politics, they revealed their incompetence, seeming to represent only the interests of

the capitalists and the landowners. Constant revelations of corruption irritated and discouraged those who might have stood
with the parliamentary liberals to oppose the system's eventual
disintegration, and many forsook the institution in disgusted
despair. How appropriate was the Marxist view of the representative organ of government—a hypocritical facade of a bourgeois state! [2] All these factors, however, are secondary to our
purpose. Even if a society suffers from the worst kind of social
and economic maladies, this does not necessarily mean that intellectuals will accept such a radical idea as Marxism. Why in
this case did they, and so enthusiastically?

During the Taishō era, history played an ironic trick on the
so-called Japanese liberals: through their failure to convey their
ethical ideals to the public in concrete terms, they produced an
intellectual milieu where Marxist ideals could be easily accepted. Devoid of social success, Japanese liberalism yielded to
Marxism, which provided liberal ideals with a specific content.
Marxism above all is a product of Europe, a product of her intellectual, social, and economic experiences. Taishō Japan was
ready to see in this dogma the explanation of many issues and
the answer to many questions. Marx resurrected the eighteenth-
century image of man from the abyss into which the romantics
in their enthusiasm for individual sentiment had driven it. No
other intellectual school stated this ideal—that man is essentially good and rational—more naively and flatly than did the
Shirakaba-ha intellectuals. Of course, Marxism also has its own
empirical pessimism, reminiscent of the pessimism of Christianity. Yet with Marxism the sin is not that of the individual, but
rather of society. The individual is a victim of the particular
form of production upon which society rests. He is, however,
given the eschatological anticipation of salvation. The naturalists would have felt relieved by such a prognosis of their plight,
for the very society that frightened them and refused to understand their individual longings was diagnosed by the Marxists
as the source of all evil. In Marx we see the survival of the Enlightenment legacy of the concepts of progress, egalitarianism,

and freedom. The hostility with which the older Japanese intellectuals responded to the primacy Marx placed on the economic aspect of man and history appeared to the younger generation of intellectuals to be no more than arrogant ignorance of the real conditions of their society. In addition, the universal aspect of Marx's dialectical materialism appealed to a nation that could hardly conceal its inferiority complex from Europe. Marx's view of history equalized all nations in its rigidly economic determinism. So did Uchimura's view of history, although this was more a religious hallucination than a concrete message. Moreover, the very feature in Uchimura's theology which is intellectually satisfying deprived the intellectual of a role to play in society. Marxism, on the other hand, inflated the Westernized Japanese intellectuals by making them philosopher-kings. It commanded that they know what ought to be done and act accordingly, in the actual world, to cure that world's ills.

In December 1918, at Tokyo Imperial University, a group of students in the faculty of law formed a new organization called the Shinjinkai (New people's society). These students resented the traditional prerogative of the faculty of law to supply competent personnel to the government bureaucracy. They believed that they should not acquiesce in social impotence. The society's charter read:

I. We will collaborate with the new movement for liberating humanity which is the cultural trend of the world, and will try to assist and further it.
II. We will engage ourselves in the rational reform movement of present-day Japan.[3]

In their journals *Demokurashī* (Democracy) and *Zenei* (Vanguard), we find pictures of Lincoln, Rousseau, and Kropotkin side by side with those of Marx, Lenin, and Rosa Luxemburg. The ideological basis of the society was a kind of radical liberalism, and its platform, in its eclectic vagueness and idealism, mirrored more the liberal sentiment of Taishō Japan than it did either Marxism or anarchism. There were, however, certain theoretical elements in the platform which were soon to be given a much sharper focus by Marxism. The idea of "liberating humanity," for example—with which the Shirakaba-ha writers, too, were obsessed—was in a social sense far from realization. Unlike Arishima, the intellectual "elite" of this group believed that they could assist, even lead, the movement for "rational reform." They still had no blueprint to follow, but they did have a faith in their ability to manipulate and remold society according to their ideals.

It was above all their impatience with the present that compelled many of them to accept more radical ideologies. One of their leading members, Akamatsu Katsumaro, for a while became a member of the Japanese Communist Party.[4] Many of them later became active associates of the army and bureaucrats during the 1930s, working with them against the political parties.[5] "It is said that the excitement of the students who applied for admission to the Society resembled that of revival meetings." "Many were enchanted by the anticipation that perhaps the next day would witness a great social transformation." "In front of you stands the ideal society of humanity. —Yes, if you only stretch your hands, you can reach it." [6]

The Russian Revolution was vividly in the background. In June 1922, Akamatsu and a few others formed the Federation for Non-Intervention in Russia.[7] By then the comments both on the revolution and Marxism became ubiquitous and profuse, and even among nonsocialists the sentiment was sympathetic.[8] All this led the young intellectuals to a dissatisfaction with the theoretical disarray of constitutional creeds, which were concerned only with the painstaking details of government process.[9] All things having been said and discussed, such ethical ideals as were proposed by the Shirakaba-ha or by Yoshino Sakuzō appeared palpably uncertain of any success in society.[10] Marxism was the intellectual and emotional answer to the dilemma. In this context, Arishima's turn to Marxism becomes understandable, despite the fact that it was also an ironic excuse for his own social impotence.

It was, then, no time for diffidence and inaction. One theme that ran through the Marxist view of Akutagawa's death was that his primary sin had been to universalize the individual anxiety that was peculiar only to the dying bourgeois class. The ideal plan for regenerating the decadent state of Japanese society, it maintained, would escape the imagination of those bourgeois intellectuals "who are afraid to let themselves go." [11] They would linger in their plight, calling it inevitable and universal. Marxism was presumably the message that could salvage the individual (even the bourgeois individual, once he is repentant) into sharing the chiliastic hope for the classless society that was coming despite the opposition of the capitalist state.

It was in this setting that proletarian literature emerged and captured a commanding position among the literary schools of late Taishō and early Shōwa Japan.[12] Just as rapidly, by the early 1930s it faded away. In retrospect, it appears that the movement itself was to blame for its rapid decline.

Unlike earlier literary figures, the proletarian authors had to be constantly concerned with their relation to politics. In fact, with a few brilliant exceptions the major contribution of proletarian literature in Japan lies chiefly in its works of literary criticism, in the ambiguous border area between art and politics. Also, the writers were necessarily conscious of their organizational role as intellectuals, a role totally unknown to an average "bourgeois" writer. The organizational principles of the Japanese Communist Party became the dictum for the intellectuals dedicated to the Marxist-Leninist cause. Although these principles often conflicted with the creative impulse of the writers, their submission to the dictates of the party is striking.

Although the sudden burst of desire among the intellectuals to be reintegrated into the social process is impressive, it is a paradox that these intellectuals embraced the ideals of Marxism, which were alien to the common Japanese.[13] From the outset, then, the Marxist intellectuals were in the difficult predicament of facing a hostile government on the one hand and, on the other, of addressing their ideas to the people, to whom purely Marxist symbols meant little. A creative writer had to face yet another difficulty, in that he had to adjust his art to the concrete needs of each historical moment. The party theoreticians would bring the potentiality of the historical moment to consciousness, and the party would carry out the mission of actualizing it in reality. It was the writer's task to translate the academic jargon of Marxism into popular and comprehensible symbols and terminologies. He stood between the party—the vanguard of class consciousness—and the ignorant people who needed to be mobilized. It is understandable that the party would demand that strict political discipline be imposed on writers. The artist would often challenge the total control of the political dicta imposed on him, claiming that art ought to have a certain amount of autonomy. The major theme of the literary controversy over the role of art in the Marxist movement centered on this problem.

The issue was never solved. The theoretical stalemate, however, led to the *de facto* submission of the artists to the political tyranny of the Japanese Communist Party. Preoccupied with the necessity for theoretical impeccability as a prerequisite for conscious proletarian artists, they steadily isolated themselves from the common strata of Japanese society. Although they left an impressive mark on the history of Japanese literature, their works remain in its annals because of their artistic excellence rather than their ideological merit. It has been a long time since the most memorable of the proletarian writers, Kobayashi Takiji, was murdered by the police in February 1933. By the time of his violent death, the party work imposed on Kobayashi changed him from a genuinely talented writer to a conscientious party member burdened by the clandestine nature of his assignments. All these writers tried to find their place in society. But their impatient desire to participate was paradoxically to result in their total isolation in the end.

Tanemakuhito: *Not as a Servant but as a Collaborator*

The first literary journal with a political and revolutionary orientation, *Tanemakuhito* (Those who sow the seeds), was published in October 1921.[14] It was the first journal to introduce the notion of the Third International. Its untitled manifesto read: "We defend the truth of revolution for our lives. Here we stand with the comrades of the world!" [15] The journal was not exclusively Marxist, however, and opened its pages to anyone disposed to the idea of social revolution. Although the dispute between the anarchosyndicalists and the Japanese Bolsheviks was going on at the time, *Tanemakuhito* appeared to be indifferent to the more sophisticated theoretical controversies that the political writers were carrying on. It was not the only radical journal published at that time, however. During the same month (October 1921), *Kaijin* (The destroyer) appeared with the declaration: "Our urgent objective . . . is to destroy altogether the idols of past art." [16] In January 1923, Hagiwara Kyōjirō (1899–1938) and Tsuboi Shigeji (1898–   ) started a journal entitled *Aka to kuro* (Red and black), championing anarchism and dadaist poetry. The latter two were closer in their aesthetic sentiment to the anarchosyndicalist doctrines of Ōsugi Sakae than to Marxist literary theory.[17]

Within this chaotic milieu of radical literary theories, Hirabayashi Hatsunosuke (1892–1931) emerged as the foremost Marxist literary critic. Born to the family of a small landlord, he was graduated from Waseda University in 1917. In January 1922 he joined the *Tanemakuhito* circle. In December 1921, Hirabayashi wrote an essay on "The Concept of Dialectical Materialism and Literature." Here he pointed out that literature, like jurisprudence, religion, morality and philosophy, is a form of social consciousness. Literature is to different degrees inevitably influenced by the class prejudices of the ruling class. Although the people tend to fail in observing it, art is a function of historical changes based on a society's economic system.

"Those same people who established social relationships which are in conformity with a particular form of production have produced principles, concepts, and categories which in turn conform to the social relationships." Hirabayashi went on to say: "These concepts and categories are no more permanent than the social relationships." Yet the supporters of the present culture are opposed to this view by maintaining that the capitalist culture is the eternal one unrelated to the material conditions of men.[18]

Admitting the ephemeral character of art, however, Hirabayashi is quick to add that it still attracts the highest esteem of man. According to him, dialectical materialism has never challenged culture per se. Rather, it challenges culture established on a particular form of production. Against the prevalent view that art is irreconcilable to the scientific view of man and history, Hirabayashi answers: "As it is possible to love while believing in the mathematical principles . . . it is also possible to create and appreciate art while believing in dialectical materialism."[19] In suggesting such reconcilability, Hirabayashi gives an ambiguous autonomy to what he calls culture per se. Superficially, his argument lacks the usual Marxist consistency. Today, a Marxist critic comments that the Achilles heel of Hirabayashi and his contemporaries who came into the revolutionary movement is to be found in their insufficient understanding of Marxism: "They did not start out with a full understanding and appreciation of the Marxist methodology."[20] Although this indictment is factually correct, it peculiarly fails to see the consistency in the argument. Hirabayashi was arguing for the total elimination of class character from both art and literature.

From the premise that material conditions determine culture [one's consciousness], and that the class struggle leaves on art the stamp of class prejudices, it should be concluded that in order to eliminate such class prejudices stamped on art we should first of all eliminate class opposition. During the period of transition, as the revolutionary factors increase in the mode of production, the revolutionary elements increase also within literature.[21]

From this observation Hirabayashi went on to conclude that the literary movement of the proletariat has significance only as a part of the larger whole, only as it collaborates with the political and labor movement of the working class. "Those who cannot be satisfied with the relative worth of this literary movement had better engage themselves in an absolute movement; shoot God, or blow down the sun!" [22]

Hirabayashi warns that the artist should not exaggerate the political role he can play in the whole movement. This is a self-conscious response to the view of such bourgeois writers as Kikuchi Kan and Kume Masao, that if an intellectual is committed to the ideal of Marxism and to the liberation of the working class, he should not remain in the negative role of an artist.[23] Hirabayashi understood the charge, but felt it his obligation to work for history. Although there is a suggestion of the need for the collaboration of artists with the political movement, Hirabayashi left it undefined how artists ought to participate in organizational terms.

Sometime in 1923, Trotsky wrote for *Pravda* an article entitled "Not by Politics Alone Do We Live." [24] Hirabayashi argued for preserving a degree of autonomy for artists. If the dictatorship of the proletariat represents only a passing phase, preceding the final culmination of history into a classless paradise wherein art will free itself from "the imprint of class prejudices," proletarian art or culture, the so-called *prolet kult,* is by definition the art of a particular class and certainly not universal. Art, despite its temporarily secondary role in the process of history, should command the highest respect, for it provides a spiritual consolation that politics is incapable of providing. In order to make art genuinely universal and representative of humanity, then, the urgent task is to change the existing form of society—a task primarily not of art but politics. Art loses its autonomy within the necessity of history, and this is a necessity that Marxism alone can reveal. Art is unable by itself to see what ought to be done socially, unless it comes into the service of politics: art becomes the handmaiden of politics until politics loses its meaning in the classless society. Then art will come into its own, genuinely free and artistic. Hirabayashi would argue that the bourgeois intellectuals who have come to know the predicament of their existence ought to renounce their class character and work for history. The people will eventually realize the falseness of the claim the bourgeois artists made of their anxiety, which has in fact no timeless quality but is only a symptom of the culture of a dying class. What had been considered Weltschmerz is merely the pain experienced by this one class. Within this logic, proletarian art is a temporary phenomenon, just as bourgeois art has been. At the same time, it is wrong to argue for the autonomy of art within this phase of history. Until the coming of the grand finale, art should remain an instrument, or at best a part, of a more significant movement carried out on the political plane.[25]

Such was the theoretical famework of the proletarian art movement until 1925. The last point, the relationship between the artist and politics, how the artist should be caught up into the political movement, was left undefined. Already, however, one can detect within Hirabayashi's logic a trend toward the total politicization of art.

There was one literary critic who, building on the basis of what Hirabayashi had done, elaborated a theory that subtly tried to preserve an independent and recognizable role for the proletarian artist. Aono Suekichi (1890–   ) was a contemporary of Hirabayashi's and a graduate of Waseda University. On Hirabayashi's recommendation he joined the *Tanemakuhito* circle in 1923, a year after Hirabayashi had joined it. In an essay entitled "Art Based on Research," written in June 1925, Aono noted that Japanese novels had merely been the collections of conscious and unconscious impressions. He located the cause of the sorry state of contemporary literature in the indolence of artists "who would not probe into the social and historical context of their subject matter." As a remedy, he suggested the idea of art based on research. The remedy appears, however, to be applicable only to the proletarian writers.

> The proletariat are the class that handles the means of producton. They are the class that in fact runs society. This is our world, the world that is denied to observation by bourgeois literature. It is the exclusive prerogative of the proletariat to analyze and describe this world. Bourgeois literature from now on will depart more and more from the scene of production and that of the class struggle. It will take refuge in the world of reflecting upon licentious living . . . On the other hand, proletarian literature ought to penetrate deeper and more meticulously into the world of economic production and that of the class struggle.[26]

It is the positive historical role of proletarian writers to see reality as it exists. Aono intellectualizes the class struggle so as to preserve a well-defined role for the artist as well as for other intellectuals. The essay concludes with the remark that the consciousness of rebellion and defiance can have solid roots only if it is articulated in well-researched terms. The realistic proletarian artists are capable of arousing the proletariat from their ignorant slumber into class consciouness.[27]

In September 1926, Aono published an epoch-making essay entitled "The Natural Growth and Consciousness of Purpose." Here he makes a clear distinction between proletarian literature and the proletarian literary movement. He attributes the emergence of the former to the emergence of the working class. In itself, to describe the life of the proletariat and the proletariat desiring their self-expression is merely to satisfy the self. As such, it is not as yet the act of a man conscious of the purpose of his class. It is sporadic and unorganized. Only when the artist becomes conscious of the purpose of the class struggle will his art become the art of his class. Aono then defines the proletarian literary movement as "the movement to implant the consciousness of the purpose in proletarian literature which was in origin spontaneous." The movement reflects the growing into maturity of the working class, and Aono calls this growth "a qualitative change." Proletarian literature seeks only the satisfaction of the self and knows of no theoretical framework in which the proletariat should act. When it becomes a movement however, it understands that its purpose is to work collectively.[28]

In January 1927, Aono again wrote on the same subject, in order to clarify the theoretical ambiguities left undiscussed in the earlier essay. "I believe simply that there is a definite limit to the natural growth of the proletariat, as pointed out by Lenin." "Left alone," he continued, "the dissatisfaction of the proletariat, their anger or hatred, can never be fully appreciated and *organized*." That is, "the consciousness of socialism can be infused only from outside." Aono believed that "our proletarian literary movement is a movement in the realm of literature to infuse this consciousness" into proletarian literature. He saw the role of proletarian literary criticism as that of sharpening theoretically the primitive feeling naturally born within the proletariat.[29]

What distinguishes Aono's otherwise banal treatment of this subject is the importance he ascribed to intellect in art. The naturalists had tried to do this and failed, confusing literary realism with the scientific method. For the first time in the history of Japanese art, intellect or reason was introduced as the guiding principle, both in art and in the improvement of one's existential lot. That which the European naturalists had suggested, but which had failed in the hands of the Japanese naturalists, was discussed afresh. But Aono, following Hirabayashi, clumsily preserved for art an independent area untouched by the scientific socialism of Marxist theory. Upon this theoretical weakness the younger Marxist intellectuals were soon to capitalize in their search for theoretical impeccability.

All these essays by Aono appeared in the journal *Bun-*

geisensen (The literary front). The publication of *Tanemaku-hito* had been discontinued soon after the Great Earthquake, but during the next spring its former contributors decided to publish a new magazine with a slightly different policy. In June the first issue of *Bungeisensen* announced its platform:

I. We stand on the common front of artistic struggle in the liberation of the proletariat.
II. The individual's activities and ideas in the movement for liberating the proletariat are left to the free choice of the individual member.[30]

Aono explained in the same issue the reasons for the discontinuation of *Tanemakuhito*. In the first place, the group had lost its cohesion and its control over its members. Second the group was bankrupt. Finally, although *Tanemakuhito* demanded uniformity in members' actions, there was a diversity of opinion among the members as to the political means by which their avowed purpose could be accomplished.[31] *Bungeisensen* limited itself to the common front in the world of literature and left its members free to choose their own political action. The political freedom of this circle arbitrarily separated the artists from the party, and was soon condemned as a political sin against the party.

In December 1925, with the *Bungeisensen* as a nucleus, the Nihon Puroretaria Bungei Remmei (Japanese Proletarian Literary Federation) was organized. It included almost all the socialist artists of Taishō Japan, and since it emphasized the absence of ideological and political conformity, its platform was vague and inclusive:

I. We pledge to create the culture of the proletarian class struggle in the period of its dawn.
II. We pledge to fight with the strength of our mutual unity in the wide field of culture against the culture of the ruling class and its supporters.[32]

The campaign activity was limited to the domains of art and literature.

The organizational principles of the federation stated here contradicted Aono's writings. Aono contended that freedom should be given to the members. He had already argued, however, that the proletarian art movement should infuse the knowledge of "purposive consciousness" into the works of proletarian literature that had spontaneously risen. Both assertions were intellectualistic. Should there not be an ideological uniformity? Otherwise the "purposive content" would lose its meaning. Marxism prides itself on the unity of theory and practice. If the party represents Marxism, how can diversity in practice be tolerated?

The very looseness of the federation's theoretical position accurately mirrors not only the mood of the early socialist authors but also the early phase of the development of the Japanese Communist Party. So-called Yamakawaism, theorized by Yamakawa Hitoshi (1880–1958) who was dominant among party members until 1926, emphasized the need to popularize Marxist ideals and to politicize the communist movement, hitherto confined to the area of the union movement. After June 1923, when the police raided the communists and broke down the party organization that had been in existence since July 1922, Yamakawa came to believe that it was fruitless to form an advanced political party in the absence of mass political consciousness. He insisted on dissolving the party and in its place proposed a common front of worker and peasant organizations. In so doing he felt it necessary to make concessions to the rightist elements within socialism. Thus the literary theories of both Hirabayashi and Aono reflected the state of Marxism in Japan before 1926. The artists, regardless of their ideological commitment and training, were recruited into the movement so long as they entertained the thought of liberating the working class from the yoke of capitalism. They offered their collaboration but refused to be subservient to the politics of the party.[33]

The climate of Marxist opinion within Japan was congenial

to those artists who would avoid party discipline beyond what they considered reasonable. Gradually, however, Yamakawaism and its ideological tolerance of diverse socialist groups were taken over by the doctrinaire rigidity of a younger Marxist, Fukumoto Kazuo. His writings, starting in 1924, came to capture the leading ideological position by 1925 and held it until he was condemned by the Comintern in 1927. Fukumoto argued that Yamakawaism was eclectic and that it neglected to emphasize the revolutionary element within Marxism. The gist of Fukumoto's argument, now called Fukumotoism, was that the Japanese Communist Party should separate the genuine Marxists from the fellow travelers and social democrats and then crystalize them into a well-organized party. Hence the well-known slogan: "Break away first before we unite." He saw that "for the time being, the struggle is to be limited to the realm of theoretical struggle." In its quest for the purification of Marxist ideology, Fukumotoism set the intellectual tone of the Marxist movement for the following two years.[34]

Fukumotoism was a possible answer to the problem posed by Aono's essay, for Aono never clearly defined the exact meaning of the expression, "the consciousness of purpose." In short, Fukumotoism implied a more thoroughly ideological as well as political discipline for the coming revolution. In addition, by arguing for ideological purification at the expense of an organizational alliance of leftists, Fukumoto's view of Marxism greatly advanced the intellectuals' position within the Marxist movement. In this context, one may retrospectively appreciate why Fukumotoism was hailed by the younger Marxist intellectuals in the universities.

From Collaboration to Servitude

As a branch of the Shinjinkai at Tokyo Imperial University, there was formed the Shakai Bungei Kenkyūkai (Society for the Study of Socialist Literature). The members included such students as Hayashi Fusao, Nakano Shigeharu, Tani Hajime,

Kusaka Eijirō, Kaji Wataru, and Kamei Katsuichirō, to name only the conspicuous few who later became (except for Hayashi Fusao, who eventually defected) leading Marxist critics and writers.[35] In the October issue of *Bungeisensen,* Tani Hajime (1906–   ) published an article entitled "The Development of the Proletarian Movement in Our Country." This essay, the result of discussions held by the more radical members of the Society for the Study of Socialist Literature who formed a subgroup, the Society for the Study of Marxist Art, incorporated the new doctrinal position of Fukumotoism. Seeing the social situation as needing ideological enlightenment, Tani defined the role of artists as essentially didactic. He accused those who tried to find refuge in the world of art of ignorance of "the present responsibility of the proletarian movement." [36] At that time the established literary circles were undergoing a series of intense vendettas. Within the theoretical framework of Fukumotoism, it was considered a necessary prelude to the formation of a genuine party that the Marxists would fight among themselves to arrive at the correct theoretical position. In addition to the purely theoretical controvery, however, the opposition between the more established proletarian writers and the new university participants intensified the struggle.[37]

At the Second Congress of the Japanese Proletarian Literary Federation, held in November 1926, the federation forced the resignations of the non-Marxist (primarily anarchist) members.[38] Marxism became the sole guiding principle of the federation. Organizationally, the executive officers were chosen from among those who were members of the Society for the Study of Marxist Art. "These young intellectuals," notes Sobue Shōji today, "were favorably disposed to theorizing, but were not acquainted with the historical experiences of proletarian literature." [39] The members of the society unrelentingly attacked the established writers, who often evaded the reality that the position of the writer should be secondary to that of the political leadership. The Japanese Communist Party was dissolved in March 1924 under the initiative of Yamakawa Hitoshi and

Sakai Toshihiko, who turned their attention to the formation of an alliance of socialist groups. In December 1926 the party was recreated, with Fukumotoism as its ideological basis. Many old-time socialists were alienated by the party's ideological intolerance, indicative of its obsession to preserve its role as the vanguard of the revolutionary movement. The political reality of the party, on the level of ideology and that of organization, was mirrored in the writers' movement as well.

To provide the ideological framework wherein a Marxist writer could write in good political conscience, Hayashi Fusao wrote an article, "The Socialist Literary Movement," which appeared in the February 1927 issue of *Bungeisensen* in the form of an editorial. Here he enumerated four points that had been widely accepted by the socialist authors during the preceding years: (1) that the vanguard meant those who were conscious of the purpose of socialism; (2) that the socialist literary movement was a movement of the vanguard; (3) that the socialist writers had to be socialists first before they could be artists; and (4) that socialist art had to be above all a work of art.[40] There is an antinomy in Hayashi's statement on proletarian realism. On the one hand, he demands that the artist renounce the idea of art for art's sake. On the other, he states the purpose of art in a nonutilitarian framework: "Socialist art pursues the artistic values." Hayashi's argument assumed, then, that a good artistic work in socialist literature was necessarily a fine piece of art. The implied presence of the artistic criterion against which all works of art ought to be measured reflects the continuation of a theme Hirabayashi had earlier stated. He saw no contradiction in his position: "The two precepts, to be a socialist first before being an artist, and for socialist art to be above all artistic, are not contradictory." [41] But the younger Marxists were impatient with such theoretical ambiguity.

Shortly after the publication of Hayashi's editorial, there appeared in *Musanshimbun* (Proletarian news) an article by Kaji entitled "Overcome So-Called Socialist Literature." Kaji wrote: "The role of art is to become a trumpet to lead the masses who are now gradually being organized." "Literature merely plays a secondary role of exposing the political realities of a bourgeois society—secondary to the politics of the proletarian movement which carries out the loftier part of organizing the masses into a revolutionary organization." Art deteriorates, in Kaji's argument, into a mere political instrument with "emotive appeal." He vehemently accused Hayashi of exaggerating the role of art in the proletarian movement. "Unless we thoroughly fight against such an ideology and isolate it," he concluded, "we can never incorporate the literary movement into the whole proletarian movement." [42]

In March, Hayashi answered Kaji in *Bungeisensen*. His article was more a plea than an argument and did not refute Kaji's thesis. He tried to explain the artistic difficulty one faced in working under a political directive, and said that Kaji had distorted the meaning of his argument.[43] In the same issue of *Bungeisensen*, Nakano Shigeharu, a contemporary of Kaji's at Tokyo Imperial University, called Hayashi's idea "the crystallization of the petty-bourgeois nature," [44] called it "empty words." Nakano reminded writers that their main responsibility as the vanguard was "to revolutionize the world. . . . Until we, in fact, dedicate ourselves to performing a social revolution the knowledge [of Marxism] will remain meaningless." [45] To achieve the revolution was the vanguard's immediate task. Thus, to assert under any guise the autonomy of the proletarian literary movement was a historical fallacy.[46]

The theme that "the literary movement cannot exist independently," and, hence that the sole purpose of the literary movement would be to serve as a part of the total proletarian movement, reflects two factors, which both had their roots in the theories of Fukumotoism. First, literate Marxists (except for Hayashi Fusao, who was ideologically less disciplined than his fellow members of the Society for the Study of Marxist Art) were critics but not writers. They had little sympathy for the older writers, whom they considered an accidental product of bourgeois literature, and felt that they required ideological training—which, in the context of Fukumotoism, meant political training. In addition, these younger Marxists had an immediate sense of eschatological hope. Fukumotoism, while arguing for confining the struggle to the realm of theoretical purification and refinement, predicted the immediate collapse of the capitalist world.[47] In such an intensely chiliastic atmosphere, the problem of the autonomy of art was only of secondary relevance. Thus the editorial, though harmless in itself, was irritating to the impatient critics who, in their overwhelming concern with politics, denounced the artists: "They miserably try to find all kinds of pretexts . . . to escape from their role at this stage of the development!" [48]

In March 1927, the internal struggle within the Proletarian Artists' Federation came to the surface. At a special session, the officers representing the *Bungeisensen* resigned from their positions, and the actual management of the federation was transferred to an anti-*Bungeisensen* group of younger intellectuals. Thereafter, the federation decided to purge the sixteen *Bungeisensen* members, but they voluntarily resigned during the next few days. This was in June. Aono Suekichi, Hayashi Fusao, Hayama Yoshiki, Kurahara Korehito, and almost all the established authors of the socialist groups resigned, and they soon formed the Rōnō Geijutsu Dōmei (Workers' and Peasants' Artist Federation).[49] The journal *Bungeisensen* continued to be the journal for the latter, among whom were some of the original founders. Meanwhile, the Proletarian Artists' Federation in July started its own journal, *Puroretaria geijutsu* (Proletarian art).[50] During that same month Akutagawa committed suicide. Indeed, the split was in conformity with the theoretical position Fukumoto had elaborated. Nevertheless, for those intellectuals who had for many years committed themselves to the most heterodox political doctrine available, the break was a cruel blow. It was natural that the proletarian authors would react to Akutagawa's death with highly charged emotion. Is it, after all, surprising that many of them felt closer to Akutagawa than to those who suddenly came to invade their art world—even though the latter were ideological allies?[51]

Meantime, in Moscow, the Comintern was holding its meeting. The representatives of the Japanese Communist Party were informed of the mistakes of both Yamakawaism and Fukumotoism, the former for its "liquidationism" and the latter for its sectarianism. It was not until 1928 however, that the entire script of the so-called Twenty-seven's Thesis of the Comintern of 1927 was translated and clarified.[52]

Immediately after the Comintern Thesis was announced, Fukumotoism subsided into sudden and quietly disgraced obscurity.[53] Its legacies, however, lingered on within the radical groups. The very frame of mind which insists on the theoretical impeccability of one's position and the categorical imperative to act in conformity with the theoretical interpretation of a given situation deprived the Marxists of flexibility, both in organizational activities and in intellectual endeavors. The cult of intellect has often prevented the socialists from comprehending the sentiment of the masses. Yet in more ways than one, Fukumotoism was a unique political experience in the political culture of Japan. It was characterized by a willingness to sacrifice personal relations to theoretical commitment and by the unrelenting discipline of behavior in terms of "scientific reasoning," requiring the optimistic reliance on *Gesinnungsethik* to be replaced by the strategy of what Weber calls *Verantwortlichkeitsethik*. Obsessed with the final goal of their activities, the liberation of the working class, the Marxists became willing realists. The realism of their behavior, however, was conditioned by the theoretical view of their existential situation. In literature, the members of the Shirakaba-ha, Mushakōji in particular, believed that by universalizing one's *Gesinnungsethik* an ideal society could be achieved. In the absence of any political strategy for arriving at an ideal society, they blindly believed in the ultimate goodness of man. Kobayashi Takiji, the most able proletarian writer, described, for instance, in

Tōseikatsusha (The life of a party member) the hero who would sacrifice the others for the party.[54] The transition was dramatically explicit. The two ethical attitudes were mutually exclusive, making it highly improbable that there would be any alliance of communists with liberals in their fight against the militarists or ultranationalists.

From October 1926, when Kurahara translated an article in *Pravda* which summarized the Comintern's Thesis, until the spring of 1928, there was a series of dazzling organizational reorientations among the socialist writers and critics. In November, the Workers' and Peasants' Artist Federation split into two groups over the question of whether their journal *Bungeisensen* should publish an article by Yamakawa Hitoshi, who, being more conscious of the Comintern's criticism of Fukumotoism than of the criticism directed against him, criticized "the sectarianism of the leftist deviationists" represented by *Musanshimbun*.[55] The group that opposed the publication, led by Kurahara, resigned from the federation on November 11. A day later, the ones who had resigned formed the Zenei Geijutsuka Dōmei (Federation of Vanguard Artists) and started their own publication, *Zenei* (Vanguard), the following January.[56] The December issue of *Bungeisensen*, bereft of its tie with the more militant Marxists, went all-out to chastize Fukumotoism for its "romantic leftism." [57] *Puroretaria geijutsu* published, also in December, an article on the recent split in the federation and expresed its sympathy for the members who had left to form the new organization. At the end of the year, the Proletarian Art Federation and the Federation of Vanguard Artists held a joint conference to discuss a merger of the two groups.[58] The project from the outset faced difficulties. For one thing, nobody knew the exact nature of the Comintern Thesis. Kurahara wrote in the January 1928 issue of *Zenei* on the "New Stages of the Proletarian Art Movement." He proposed the "popularization of art and the formation of the common front of leftist artists." At this point he opposed both Fukumotoism and Yamakawaism, and saw the unification of the socialist and radical writers as the primary objective of the proletarian artist' movement.[59]

As the conditions for the formation of the common front, Kurahara suggested that:

(1) The organization will include all agrarian artists' organizations as well as leftist petty-bourgeois artists' groups, with the existing proletarian artist organizations as a nucleus.

(2) Each group that joins the common front will maintain its organizational and ideological autonomy.[60]

Nowhere did he allude to the necessity for collaboration between the Federation of Vanguard Artists and the Proletarian Art Federation. Sobue correctly saw that there was a basic difference between Kurahara, who foresaw the unique problems an artist would face in a political movement, and Kaji Wataru, who would ignore the difficulties by making the artists mouthpieces of the party.[61] What prompted the final unification of the leftist writers was the March 15 incident (immortalized in Kobayashi Takiji's novel, *3/15/1928*), when the government arrested more than fifteen hundred leftist activists.[62] The next day, the two groups issued a joint declaration and on March 25 formed the well-known NAPF (Nippona Proleta Artista Federatio).[63] In May 1928 the NAPF started its new journal, *Senki* (The fighting flag). It ceased publication in December 1931, a date that marked the virtual ending of the legal literary works of the regular Marxists. Already the Japanese Communist Party and the revolutionary labor organization had been declared illegal, and the journal was the only legitimate means by which the party could express its directives under a literary guise. The *Bungeisensen* group (Workers' and Peasants' Artist Federation, or *rōnō-ha*) was excluded from *Senki's* editorial board—a fusion of the *Puroretaria geijutsu* and the Zenei groups, despite the former's pretension of being a common-front organization.[64]

In the first issue of *Senki,* Kurahara, the theoretician for the NAPF, wrote an article on "The Road to Proletarian Realism," in which he defined realism as "the artistic style of a rising class." But he criticized the existing form of realism, naturalism, as being essentially based on the asocial individual who was defined more by such factors as heredity. Such individualism based on "the biological self," Kurahara argued, was the basic principle of bourgeois society, obscuring the social nature of the individual self. Flaubert and Maupassant were examples of this individualism. Naturalism, where "the literary topic is confined to the individual life," had the objectivity of the natural sciences but lacked the quality of the social sciences. Kurahara went on to remark that such a writer as Zola could only be a humanitarian. He could appeal to a sense of justice or to the people's sentiment, but could never transcend the given social situation. In place of the biological emphasis of bourgeois realism (naturalism), Kurahara proposed that writers stress the social dimension of the individual life and the possibility of social improvement. This was considered the realism of working-class writers, proletarian or socialist realism. It was based on a "clear view of class" and chose its subjects "with the eye [consciousness] of the vanguard." Within such a literary framework, according to Kurahara, an incident would change "from natural [spontaneous] to willed [historical] necessity, from the accidental to the inevitable." The writer now could manipulate historical situations in order to bring about the classless paradise. It was his thesis "not to suggest that the proletarian writer should either distort or give a revolutionary embellishment to his literary materials, but that he should discover the objective reality that would correspond to his consciousness of the proletarian class." In the postscript to this issue of *Senki* was the statement: "The proletariat cannot rely on the fellow travelers." It was the consciousness of the proletariat, and that alone, which was to guide the new movement of socialist realism.[65]

In the same month (May 1928), Aono wrote in *Bungeisensen*

for the *rōnō* group that the time had come to draw up the criteria for "judging the significance of a work of art." He felt that there would emerge a "more precise appreciation" in proletarian literature than had previously been available, and complained about the crude way in which socialist artists had been criticized or appreciated. "Besides the social categories," he wrote, "we have as yet no criteria to judge a work of art on its own artistic merits." [66] The complaint legitimately reflected the state of the *rōnō* group, for by then its members, including such authors as Hayama Yoshiki, Maedagawa Kōichirō, and Kobori Jinji, had produced some of the finest works of proletarian art.[67] They urgently felt the need for a more literarily oriented criticism. Such a need, implying the autonomous role of art, was at once refuted by those who could see nothing but the political needs of their time. In July Kaji wrote in *Senki* "We study the history of art. Yet it is not to learn the perfected techniques of the past art works but to know how the latter have rationally served the society the proletariat are to destroy . . . We have a long way to go before we perfect our art." If art is understood only in its *ideological* nature, as it is in Kaji's argument, it can never rise above the level of subservience to a class. Moreover, Kaji confused the universal or classless art to be perfected in the ideal communist society with proletarian art. "We have a long way to go before we perfect our art." This statement crudely solidified the transitory nature of proletarian art, neglecting the realistic and urgent need for a more artistically oriented criticism, as advocated by the more firmly established socialist authors. "We have to criticize severely," continued Kaji, "the artistic nature of the artists."

Kaji felt that "Marxism has become an intellectual embellishment of modern man . . . the rapid rise of the proletariat, the radicalization of the class struggle, and the instability of society have led the intellectuals to a more critical mentality." He argued that "the profusion of the petty bourgeoisie within the leftist movement" was dangerous. This class would necessarily carry within itself the mentality that would plague the movement of the proletariat. Kaji's fear alienated many and also reflected the remnants of Fukumotoism among many theoreticians.[68]

Kurahara stood somewhere between Aono and Kaji as far as the relation between art and politics was concerned. If art is merely the tool of politics, only political dictates can determine the value of a work of art. Kurahara accepted this premise as the basis of literary criticism for revolutionary writers. For example, commenting on the role of a Marxist critic, he wrote that a painter should not be satisfied with merely painting scenes of a strike or from the life of a worker. "We have to come to grips with more revolutionary and more politically potent moments in life." "The basic theme of our art ought always to be the class struggle . . . The class struggle exists everywhere in our life. Whenever we deal with it, we have to choose the subject matter that has positive significance for the coming revolution." [69] Kurahara's view should be understood in terms of the emotional background of the revolutionary intellectuals, which consisted of two factors, one organizational and the other ideological. It was not until September 1929, three years after Kurahara started working for the intellectual wing of the Communist Party, that he was admitted to the party.[70] Party membership involved a great risk but was an immense honor. Kawakami Hajime, once an eminent professor of economics at Kyoto University, recorded that he accepted admission to the party with joyful tears.[71] The terrible brutality of the police against the communists intensified the latters' sense of heroism. The veil of secrecy under which the party members had to operate and the unquestioned authority of political theoreticians within the party strengthened their sense of political loyalty. In addition, we may note among them the messianic fervor that the revolution was coming any moment, that the time was ripe. Against this background, the role of the artists could be easily visualized as a secondary factor in the great political work of the party.

Kurahara, however, did not take a simple view of the former

members of the Society for the Study of Marxist Art. Kaji and Tani considered art a didactic instrument of the party and believed that the artists' conception of their own unique problems was an indication of their petty-bourgeois nature.[72] Kurahara, on the other hand, tried to solve the innumerable difficulties that artists encountered in their attempt to write under the party's directives. In his effort to understand these difficulties, we see the close relationship between Kurahara's critical writings and the works of Kobayashi Takiji.[73]

In October 1928, Kurahara published an article in *Senki* on leftist "liquidationism." He repeated the assumption: "All arts are necessarily agitation. And the proletarian arts are the arts of conscious agitation. For this reason, the proletarian art movement is *in the broad sense* of the term a political movement . . . the art program is always a political program. This is the ABC of proletarian art criticism." He then went on to say that "the problem does not exist here. The real question is what kind of agitation." In this observation, Kurahara made a subtle distinction between those art forms used purely for the purpose of propaganda and those from which a genuine proletarian art might emerge.[74]

What was meant by the second category of art is ambiguous, but Kurahara tried to articulate his thought as follows:

> As opposed to the first category of art, proletarian art in the genuine sense of the term does not necessarily agitate the masses directly to a definite social action. While the works of art oriented directly toward agitation often lose their meaning once the mission is completed, genuine works of proletarian art over a long period of time enrich and give a unity to the thought, will, and sentiment of the masses.

Kurahara accused Nakano and Kaji of having confused the two categories of proletarian art. What lurks behind Kurahara's argument is the mission of art, even if it is still defined by the wider political objective of the revolution. Beyond its role as the temporary instrument of the day-to-day strategies of the party, art was given its own raison d'être. At one place in this article, Kurahara comes very close to the theoretical position of Aono. Admonishing the extreme view of Kaji, who in utter distrust tried to eliminate all petty-bourgeois elements from the art movement, Kurahara wrote:

> We have to criticize concretely the petty-bourgeois nature of an art work, and eventually try to educate the artist to be a real proletarian artist . . . Without doing so, merely to exaggerate the danger of the petty bourgeoisie and to agitate against those who try to come into our camp, vaguely crying "overcome the petty-bourgeois nature," will disturb the artists and will bear no fruit.

Kurahara pleaded for establishing artistic criteria for proletarian art. If there was no longer any universalized value in art, there should at least be a set of artistic criteria for the appreciation of works of art within the given historical situation. He also criticized the proletarian art movement for its abstracted and exaggerated fear of the petty bourgeoisie. In conclusion Kurahara wrote: "No matter what the others would say, we have to study 'the work.'" "Our task is to engage ourselves in the hardship of construction for the sake of destruction." To him the hardship of construction meant the creation of the criteria to be used in the world of art.[75]

1929 was perhaps the proletarian writers' most prolific year. The statistics indicate the increasing circulation of *Senki,* as well as a wider participation by the proletarian writers in such major "bourgeois" magazines as *Kaizō* and *Chūōkōron.*[76] Within this milieu, Kurahara stipulated the mission of proletarian art criticism as follows:

(1) To create genuine Marxist literary criticism to be applied concretely to concrete works, the task the NAPF had neglected.

(2) To apply theoretical and abstract controversies to concrete situations of agitation and "massization" [*taishū-ka*] of art.

(3) To struggle against the opposing literary views of both the non-Marxist leftists and the bourgeois writers.[77]

During 1928, Kurahara and a few others had been engaged in the *keishiki-naiyō ronsō* (form and content controversy). The Marxists argued that it was the content of a literary work that would finally determine its artistic quality.[78] The content was given by the social situation: a proletarian writer would consciously choose for his artistic material the right content, which would assist the revolutionary situation. The opposing view was represented by Yokomitsu Riichi (1898–1947), who thought that it was style and form that in the final analysis determined literary excellence. The new school, the Shinkankaku-ha (New Sensibility School), arose in conscious opposition to the theoretical tryanny of the proletarian literary movement.[79] Kurahara pronounced that the group was the last "theoretical castle of the declining bourgeois literature," for "it denied the ideological content of literature and defended the negative and paralyzing literature of the decadent class."[80] As far as perfection of theory was concerned, Kurahara came out better. Yet these "decadent bourgeois writers" have immortalized themselves in the history of Japanese literature through the works of such writers as Kawabata Yasunari (b. 1899) and Yokomitsu.[81]

It was, however, in the domain of vendetta that Kurahara's literary activity excelled. To redress the "abstract" nature of proletarian art criticism, he proceeded to work on the subject in conscious opposition both to the extreme politicism of Kaji and to the "autonomy of art" idea of the *rōnō* writers. The result was confusion rather than clarification. Yet the writers seem to have benefited from this confusion more than they would have from an articulated servitude or a diffident independence. Through the years after 1928, one theoretical issue smoldered, that of "artistic value versus political value." This polemic was first proposed by Hirabayashi Hatsunosuke, who had been silent for some years.[82] It was Kurahara's assertion that, in art, what is good for politics determines the very goodness of the art. Hirabyashi contended that if the criterion of good and bad was reintroduced, as the Marxists proposed, artistic criteria were returning to the prenaturalist stage, for naturalism had altogether eradicated morality from the realm of art. Besides the legitimate question of whether Japanese naturalism had in fact eradicated the moral category from art, there remained the need, according to Hirabayashi, to define for the interested writers a new kind of critical category corresponding to the political dictates of Marxism.[83] Kurahara answered the question in a series of articles which appeared in *Asahi* in the fall of 1928. Here he flatly stated that "there is only one criterion in judging a social phenomenon"—namely, whether it has a positive significance for society. If it does, then it has value; if not, it is devoid of value. Kurahara invoked history as the sole judge of all social phenomena of which art is a part. In so doing, however, he juxtaposed art to science and wrote: "It is clear that, just as science has to have scientificity [scientific validity], a work of art has to have the quality of being a work of art." Yet "to have the quality of art is after all . . . not a value in and of itself. It is 'pre-value'" 'Hence, it does not necessarily mean that a piece of art with artistic quality is of value." [84] Value is a social and historical category. Kurahara neatly separated the artistic quality of a work of art and its historically determined value, and said that a proletarian might absorb from previous authors their artistic qualities but not their social values. Then Kurahara answered such questions as whether the *Communist Manifesto* is a great work of art and whether "if ideological discipline is the prime prerequisite of an artist, Lenin ought not to have been the greatest artist." [85] This point was carried to its logical extreme by Nakano Shigeharu in an article entitled "In Art There Is No Such Thing as Political Value." If an author wrote an article according to party command and turned in an unfortunate piece, Nakano wrote, "Hirabayashi would say, 'The artistic quality of the work is dismal. Its political value, however, is noble. This is a misfortune of art. . . . But even in the name of art, we cannot refuse the policy for the happiness of humanity.' " Nakano continued: "If I were to judge the case, I would say, 'This is a distasteful work . . . If he is a Marxist, he should find his work elsewhere but not in the realm of art . . . Probably, it was a political fact that he obeyed the command of the party. He, however, did not carry out his mission well.' " [86]

If all this sounds pedantic, the confusion nevertheless produced a sphere in which proletarian artists could enjoy at least some artistic freedom and pride. Within this context, we might understand the intense admiration with which Kobayashi Takiji regarded that most bourgeois of bourgeois writers, Shiga Naoya, as the muse of Japanese prose.[87] The tight and irritatingly political nature of the control over artists which the members of the Society for Marxist Art tried to wield was gradually diluted.

The House of the Left Divided

Kurahara and *Senki* took their theoretical controversy with the *rōnō* group and its *Bungeisensen* as seriously as they took their opposition to the bourgeois writers. What then were the major differences and similarities between the two groups vis-à-vis the role of art? The representative theoretician of the *rōnō* group, Kobori Jinji, whose wife was the writer Hirabayashi Taiko, wrote an article in July 1929 in which he defined the theory of the *rōnō* literary members. Kobori, too, argued that the primary purpose of the proletarian art movement was to serve the "establishment of the proletarian political hegemony and the realization of the classless society." He observed that "through literature, the propagation of individualism, the life pattern of the naturalists and that of the hedonists have interfered with the development of the class consciousness of the proletariat." The tendency was assisted above all by the development of new methods of communication, which enabled "the capitalist class to place the masses under their intellectual and emotional influence."

Kobori warned against the "undue appreciation of the role of the intellectuals," especially their role in art; for "although the intellectuals are capable of proletarian thinking, they are not able to feel as the proletariat does." It was wrong, according to Kobori, to deduce from the contributions of Marx and Engels to the social sciences the role that intellectuals might play in the realm of art. "Emotion is a far more immediate derivative of one's circumstances than intellect is. Therefore, the sentiment and the emotion of the proletariat are almost exclusively dependent on the unique circumstances under which the proletariat lives." The depreciation of the bourgeois intellectuals reflected the primarily working-class background of the *rōnō* writers. By seeing a distinction between intellect and emotion, however, Kobori did not yield any autonomy to art. Rather, he argued against the confusion of political, economic, and artistic activities within the proletarian movement, and proposed a "division of labor" for the attainment of the universal goal. Only within politics did he see art as having its raison d'être. The implied separation of politics and art under the idea of the division of labor was undercut by Kobori's identification of artistic and political value. A good work of art is necessarily determined by its content and necessarily plays the political role of "radicalizing the class struggle." There is a surprising similarity here between Kobori and Nakano, who argued that "only a good piece of art can be of efficient use for the proletarian movement."

Kobori also argued against "the theory of the 'massization' of art" proposed by Hayashi Fusao. Hayashi had proposed a dichotomy, in essence similar to that of Kurahara, between literature for the masses and literature for the vanguard. This dichotomy was irritating to an intellectual like Kobori, who had already suffered from the tyranny of intellectuals in the movement. It was equivalent to suggesting that proletarian literature should address itself to two different levels, one for the masses and the other for conscious intellectuals, whom Kobori heartily depreciated. He observed in *Senki:* "The ill influence of bourgeois literature is constantly reproduced." "The alpha and omega of the proletarian literary movement," therefore, "is to speak clearly to the working class, and to recruit the new artistic talent born of this class." These two objectives alone "would ensure the class character of the proletarian art movement and would make possible the steady development of our movement." "Exceptionally, there are a few intellectuals who in their thoughts and emotions can approximate those of the proletariat. Still, however, we should not try to find a reservoir of proletarian writers outside of their own class." "With the increase in the number of writers with a working-class background, the quality of our literature will steadily rise."

One of Kobori's finest contributions was that he fully appreciated the artistic legacies of the past. Within the historical limitations of bourgeois society, bourgeois art had produced fine literary works. For the impatient Marxists, the task of searching out the best in the past was a vain effort. Kobori, however, found that there was something in art that transcended its merely ideological character. He pointed out that the distinction between popular novels and those of purely artistic quality reflected the schizophrenic nature of post-Meiji Japanese society, particularly Japan since the 1910s. The popular novels, with their quick pace, imaginary themes, and ideal visions, appealed to the wishful mentality of the dissatisfied masses. On the other hand, there was pure literature "which revealed the conservative mentality fearful of change. At times, however, we find works fiercely antagonistic to the existing form of social institutions . . . They are written, however, merely for the satisfaction of the egoistic sentiment." Kobori, then, saw the distinction between popular literature and literature of artistic quality, which parallels Nakano's distinction between literature for the masses and that for the vanguard, or Kurahara's distinction between literature for pure agitation and literature that possessed genuine proletarian artistic quality. Thus the proletarian art movement was ready to proceed to create its own finest work, for only such work could serve the best interests of the larger movement for the liberation of the proletariat. It had to sacrifice mere agitation for genuine art. The proletarian art of Kobori, borrowing the image of the schizophrenic nature of bourgeois art, escapes total politicism.[88]

Kobori refused to abide by the political directives of the Communist Party. Paradoxically, however, he was far more optimistic about the potentiality of the Japanese proletariat than were the members of the NAPF. He was more militant about the independence of its writers, precisely because he saw that the proletarian writers had become competent enough to carry out their mission without wholly relying on the bourgeois intellectuals.

But if these features of Kobori's thinking marked the differences between the *rōnō* group and the NAPF, the similarities were far more striking: their discontent with the existing form of Japanese society, their dedication to the basic precepts of Marxism, their willingness to accept the placing of political objetives above art, their fear of the bourgeoisie, their preoccupation with bettering their knowledge of Marxism, their confidence in the future. All these similarities and more, however, did not allow them to collaborate. The impossibility of mutual cooperation on any level had been a foregone conclusion. The simple and strict relationship the Marxists made between theoretical perfection and organizational success led them to hesitate to work with anyone who had the slightest doubt about the party.

Unable to collaborate even with the *rōnō* intellectuals, the NAPF was gradually isolated within Japanese society. In 1929 the two classics of the genre appeared. Kobayashi Takiji's *Kanikōsen* (A crab ship) and Tokunaga Sunao's *Taiyō no nai machi* (A town without the sun) are irrefutable proof of the excellence of the proletarian literature of the late 1920s. Our admiration for these work and others has its roots not in their ideological consciousness but in the meticulous craftsmanship they commanded, their careful realism, social consciousness, and courage in portraying life as they saw it in the face of the cruelest persecution. After 1929, however, proletarian literature experienced a sharp decline. This was attributable largely to the government's policy of suppressing leftist organizations. At the same time, the Marxists' failure to communicate with the masses cut them off from the public. The ambiguous relationship between artists and theoreticians paralyzed the creative potentialities of many young writers, prompting a number of them to turn away from the movement.

In 1931 the NAPF published its own statement of self-criticism. Recognizing the literary achievements of 1929 and 1930, it saw certain trends unfavorable to the creative intellectuals. The worst of them was "the tendency to demand the presence of a revolutionary situation in all subject matter treated." The article went on to say that "the trend led to the general stagnation of subject matter." Art had become both superficial and stereotyped. In order to rectify the mistake, the NAPF decided "to emphasize more the creative nature of the proletariat." Thus the problem originally raised by Hirabayashi had still not been solved as late as 1931. "We have not as yet overcome the difficulty the Marxist writers face." [89] To comply with the command to portray the revolutionary potential in any situation, a writer would invariably produce a protagonist who was a member of the proletariat; with an incredible understanding of Marxist ideology, he would correctly act in conformity with the historical needs of the moment. This protagonist would symbolize the consciousness and the strength of the working class and would endure all hardships. Temptation to apostasy and the cruelty of the police became tediously common themes. The story invariably ended on a hopeful note which belied the gloomy beginning. Hence, "proletarian realism" is a misnomer. It is more a reversed romanticism—the romantic longing for a better future—a genre of historical novel with no tolerance for diversity. There is only one truth within a given situation as it is judged against the scale of

Marxian dialectical materialism, and the protagonists never failed to comprehend this truth. The NAPF became aware that such a trend would breed less than imaginative literature.

Just as the writers and critics recognized that tolerance within the proletarian literary movement was necessary for writers, the communist groups faced increasing and increasingly ruthless government persecution. The writings of the proletarian writers were fatally censored and cut. Almost every issue of *Senki*, upon publication, was prohibited from public sale, and this was the only remaining legal publication over which the Communist Party had control. In the circumstances, organizationally and ideologically the party became fearful of any deviationist tendencies among its members and sympathizers, and ideological control was tightened.[90] The political leaders' policies encouraged destructive tendencies within Japanese society, for a chaotic situation was exactly what they wished to create. During the months of the Manchurian incident, the writers were left alone, while the leaders of the party refused to collaborate with the liberal and the other socialist groups opposed to the war on the continent.[91]

The proletarian authors experienced still another misfortune in their failure to draw fruitfully upon the literary legacies of Japan. Maruyama Shizuka, a contemporary literary critic, complains legitimately that, whereas Kurahara allowed the proletarian authors to learn from Western writers, he made no reference to the Japanese classics.[92] Kurahara, indeed, wrote: "Without studying the past literature, without absorbing critically the literary legacies of which we are the heirs, it is impossible to carry out the struggle for the development of the language . . . and literary techniques." "From realists and romantics, from Heine, Tolstoy, and from a part of Dostoevsky and from Flaubert and Stendhal," Japanese literature and art can benefit. "There is nothing sectarian about Marxism. For it has developed not from the total rejection of the achievement of man's thought in the past but from the dialectical transcendence of them all." [93] Maruyama, however, points out the conspicuous absence in the literary criticism of the 1920s of attention to such Japanese classics as *Mannyōshū, The Tale of Genji, The Tale of the Heike,* and Chikamatsu.[94] Nor was there a proper appreciation of such modern Japanese literary figures as Futabatei Shimei, Kunikida, Shimazaki, or Natsume. The critics ignored, but not with impunity, the social and literary power of their immediate predecessors.[95]

It is symbolic that the Marxist critics made no significant reference during these years to the Japanese classics. Marxism was a European idea, and the Japanese Marxists, especially the major theoreticians, were intellectually and even emotionally better trained in the history of the West than in their own. Perhaps we may attribute to this factor a part of the failure of the proletarian intellectuals to communicate with the masses, engrossed as the latter were with indigenous social symbols. The liberals of the period, if we recall the experience of the Shirakaba-ha and of a figure like Watsuji Tetsurō, deftly returned to the Japanese past. Impatiently, the Marxists refused to acknowledge the liberal intellectuals in their society. Here they committed the same error as the anarchists, although the Marxists had a far better vision of their future and a better sense of political strategy. Many intellectuals now came to feel that Natsume or Nagai better approximated their own experiences than did the proletarian writers, and they turned away from the latter. During the 1930s, scholarly controversies were conducted in academic secrecy. The world of art and letters welcomed the Marxist apostates, who now tried to find their literary rehabilitation in various movements ranging from nihilism to enthusiastic nationalism.[96]

What prompted the frustration of the proletarian writers was the hesitancy of party members to allow their writers to contribute to "bourgeois" publications. In the June issue of *Senki,* the Central Committee of the NAPF published a directive to its members on this problem.[97] Contributing to bourgeois publications was considered dangerous, for it could lead to the corruption of party ideology and the relaxation of organizational discipline, as well as to an increase in the circulation of such publications.[98] There were two conditions under which a member might publish his work in journals other than those which were the organs of the NAPF:

(1) If the NAPF could control the editorial phase of the publication of the journals and books to which a member might contribute.
(2) If an individual member worked for his livelihood only on the technical side of the publication.[99]

Basically, the argument for the restrictions was based on an old resolution adopted by the Russian Social Democrats in November 1907. The entire text of this resolution was translated in the same issue of *Senki*. The main theoretical features consisted of three points:

(1) The participation of the social democrats in the liberal and liberal democratic publications would harm Marxism. It would lead to ideological and organizational corruption.
(2) When the editorial power is in the hands of those who are hostile or skeptical toward Marxism, no social democrat should be allowed to contribute to the publication, lest it should strengthen the opposing views.
(3) The complete and total control of the writings by the party members should be mandatory.[100]

Now, with the severe restrictions imposed on party members and sympathizers in the matter of contributing to ordinary and legal publications, with the increasing government surveillance, and with an indifferent and hostile public, the Marxist intellectuals formed an island within Japanese society, a closed society within a closed society.

Meantime, between July 1930 and February 1931, Kurahara was in the Soviet Union. Originally the party had intended to send him there for a long period of time, but in October 1930 he had to change his plans because of the collapse of the party leadership.[101] From the spring of 1931 to April 4, 1932, when the police finally located him in hiding, Kurahara wrote a few important articles to answer the various needs of both the party and the writers. In June 1931, he wrote an essay entitled "The Organizational Problems of the Proletarian Art Movement" and subtitled "The Necessity for the Reorganization of Factory and Village to Make Them the Basis of Operations." The article attributed the proletarian writers' failure to establish solid roots in the working class to their organizational defects. "The reorganization of the NAPF" was to be based on "the thorough democratization of the organization." "How can the proletarian art movement which is now bolshevized be implemented in organization? Is it through the bolshevization of the NAPF? No. Indeed, the opposite is required. The policy of bolshevization of the art movement has to be accompanied by thoroughly democratizing its organization." Kurahara warned against the "excessive control, unnecessary secrecy, the failure to reflect the opinions among the rank-and-file members of the NAPF." Proceeding from the precept that democracy within the party is indispensable for its political and intellectual growth, Kurahara pointed out the danger that without more freedom within the artistic establishment, "the excess in control and centralism" would lead to the "corruption of the organization and to the sectionalism of a few ideologically well-disciplined intellectuals."

Kurahara pleaded that the basis for contact with the masses be widened. This basis was to be found in the factories and villages. To perpetuate the movement, the NAPF was to avail itself of all legal means for the purpose of propagating party policies. The democratization of the NAPF itself, as well as its search for a wider basis of communication with the masses, were basically conditioned by the bolshevization of the party. Kurahara proposed that writers should not be deceived by the apparent relaxation of ideological and organizational discipline.

By suggesting that the existing readers of *Senki,* for example, should open their doors to more workers, those who had hitherto been either indifferent or "bourgeoisized," and that the workers and peasants hitherto unorganized ought to be brought into specific artistic organizations, Kurahara in fact confused the theoretical issue he had once solved. In other words, his aim in this essay was to make the art movement essentially a movement for agitation and a didactic instrument for the political indoctrination of the masses. This time he remained silent on the concrete literary needs of true writers.[102]

The practical conclusion of all this was to fight the opportunism of nonpolitical and exclusively cultural tendencies which Kurahara considered still existed within the movement. He felt that the proletarian cultural movement has developed in Japan within the realm of art. Organizationally, the NAPF is not sufficient for those working in the movement to act as a genuine wing of the communist movement in this country. In theory, he was approaching the viewpoint of Kaji and Tani rather than his own position of two years earlier, when he had tried to give an artistic role to artists. At no point did the NAPF ever give serious thought to making art independent of politics. Katsumoto Seiichirō, another NAPF theoretician, then visiting in Berlin, complained that Kurahara's view "would confine the responsibility of the artist movement to the cultural activities of labor unions and peasant organizations." Katsumoto's complaint graphically expressed the predicament in which proletarian writers found themselves in the early 1930s.[103]

This was the final politicization of art both in theory and practice. In the last two issues of *Senki* Kurahara wrote his "Thought on the Method of Art." The underlying thesis of these essays was that, while allowing the artists to see the complexity of human experience, it was necessary to impose on artists a monolithic writing method, based on a thorough understanding of dialectical materialism.[104] Epistemological training in dialectical materialism became the categorical imperative for an artist, for this method alone would ensure him of a place in history. The artists were paralyzed under a crippled party which would not admit its own death. Japanese history after 1930 has left its wishful servants behind.

Conclusion

Politics are the public actions of free men; free men are
those who do, not merely can, live both publicly and
privately. Men who have lost the capacity for public action,
who fear it or despise it, are not free; they are simply
isolated and ineffectual. Aristotle once wrote, in a terrible
phrase for all times, that the man who seeks to dwell outside the *polis* or the political relationship is "either a beast
or a god."

> B. R. Crick
> Inaugural Lecture
> University of Sheffield
> 1966

Natsume Sōseki once described the experience of modern
Japanese intellectuals in search of meaning as a "hell of loneliness." In *Kōjin* (Passers-by) he wrote: "I have no other course
for my future but to become insane, to die, or to embrace religion." [1] The three choices were the alternatives to existing in a
hostile society. The intellectuals were heirs to the legacy of the
revolutionary restoration. Deep in their hearts they were
trapped by the historical paradox that modern Japan was born
not so much of the victory of the new forces over the old as of
the skillful self-transformation of the old forces themselves. To
reject parts of the new Japanese society, then, often meant to

reject the whole of it. Whatever solution they sought, be it independence, freedom, or emancipation, they tended to locate it elewhere than in their own society, for they found it difficult to recognize such ideals as social categories.

Mushakōji apotheosized the individual only in the realm of art, claiming that "literature has to deal with life. Yet there is no necessity to interfere with society. Nay, it would be even closer to the truth to say that in literature there should not be any interference with it." [2] Akutagawa acknowledged, though grudgingly, that it was utterly impossible to isolate oneself from society, and he proceeded to the most radical form of social alienation. Arishima impugned the artistic arrogance of his fellow Shirakaba-ha intellectuals, and found in Marxism the justification for his critical thought as well as an excuse for his own social impotence. Whereas Akutagawa believed that those committed to art were socially castrated by their own artistic commitment, Arishima invoked history to explain his alienation. In both cases, the hell of loneliness found no remedy. Uchimura's religious solution, which appealed to many young intellectuals, demanded that they bear with the hell of this world in anticipation of otherworldly blessings. The naturalists did have the courage to suspend themselves in limbo between society and their artistic world. Often, like the Shirakaba-ha writers, they made remarkably acute critical comments on their society. Shimazaki himself, however, confessed that he had no vision of the future.[3] The anarchists had their own solution for ameliorating the evils of their society. Few of them, however, went beyond the idea of destroying it.

The younger Marxist writers succeeded in removing many of the causes of the anxiety suffered by their intellectual predecessors. From the Marxist theory of history they learned their historical role—a role that naturalists and Arishima had craved. Under Marxism, the individual was elevated to a level where he could command history instead of having to await divine intervention to remedy society's ills. Marxism taught that the identity of thought and action was possible, and it challenged the fatalistic resignation of the naturalists. It awakened the indifferent and dormant intellectuals to an awareness that all was not well with their society and that something could be done. Based on faith in the rational worth of man, the essence of European radicalism—that man can manipulate his social and moral lot—finally found its way to Japan.

The misfortune was not that Marxism taught the intellectuals to share the burden of society, but that it gave them an exaggerated sense of their own worth. Having become the most faithful servants of history, furthermore, they were in the end enslaved by their own conception of it. In Marxism, politics should be merely a means toward the ultimate end of bringing about a communist society. Yet as used by these Marxists politics eventually made instruments of the individuals in the movement.

Raymond Aron has observed that "the intellectual will lose interest in politics as soon as he discovers its limitations." This remark portrays with stunning accuracy what happened to many of the Japanese Marxist writers after the nineteen-twenties. Aron continues: "If [the disillusioned intellectuals] alone can abolish fanaticism, let us pray for the advent of the sceptics." [4] Instead of becoming political skeptics, however, many of the disillusioned Japanese intellectuals turned to nationalistic fanaticism, artistic anarchism, or nihilistic escapism. Their faith disillusioned them. Their society alienated them. The hell of loneliness remained.

Preoccupied with their own philosophical, religious, or aesthetic pursuits, the prewar Japanese intellectuals on the whole failed to see a paradoxical, yet simple, fact about constitutional government. This form of government does not invade the inner life of man; it philosophically assumes the plurality of individual values and faith and has the strength to permit political indifference, on the one hand, and to invite criticism or even hostility on the other. It institutionally and legally guarantees freedom of choice for man in his social, political, and intellectual life. Yet in times of crisis, when it faces challenges from impatient foes, it can not survive without the conscious and sympathetic support and participation of those who benefit from it. Such a simple truth often eludes the most intelligent and sensitive of men.

Notes

Bibliography

Glossary

Index

Notes

I. THE REVOLUTIONARY RESTORATION

1. Akutagawa Ryūnosuke, "Shuju no kotoba" (Words of a dwarf), *GNB*, XXVI, 191.

2. Maruyama Masao, "Nihon no shisō" (Japanese thought), in *Gendai shisō* (Tokyo, 1957), XI, 3–48. In what is undoubtedly one of the most brilliant critiques of Japanese intellectual experiences, Maruyama points out the danger of the tyranny of an idea which is accepted uncritically, and pleads for the strength of the individual to bear the burden of dealing with ambiguous realities without resorting to an easy, all-embracing solution or to despair.

3. Funayama Shin'ichi, *Nihon no kannen ronsha* (Tokyo, 1956), pp. 222–223.

4. *Nishida Kitarō zenshū*, Iwanami ed. (1948–1953), appendix, V, 49.

5. *Ibid.*, appendix, I, 59.

6. *Ibid.*, p. 101.

7. Miyajima Hajime, *Meijiteki shisōkazō no keisei* (Tokyo, 1960).

8. *Nishida Kitarō*, appendix, I, 148.

9. See Miki Kiyoshi, *Dokusho to jinsei* (Tokyo, 1948), pp. 2, 39. See also Kurata Hyakuzō, *GNB*, LXIV, 307–317. In this short essay, Kurata introduces Nishida's *Zen no kenkyū* to the public. Although the essay was written in November 1912, it was first published in 1921 in Kurata's *Ai to ninshiki tono shuppatsu* (Beginning of love and understanding). Through this collection of essays many Japanese were introduced to Nishida's work. See also Miyajima, pp. 11–12.

10. *Zen no kenkyū*, Iwanami ed. (Tokyo), p. 52.

11. *Ibid.*, p. 64.

12. *Ibid.*, pp. 60–61. Nishida himself feels that "art understands the real nature of existence" better than scholars and scientists, who abstract their experiences.

13. *Ibid.*, in *Nishida Kitarō*, I, 67–71. Here Nishida speaks of the order and harmony of the universe. In it he sees no accidental event. "Hegel said what is real is rational, and what is rational is real . . . From a certain point of view it is a refutable truth . . . What we consider accidental appears so due to our ignorance." This is not so much a conservative thought as a quiescent attitude, taking things as they come. See also Judith Shklar, *After Utopia* (Princeton, 1957), p. 12.

14. *Zen no kenkyū*, pp. 169, 170.

15. Letter to Nishida Sotohiko (Mar. 12, 1950), in *Nishida Kitarō*, appendix, VI, 108.
16. *Ibid.*, IV, 6.
17. Letter, in *ibid.*, Appendix, VI, 47.
18. "Junsuikeiken sōgo no kankei oyobi renraku ni tsuite" (On relationship and contact among pure experiences), in *Nishida Kitarō*, appendix, II, 67.
19. *Ibid.*, X, 331.
20. Letter, in *ibid.*, appendix, VI, 92–93.
21. "Zoku shisaku to taiken igo" (Since *Thoughts and Experiences, Continued*), in *ibid.*, XII, 271.
22. *Zoku shisaku to taiken, ibid.*, p. 93.
23. See Minobe Tatsukichi, *Kempō satsuyō* (Tokyo, 1923). Cf. Ienaga Saburō, *Minobe Tatsukichi no shisō-shiteki kenkyū* (Tokyo, 1964), which is a brilliant analysis of Minobe's ideas on law, society, and politics.
24. Watsuji Tetsurō, *Son'nōshisō to sono dentō* (Tokyo, 1943), pp. 57, 60.

II. UCHIMURA KANZŌ

1. Ōhara Kokingo, "Hokuchi kigen" (Warnings from the north), quoted in Maruyama Masao, *Nihon seiji shisō-shi kenkyū* (Tokyo, 1956), p. 340.
2. "Shitsubō to kibō: Nippon koku no sendo" (Disappointment and hope: The future of Japan), in *Uchimura Kanzō zenshū* (Tokyo, 1932–1933), XIV, 228–229.
3. "Warera no Kirisutokyō" (Our Christianity), in *ibid.*, XIII, 36.
4. "Kōkoku to bōkoku" (Prosperous countries and ruined countries), in *ibid.*, I, 667–668.
5. *The Japan Christian Intelligencer*, in *ibid.*, XV, 592. When a then well-known missionary, J. Cook, came to Japan in 1882, he noted that the real obstacles to Christianity in Japan were of European origin. See Otis Cary, *A History of Christianity in Japan* (New York, 1909), p. 161. See also Sumiya Mikio, *Kindai Nihon no keisei to Kirisutokyō* (Tokyo, 1950), p. 63. Sumiya observes that by the 1880s such books as Paine's *Age of Reason*, Ingersoll's *Lecture on God*, Draper's *Conflict Between Science and Religion*, Do's *The Intellectual Development of Europe*, and works by J. S. Mill had been translated, thus forming the basis for a formidable intellectual opposition to Christian theology in Japan.
6. Ernst Troeltsch, *The Social Teaching of the Christian Churches* (New York, 1931), p. 732.

7. "Epesosho kenkyū" (A study of Ephesians), in *Uchimura,* VII, 386.

8. *Alone with God and Me,* in *Uchimura,* XV, 370–466.

9. "Tanjū sūteki" (A few drops of bile), in *ibid.,* II, 399.

10. *Alone with God and Me, ibid.,* XV, 462, 464.

11. "Kyōkai shomondai" (Various problems of churches), in *Uchimura,* IX, 238–239.

12. *Ibid.,* p. 239.

13. *Alone with God and Me, ibid.,* XV, 392.

14. Cf. Shigefuji Takeo, *Makkusu Uēbā kenkyū* (Tokyo, 1949), p. 75.

15. "Shidō" (Samurai's code), in *Yamaga Sokō zenshū* (Complete works of Yamaga Soko), vol. 7, quoted in Shigefuji, pp. 23–24, 182.

16. In his autobiography, *How I Became a Christian* (*Uchimura,* XV, 15), Uchimura writes: "I alone was left a heathen; the much detested idolator, the incorrigible worshiper of wood and stones. I will remember the extremity and loneliness to which I was reduced then. One afternoon I resorted to a heathen temple in the vicinity said to have been authorized by the government to be the guardian god of the district. At some distance from the sacred mirror which represented the invisible presence of the deity, I prostrated myself upon coarse dried grass, and . . . prayed . . . and beseeched that guardian god to speedily extinguish the new enthusiasm in my college, to punish such as those who obstinately refused to disown the strange god, and to help me in my humble endeavor in the patriotic cause I was upholding, then."

17. Maruyama Masao, *Nihon seiji,* p. 30.

18. *Alone with God and Me,* in *Uchimura,* XV, 446, 538.

19. "Sanjō no suikun ni tsuite: Torinozokubeki mittsu no gokai" (About the Sermon on the Mount: Three misunderstandings that should be corrected), in *ibid.,* V, 79.

20. Karl Mannheim, *Ideology and Utopia* (New York, 1936), p. 112.

21. "Yotei no kyōgi" (The doctrine of predetermination), in *Uchimura,* VIII, 720.

22. "Shinja to gensei: Mataiden goshō jūsan jūroku setsu no kenkyū" (Believers and this world: A study of Matthew, 5:13–16), in *ibid.,* V, 97.

23. "Shin no dendōshi" (A true evangelist), in *ibid.,* IX, 296.

24. Cf. Marianne Weber, *Max Weber: Ein Lebensbild* (Tübingen, 1926), p. 382.

25. "Mukyōkai shugi no zenshin" (Advancement of the doctrine of no-church), in *Uchimura,* IX, 216.

26. Tamura Naoomi, *Bokushi ni natte kara* (Since I became a pastor), quoted in Sumiya, *Kindai Nihon*, p. 20.

27. *Uchimura*, XV, 65.

28. Ishihara Ken, "Meiji Nihon ni okeru Purotesutanto kyōkai" (Protestant churches in Meiji Japan), *Fukuin to sekai* (Gospel and the world; August 1946), pp. 21–23. Ishihara gives the following figures for the percentage of churches that were financially self-supporting:

Year	Percentage
1882	14.7
1885	15.6
1888	23.0
1894	21.4
1902	17.0

29. *Alone with God and Me.*, in *Uchimura*, XV, 452–454.

30. *Ibid.*, p. 398.

31. See Kuyama Yasushi *et al.*, *Kindai Nihon to kirisutokyō* (Tokyo, 1956), p. 133.

32. "Kirisuto shinto no nagusame" (Consolation of Christian believers), in *Uchimura*, I, 28.

33. "Seisho kenkyūsha no tachiba yori mitaru kirisuto no sairin" (The second coming of Christ viewed by a Bible researcher), *ibid.*, IX, 639–641.

34. *Ibid.*, p. 760.

35. *Ibid.*, p. 641.

36. *Ibid.*, p. 640. It was in a copy of the *Sunday School Times* which Uchimura received in 1916 from an American friend that he found a suggestion of this doctrine.

37. "Seisho no shōmei: Kirisuto sairin ni kansuru omonaru seigo" (Proofs in the Bible: Some of the important holy words concerning the second coming of Christ), *ibid.*, p. 643, "Iesu no shūmatsu kan: Mataiden dai nijūyon shō no kenkyū" (Eschatology of Jesus: A study of Matthew, chap. 24), *ibid.*, p. 678.

38. "Shichifuku no kai" (An explanation of the seven blessings), *ibid.*, pp. 656–657.

39. "Kirisuto sairin no yokkyū: Roma sho hasshō jūyon, nijūsan setsu no kenkyū" (Desire for the second coming of Christ: A study of Romans, 8:14–23), *ibid.*, p. 741.

40. *Ibid.*

41. Mannheim, p. 112.

42. "Nisshin sensō no gi" (Meaning of the Sino-Japanese War), *Uchimura*, II, 212–221.

43. Quoted in Tabata Shinobu, "Uchimura Kanzō ni okeru hei-

washugi shisō no tenkai" (The development of pacifism in Uchimura Kanzō), *Shisō*, No. 353:27 (Nov. 1953).

44. "Tanjū yoteki" (More drops of bile), *Uchimura*, II, 420.

45. On Fukuzawa Yukichi's pacifism, see Tabata, and also a letter to Mr. D. C. Bell (June 6, 1895), in *ibid.*, XX, 290.

46. "Heiwa no shukufuku" (The blessing of peace), *ibid.*, V, 89, "Jinsei mondai kaishaku no hōhō" (Method of understanding life's problems), *ibid.*, XIV, 275, "Heiwa naru" (Accomplishment of peace), *ibid.*, p. 380.

47. "Kinji zakkan" (Miscellaneous impressions of the present), *ibid.*, p. 304.

48. "Hisenshugisha no senshi" (The death of a pacifist in battle), *ibid.*, p. 363.

49. "Senji ni okeru hisenshugisha no taido" (The attitude of pacifists in wartime), *ibid.*, p. 330.

50. Another type of compromise would be to find some mystical value in identifying oneself with the people when one faces the dilemma between one's ideal and the reality the people demand. For the parallel case of Emil Lask (1875–1915), see Marianne Weber, p. 538. The latter gives an interesting case of an intellectual consciously trying to mitigate the gap between the masses and the intelligentsia, although his was a negative solution.

51. "Kinji zakkan," *ibid.*, p. 304.

52. "Noa no daikōzui o omou" (Thoughts on Noah's flood), *ibid.*, p. 479.

53. See Ishida Takeshi, *Meiji seiji shisō-shi kenkyū* (Tokyo, 1954), p. 39. The system of the new state ethics was outlined in terms of the divine authority of the emperor through the promulgation of the rescript. Ishida correctly points out that the rescript contains two basically contradictory components which were rather clumsily compromised: one was the effort to inculcate people with the notion that they should submit themselves to the existing hierarchical system of authority by glorifying the traditional virtues of filial piety and loyalty; the other was the effort to arouse in the people a desire to unite horizontally so as to form an emotionally unified and patriotic nation. It is the latter component that is indicative of the enlightened aspects of the rescript.

54. "Bungakuhakushi Inoue Tetsujirō kun ni teisuru kōkaijō" (An open letter to Inoue Tetsujiro, Doctor of Literature), in *Uchimura*, II, 180, 183, 184.

55. For his theological advocacy of "patrimonial ethics," see "Shinja to gensei," *ibid.*, V, 97–98.

56. Quoted by Uchimura in his open letter to Inoue Tetsujiro written in 1893, *ibid.*, II, 181.

57. "Ōshūsensō to Kirisutokyō" (The First World War and Christianity), in *ibid.*, XIV, 480.

58. *How I became a Christian*, in *ibid.*, XV, 152.

59. "Nōmin kyūsaisaku toshite no kirisutokyō dendō" (Christian missionary work as a relief measure for the agrarian population), *ibid.*, XIV, 299.

60. *Ibid.*, II, 181.

61. "Mōze no jukkai to sono chūkai" (The Ten Commandments of Moses and annotation), in *ibid.*, III, 294–296.

62. Kuyama, p. 260.

63. *Ibid.*

64. *Ibid.*, p. 259.

65. "Kōdokuchi junyūki" (A report of travel through the copper-poisoned district), in *Uchimura*, XIV, p. 67, 68.

66. "Noa no kōzui" (Noah's flood), *ibid.*, III, p. 164.

67. "Mōze no jukkai to sono chūkai," *ibid.*, III, 300–301.

68. Akamatsu Katsumaro, *Nihon shakai undō-shi* (Tokyo, 1949), p. 98.

69. *Ibid.*, p. 103.

70. "Kirisutokyō to shakaishugi" (Christianity and socialism), in *Uchimura*, XIV, 264.

71. "Kinji zakkan," *ibid.*, p. 301.

72. "Gariraya no michi" (Road to Galilee), *ibid.*, V, 562.

73. "Risōdan wa nan de aru ka" (What is Risōdan?), *ibid.*, XIV, 92.

74. "Kokka to katei to kojin" (A nation, a family, and an individual), *ibid.*, pp. 15–16.

75. *Ibid.*, XVII, 17.

76. "Kirisuto shinto no nagusame," *ibid.*, I, 60–61.

77. "Tanjū sūteki," *ibid.*, II, 399.

78. "Tanjū yoteki," *ibid.*, p. 421. Katsu Kaishū, as military commissioner of the Tokugawa bakufu, surrendered the city of Edo and the Tokugawa political hegemony and thus preserved the city (present-day Tokyo) from possible destruction.

79. "Yorozu" (A myriad), *ibid.*, p. 431.

80. "Tanjū sūteki," *ibid.*, p. 400.

81. "Yohai no hossuru kaikaku" (The reforms I desire), *ibid.*, pp. 541–542.

82. Uchimura was bitterly opposed to those who tried to justify the materialistic motives of such a man as Fukuzawa Yukichi. "Shakai no kyūsai" (The relief of society), in *Uchimura*, XIV, 411.

83. "Kyūanroku" (A record of search for peace), *ibid.*, I, 145.

84. *Heimin shimbun* (People's news; Nov. 29, 1903), quoted in Ienaga Saburō, *Nihon kindai shisō-shi kenkyū* (Tokyo, 1953), p. 244.
85. "Shokan oyobi kansō" (Impressions and thoughts), in *Uchimura*, II, 662–663.
86. *Ibid.*, XX, 336.
87. Quoted in Ienaga, *Nihon Kindai shisō*, p. 251.
88. "Hibi no shōgai" (Daily life), in *Uchimura*, XVII, 337.
89. *Ibid.*, XVIII, 12.
90. "Hibi no shōgai," *ibid.*, XVII, 49–50.
91. Ienaga, *Nihon kindai shisō*, p. 257.
92. Quoted in *ibid.*
93. "Denmaruku koku no hanashi" (Stories about Denmark), *ibid.*, XIV, 703–715.
94. This mood of anti-industrialism prevailed among many intellectuals who disliked their nation's preoccupation with material prosperity. See, e.g., *(Nagai) Kafū zenshū* (Tokyo, 1948–1953), "the whole Meiji culture is conveniently based on vanity . . . Hundreds of modern Parliaments, hundreds of modern churches and hundreds of modern schools are merely miscellaneous imported European goods."
95. See Chapter III, n. 1; see also Edward Seidensticker, *Kafū the Scribbler* (Stanford, 1965), pp. 45–47.
96. *Uchimura*, I, 663–664.
97. G. W. F. Hegel, *Philosophy of History*, tr. J. Sibree, as quoted in George Sabine, *A History of Political Theory* (New York, 1954), p. 630.
98. Sabine, p. 631.
99. "Kirisutokyō to aikokushin" (Christianity and patriotism) in *Uchimura*, XIV, 561.
100. *The Philosophy of Hegel*, ed. and tr. Carl J. Friedrich, p. 145.
101. "Nipponkoku to Kirisutokyō" (Japan and Christianity), *Uchimura*, XIV, 627–643.

III. THE ANARCHISTS

1. For this episode, see Itoya Toshio, *Daigyaku jiken* (Tokyo, 1960). For the complete bibliography see *ibid.*, pp. 239–265. Also *GNB*, appendix, I, 157. In his short story "Hanabi" (Tokyo, 1924), in *(Nagai) Kafū*, XII, 215–227, Nagai describes how he came to feel his social impotence as he witnessed the trial and the execution of the anarchists. Yet Tokutomi Roka and some other prominent intellectuals protested the government measure stifling the intellectual activities of the Japanese.

2. Suzuki Fujiya in the April issue of *Kokka shakaishugi* (National socialism), quoted in *KNS, I,* 216.

3. Arahata Kanson, *Kanson jiden* (Tokyo, 1960), pp. 226–240. For the materials on the Japanese radical movement after 1941, see Watabe Yoshimichi, et al., *Nihon shakaishugi bunken kaisetsu* (Tokyo, 1958), pp. 80–122.

4. *Kindai Nihon shisō-shi,* vol. 4 (a chronological chart of major publications since 1858; Tokyo, 1957).

5. For the details, see *Tenkō* (Tokyo, 1959), pp. 69–71; Shinobu Seizaburō, *Taishō seiji-shi* (Tokyo, 1954), pp. 79–804; Karasawa Tomitarō, *Gakusei no rekishi* (Tokyo, 1955), pp. 216–257.

6. Mori Ōgai, indeed, was the intellectual closest to the ruling elite. Yet he was critical of the crude method the government used to handle the anarchosyndicalists. For his concern with socialism see *KNS,* I, 162–168; Katō Shūichi, *Ōgai,* in *NB,* XV, 34. Also *GNB,* appendix, I, 298. For his feeling toward General Yamagata Aritomo, see "Kokian ki," in *Ōgai zenshū,* Iwanami ed. (Tokyo, 1954–1956), XVIII, 432–433.

7. *Ōgai,* XX, 518–525 (his correspondence on socialism, revealing his knowledge of the subject).

8. On Kōtoku Shūsui, see Tanaka Sōgorō, *Kōtoku Shūsui* (Tokyo, 1955). For a selected compilation of Kōtoku's own works see *Kōtoku Shūsui sensho* (Tokyo, 1950). For his diary and letters, see *Kōtoku Shūsui: Nikki to shokan,* ed. Shioda Shōbei (Tokyo, 1954). Attention to Kōtoku's political thought is indispensable for understanding the radical antiparliamentary mood and thinking of the left.

9. Minobe Ryōkichi, *Kumonsuru demokurashī* (Tokyo, 1959), pp. 26, 28. The special attorneys were Abe Isoo, Yoshino Sakuzō, Sasaki Sōichi, Miyake Setsurei, Anezaki Masaharu, Takano Iwasaburō. All of them were opinion leaders of Taishō Japan as well as some of its best legal minds. For an interesting account of the background, see Ōuchi Hyōe, *Watakushi no rirekisho* (Tokyo, 1951), pp. 157–170.

10. Quoted in Minobe Ryōkichi, pp. 31–32. Also *Ōgai,* XXII, 222. Mori recognizes certain merits of Kropotkin's thought, although he is critical of Morito.

11. Tazoe Tetsuji was a representative leftist theoretician for parliamentarism. See Kishimoto Eitarō et al., *Katayama Sen* (Tokyo, 1960), pp. 257–288. Katayama and other parliamentary socialists originally thought that it would be possible to push social legislation through the Diet. Katayama argued that the abolition of private property was easier in Japan than it would be in Europe, for in Japan there were no recognized natural rights other than those prescribed by law. Hence, if the people agreed, it was possible to abolish private property rights through the Diet.

12. *KNS*, I, 147–148. Cf. Tazoe Tetsuji, "Shakaitō, museifutō bunretsu no kekka," (The consequences of the split of the socialist and anarchist parties), *Shakai shimbun* (The Socialist news) (Nov. 17, 1907).

13. *Chokusetsu kōdō*. See "Shakai seisaku to shakaishugi" (Social policy and socialism), *Ōsaka heimin shimbun* (The Osaka people's news) (Aug. 20, 1907), quoted in *KNS*, I, 149–150. See also "Chokusetsu kōdōron" (A theory of direct action), *Ōsugi Sakae zenshū* (Tokyo, 1923), II, 725–728.

14. *KNS*, I, 217.

15. For the movement for universal male enfranchisement, see Shinobu Seizaburō, pp. 489–609. This is the most thorough treatment of the subject matter, as well as of its political, social, and economic background.

16. For an interesting account of the militarist political ideals of the 1920s and 1930s, see Ikeda Sumihisa, "Seinen shōkō to kakushin shisō," (The young officers and radical ideas), in *Himerareta Shōwa-shi* (Tokyo, 1956).

17. Maruyama Masao, *Kōgiroku* (notes taken by students at Tokyo University in 1958–1959 and mimeographed).

18. See Togawa Yukio, *Ansatsusha* (Tokyo, 1958), e.g. pp. 171, 261.

19. Maruyama Masao, *Gendai seiji no shisō to kōdō*, vol. I (Tokyo, 1956). About the absence of any concrete plans, see *ibid.*, pp. 55–58. Maruyama writes of the careful planning for carrying out a coup d'état by the rightists and militarists, and of their failure to provide any plan to be carried out thereafter.

20. "Minshushugi no jakumetsu" (The annihilation of democracy), in *Ōsugi*, I, 556–570.

21. "Kojinshugi to seijiundō" (Individualism and political movements), *ibid.*, pp. 363, 347–370.

22. "Shakaiteki risōron" (A theory of social ideals), *ibid.*, II, 624–628.

23. "Yajū" (A wild beast), *ibid.*, pp. 764–765.

24. There were two separate series of *Kindai shisō*, Oct. 1911–Sept. 1914, and Oct. 1915–Jan. 1916. The anarchists Ōsugi and Arahata started this journal "for our genuine friends, i.e., the working class." See *Kindai shisō*, 1.1:1. Ōsugi writes of his "own instinct which is forever socially restless."

25. On Ōsugi's individualism, see Arahata, pp. 228–229. Arahata reproaches Ōsugi for his abstract individualism, See also Ōsugi's own essays, e.g., "Sei no sōzō" (Creation of life), *Ōsugi*, I, 50–58, and "Yuiitsushya" (The only one), *ibid.*, pp. 120–129. Here Ōsugi writes of his understanding of such figures as Stirner and Bergson.

26. "Beruguson to Soreru" (Bergson and Sorel), *ibid.*, pp. 406–430.

27. "Saikin shisōkai no keikō" (Recent trends in the world of thought), *ibid.*, p. 109.
28. See Ōi Tadashi, *Nihon kindai shisō no ronri* (Tokyo, 1958), pp. 170–179.
29. See Chapter V below, on Arishima Takeo.
30. "Boku wa seishin ga suki da" (I am fond of spirituality), *Ōsugi*, II, 743.
31. "Mudabana" (An abortive flower), *ibid.*, pp. 766, 767.
32. "Chishiki kaikyū ni atau" (To the intellectual class), *ibid.*, pp. 660–663.
33. Joseph Schumpeter, *Socialism, Capitalism and Democracy* (New York, 1950), pp. 153–155.
34. For Ōsugi's comments on his contemporary labor leaders, see "Rōdō undō to chishiki kaikyū" (The labor movement and the intellectual class), *Ōsugi*, II, 664–672; see also "Kagawa Toyohiko ron," "Kagawa Toyohiko ron zoku," and "Suzuki Bunji ron," in *ibid.*, pp. 689–711.
35. *Ibid.*, p. 671.
36. "Kakumei no kenkyū" (The study of revolution), *ibid.*, V, 702.
37. "Torotsukī no kyōdōsensenron" (Trotsky's theory of the united front), *ibid.*, II, 482–489.
38. *Ibid.*, pp. 487–488; "Nihon dasshutsuki" (My escape from Japan), *ibid.*, III, 371–417.
39. For their failure to collaborate, see *ibid.*, III, 399. On Ōsugi's suspicions about Bolshevism, see *ibid.*, pp. 369–394.
40. "Kumiai undō to kakumei undō" (The union movement and the revolutionary movement), *ibid.*, II, 663.
41. "Sei no sōzō," *ibid.*, I, 51–57.
42. Quoted in Ōi, p. 176.
43. "Minshū geijutsu no gikō" (The technique of popular arts), *Ōsugi*, I, 627.
44. "Rōdō undō to rōdō bungaku" (The labor movement and labor literature), *ibid.*, p. 651.
45. Nicholas Berdyaev argues in his *Slavery and Freedom* (New York, 1950), that socialism is not an inevitability (as Marxism implies) but a possibility for man to create, emphasizing the existential element necessary for any creative action. Therefore, accepting the Marxist analysis of capitalism, he criticizes the fatalistic content in the prediction Marx made of history.
46. "Sei no sōzō," *Ōsugi*, I, 53–54; "Beruguson to Soreru," *ibid.*, p. 406.
47. "Jiyū no maebure" (A forerunner of freedom), *ibid.*, II, 746. "Sei no kakujū" (Expansion of life), *ibid.*, I, 39.

48. "Atarashiki sekai no tame no atarashiki geijutsu" (New art for a new world), *ibid.,* pp. 607–608.

49. H. Stuart Hughes, *Consciousness and Society* (New York, 1958), pp. 172, 173.

50. See E. A. Shils's "Introduction" to Georges Sorel, *Reflections on Violence,* tr. T. E. Hulme and J. Roth (Glencoe, Ill., 1950), pp. 13–29.

51. "Sei no sōzō," *Ōsugi,* I, 57.

52. On the anarchist literary movement, see Takami Jun, *Shōwa bungaku seisui-shi* (Tokyo, 1958), I, 71–98.

53. Kambara Tai, "Mirai-ha no shōri" (The victory of futurism), *Shisō* (April 1922), pp. 109–120; (May 1922), pp. 143–154; (June 1922), pp. 163–169.

54. Katō Kazuo, "Ōinaru katei" (The great process), *GNB,* XCIV, 201.

55. E. H. Wilkins, *A History of Italian Literature* (Cambridge, Mass., 1954), p. 484.

56. *Ibid.,* p. 485.

57. "Atarashiki sekai no tame no atarashiki geijutsu," *Ōsugi,* I, 608–609.

58. *Asahi* (Sept. 25, 1923).

59. See Irving Howe, *Politics and the Novel* (New York, 1957), pp. 210–211.

60. Georges Sorel, *Réflexions sur la violence* (Paris, 1919), p. 32, quoted in William Y. Elliott, *The Pragmatic Revolt* (New York, 1928), p. 128.

IV. NATURALISM

1. Roger Martin du Gard, *Jean Barois,* tr. S. Gilbert (Paris, 1913), p. 256, quoted in Hughes, p. 31.

2. Arnold Hauser, *The Social History of Art* (New York, 1958), IV, 85.

3. *Ibid.,* p. 86. See also Emile Zola, *Le roman expérimental* (Paris, 1880).

4. Mannheim, p. 79.

5. A. R. Hall, *The Scientific Revolution* (New York, 1958), p. ix.

6. G. H. Mead, *Thought and Movement in the Nineteenth Century* (Chicago, 1936), p. 41; *ibid.,* pp. 25–50. See also Kant's "Metaphysical Foundations of Morals," in *The Philosophy of Kant* ed. and tr. Carl J. Friedrich (Modern Library ed.). Here and elsewhere Kant explains the relationship between necessity and freedom, which later develops into his theory on pure and practical reason. For the political rele-

vance of Kant's thought on freedom, see L. Krieger, *The German Idea of Freedom* (Boston, 1957), pp. 86–125.

7. A letter to Morita Sōhei, in *Sōseki zenshū* (The complete works of Natsume Sōseki), Iwanami ed. (Tokyo, 1928–1929), XVIII, 305.

8. Shimamura Hōgetsu, "*Hakai hyō*" (A comment on *Hakai*), *Waseda bungaku* (The Waseda literature; May 1906), quoted in Kawazoe Kunimoto, *Nihon shizenshugi no bungaku,* in *NB,* XI, 25.

9. For the contemporary commentaries written on *Hakai* in 1906–1907, see Hirano Ken, *Shimazaki Tōson* (Tokyo, 1957), pp. 23–24.

10. Hasegawa Tenkei, "Handō no genshō" (Phenomena of reaction), *Taiyō* (The sun; May 1906), quoted in Hirano, *Shimazaki,* pp. 27–28.

11. *Ibid.,* p. 31.

12. Ino Kenji, *Kindai Nihon bungaku-shi kenkyū* (Tokyo, 1953), p. 118.

13. Kamei Katsuichirō, *Shimazaki Tōson* (Tokyo, 1938), p. 58. This view is modified in Kamei's postwar work, also entitled *Shimazaki Tōson* (Tokyo, 1957). While acknowledging the socially pregnant character of *Hakai,* however, Kamei maintains that the work in essence deals with Shimazaki's own problem of facing the hostile world. Kamei's work on Shimazaki is a judicious documentation, revealing the continuity of the "romantic elements" in Shimazaki's work. For a balanced view, see Yoshida Seiichi, *Shizenshugi no kenkyū* (Tokyo, 1958), pp. 77–95.

14. Hirano, *Shimazaki,* pp. 30–34; also Kataoka Yoshikazu, *Shizenshugi kenkyū* (Tokyo, 1957), p. 63.

15. "Warazōri" (Straw sandals), *Shimazaki Tōson zenshū,* Shinchōsha ed. (Tokyo, 1950), IX, 112.

16. See Noma Hiroshi's note to the Iwanami edition of *Hakai* (Tokyo, 1957), which shows the inevitable limitations of *Hakai* as social criticism. See also the Chikuma edition of the complete works of Shimazaki, vol. 4 of which includes a note of protest presented by the Buraku Kaihō Dōmei (Federation for the Liberation of *Eta*). A cursory glance at *Hakai* at once shows the author's prejudice toward this caste. The recurrence of such expressions as "slow," "unintelligent," "nonresponsive," and the like, indicates his uncritical acceptance of the popular view of the *eta.*

17. "Rūsō no *Zange* chū ni miidashitaru jiko" (Discovery of self in Rousseau's *Confessions*), *Shimazaki zenshū,* XIV, 13–15.

18. Shimamura Hōgetsu, in *Waseda bungaku* (Oct. 1907), quoted in Kawazoe, *Nihon shizenshugi,* pp. 28–29.

19. Tayama Katai, *Futon,* in *GNB,* IX, 31–58, esp. p. 58.

20. Nakamura Mitsuo, *Fūzoku shosetsu-ron* (Tokyo, 1959), typifies

this view. Nakamura accuses Tayama's *Futon* of having diverted the socially pregnant potentiality of *Hakai* toward the creation of the genre of the *shishōsetsu* (I-novel).

21. *Arashi* (Storm), *Shimazaki zenshū*, vol. II. For the argument presented here see *ibid.*, pp. 52–143; also Akutagawa Ryūnosuke, *Aru ahō no isshō* (Life of a fool), in *GNB*, XXVI, 314. Akutagawa calls the protagonist of *Shinsei* "a cunning hypocrite." Some uninhibited praise has been given to this novel; see Hirano, *Shimazaki*, pp. 136–138; also Masamune Hakuchō, *Sakka-ron* (Tokyo, 1948), pp. 281–284.

22. Iwanaga Yutaka, *Tayama Katai kenkyū* (Tokyo, 1956), pp. 223, 244.

23. Tayama Katai, in *Waseda bungaku* (Sept. 1908), quoted in Iwanaga, p. 246. On Tayama's literary method, see also his articles in *GNB*, IX, 391–402.

24. Shirayanagi Shūko, "Paionia no akusen" (The hard battle of a pioneer), *GNB*, XCIV, 85.

25. *Ibid.*, p. 86.

26. *Ogai*, II, 209–334.

27. *Ibid.*, pp. 331, 334. For his critical comments on naturalism and literary methods, see also "Maihime" (Dancing girl), *ibid.*, pp. 11–19; and "Wasedaha ron" (Discussion on the Waseda group), *ibid.*, XV, 463–465.

28. "Igaku no setsu yori idetaru shōsetsu ron" (A discussion of the novel derived from theories of medicine), *ibid.*, XII, 1–2.

29. Quoted in Katō Shūichi, *Ogai*, *NB*, XV, 24.

30. Uozumi Setsurō, "Jikoshuchō no shisō toshite no shizenshugi" (Naturalism as the idea of individualism), *GNB*, XCIV, 103.

31. Ishikawa Takuboku, "Jidai heisoku no genjō" (On the contemporary frustration), *GNB*, XV, 209. Nakano Shigeharu, a Marxist writer and critic, has a fine piece dealing with Ishikawa's attitude to naturalism and other social and intellectual issues. Originally written in 1926, the article is "Takuboku ni kansuru danpen" (Jottings about Takuboku), *ibid.*, pp. 390–394. Elsewhere Ishikawa comments on naturalism that "because naturalism demands neither ideals nor solutions, and because it sees things as they are, it does not challenge the state . . . For the same reason, won't naturalism's fight against the hypocrisy of the old morality be a meaningless defiance?" "Kiregire ni kokoro ni ukanda kanji to kaisō" (Random thoughts and reflections; Nov. 1909).

32. On the tyrannical predominance of naturalism, see *Tanizaki Jun'ichirō zenshū*, Chūōkōron ed. (Tokyo, 1958–1959), XVI, 245.

33. Takami, *Shōwa bungaku*, pp. 9–14. Among the thirty-three contributors there are a few who had already expressed their interest

in socialism. A month later, in December 1920, the Nihon Shakaishugi Dōmei (Federation of Japanese Socialist) was formed. It included many eminent intellectuals.

34. Quoted in Takami, *Shōwa bungaku,* p. 14.

35. "Mune o hirake" (Open your heart), *Shimazaki zenshū,* XIV, 237–238. On the same page, Shimazaki writes of the evil of the "excessively analytical attitude . . . in the recent months toward human and social life."

36. *Asahi* (Jan. 1, 1925).

37. Takami Jun most graphically describes the emergence of socialist literature. If his artistic approach does not suffice for those concerned with the details of its beginning, they should consult, e.g., Nishida Masaru, *Nihon kakumei bungaku no tembō* (Tokyo, 1958), pp. 130–159, or Sobue Shōji et. al., "Puroretaria bungaku," in *NB,* vol. 13. For a more detailed discussion, see Chapter VII below.

38. *Shimazaki zenshū,* XV, 104. For the author's notes on the novel, see *ibid.,* XVII, 6–7, 10–124.

39. Hirano, *Shimazaki,* pp. 162–163.

40. For biographical information on the naturalists, see *GNB,* each volume of which contains a biographical note on the author at the end. In many instances the biographical notes were written by the authors themselves. When, therefore, sources are not indicated, such information is taken from *GNB.*

41. *Shimazaki zenshū,* vols. 7–8.

42. On Shimamura Hōgetsu, see Kawazoe, *Nihon shizenshugi,* pp. 71–196.

43. Kunikida Doppo, *Ikanishite yo wa shōsetsuka to narishika* (How I became a novelist), quoted in Miyajima, p. 190.

44. Kunikida Doppo, in *Gendai Nihon bungaku zenshū* (Tokyo: Kaizōsha, 1927), XV, 293, 298–299, 316.

45. The discovery was made by Kawazoe (*Nihon shizenshugi,* pp. 101–113). Kawazoe argues that Shimamura had had no interest in politics, and that his registration in the Department of Politics at Waseda University was more or less a gratuitous act to please his foster father.

46. *Shimazaki zenshū,* IV, 338.

47. See Miyajima, pp. 201–229.

48. Kunikida Doppo, "Aza mukazaru no ki" (On not betraying), *GNB,* LVII, 309.

49. On this phase of the naturalists, see Miyajima, pp. 229–273; and Kamei, *Shimazaki Tōson,* pp. 9–75. These two authors appreciate differently the "romantic phase" of Shimazaki. The former suggests that Shimazaki makes a significant break, whereas Kamei sees in Shimazaki's later works the continuity of the romantic themes he

cherished in his early life, as evidenced by the frequent use of such terms as "longing," "life as a journey," "love," and "the self." Hirano Ken also argues for the apparent break Shimazaki made after *Hakai*. Nakamura Mitsuo, in *Fūzoku shōsetsu-ron* (Tokyo, 1950), has the same view, emphasizing *Futon's* influence on Shimazaki.

50. Kunikida, "Aza mukazaru no ki," *GNB*, LVII, 309.

51. For a detailed discussion of these writers' experience with Christianity, see, e.g., Kuyama et al., pp. 147–167; also Masamune Hakuchō, *Uchimura Kanzō* (Tokyo, 1948).

52. Kawazoe, *Nihon shizenshugi*, pp. 161–164. Kawazoe uses Shimamura's diary to show how deeply the latter was interested in the religious background of England, where he studied. Shimazaki's interest in and infatuation with Christianity is also described in fictional form in his *Sakura no mi no jukusuru toki*, in *Shimazaki zenshū*, IV, 257–263, 289–301.

53. Kuyama et al., pp. 1–19; also Sumiya, *Kindai Nihon*.

54. Kuyama et al., p. 153. This observation was made by Kamei Katsuichirō, a participant in the forum dealing with the problematic relation between Christianity and modern Japan.

55. *Shimazaki zenshū*, IV, 314.

56. Masamune Hakuchō, *Uchimura*.

57. Kamei, *Shimazaki* (1938), pp. 26–33.

58. See Chapter I above, on Uchimura.

59. Carl Becker, *The Heavenly City of the Eighteenth Century Philosophers* (New Haven, 1932), pp. 27–28.

60. For the coming of naturalist works from Europe to Japan, see Yanagida Izumi, *Meiji shoki no honyaku bungaku* (Tokyo, 1935), pp. 257–290.

61. Mori *Ogai* was the first to use the term "naturalism" *(shizenshugi)* in 1889. *Yomiuri* (Jan. 1889).

62. "Shōsetsu no jissai-ha o ronzu," (A comment on literary realists), *Jogaku zasshi* (May 1891).

63. See Tayama Katai, *Tōkyō no sanjūnen* (Tokyo, 1921).

64. Letter of Nov. 9, 1902, to Tayama Rokuya, *Shimazaki zenshū*, XIX, 58.

65. Aizu Tsuneji, in *Shimazaki Tōson dokuhon:Bungei* (Tokyo, 1958), quoted in Miyajima, p. 233.

66. *Shimazaki zenshū*, XIX, 52–53, 55, 58. See also Shimazaki's letters written between 1899 and 1905, which show how closely and with what enthusiasm he read such European authors as Turgenev, Balzac, and Zola.

67. *Shinkatamachi yori* (From Shinkatamachi), *Shimazaki zenshū*, XIV, 14, 26.

68. *Ibid.*, p. 7.

69. *Nochi no Shinkatamachi yori* (Later, from Shinkatamachi), *ibid.,* pp. 149–150.

70. "Shizen kara geijutsu o eru: 'Shingikō to iukoto' eno kaitō" (Obtaining art from nature: An answer to "what is called a new technique"), *ibid.,* XVII, 335.

71. Hirano, *Shimazaki,* p. 46. Also "Ie okugaki" (Postscript to *Family*). *Shimazaki zenshū,* XVIII, 196.

72. *Ibid.,* XIX, 122.

73. "Haru o machitsutsu" (Waiting for the spring), *ibid.,* XV, 11–25, 96–97; *Shisei ni arite* (In the city), *ibid.,* pp. 264–266; *Momo no shizuku* (Drops from a peach), *ibid.,* pp. 392–398; "Bashō no isshō" (The life of Bashō), *ibid.,* XIV, 123–124.

74. See Katayama Koson, "Shizenshugi dakkyakuron" (On getting rid of naturalism), and "Hōgetsu no niseshizenshugi" (Hōgetsu's pseudo naturalism), *GNB,* XCIV, 94–95. Here Katayama criticizes Hōgetsu as a "pseudo-naturalist." The articles were written in 1910.

75. Masamune Hakuchō, *Shizenshugi seisui shi* (Toyko, 1948), p. 206.

76. Yoshida, *Shizenshugi.* On *heimen byōsha,* see *ibid.,* pp. 15–16, 171–173, 222, 328; on *mushisō mukaiketsu,* see *ibid.,* p. 346. Also Hasegawa Tenkei, *GNB,* XCIV, 71–77. In this essay, "Genjitsu bakuro no hiai" (Disillusionment with the exposure of realities), Hasegawa argues that the ultimate reality of life has no solution for life's miseries. Hence it is impossible to find peace through literature, whose primary purpose is to depict such realities of life rather than to find a solution for them.

77. *Iikura dayori* (Letters from Iikura), *Shimazaki zenshū,* XIV, 317.

78. Masamune *Sakka ron,* pp. 282–283.

79. Kume Masao, "Shishōsetsu to shinkyō shōsetsu" (I-novels and novels of the state of mind), in Hirano Ken et al., *Gendai Nihon bungaku ronsō shi* (Tokyo, 1957), I, 109.

80. "Nenpu" (Chronology [of Satō by Yoshida Seiichi]), *GNB,* XXX, 426.

81. *Denen no yūutsu* (The pastoral melancholy), *ibid.,* pp. 13, 28, 29.

82. "Ichinichi" (One day), and "Awaremubeki mono" (Those who should be pitied), *Shimazaki zenshū,* XIV, 51.

V. THE SHIRAKABA-HA

1. For the literary controversy that followed upon the publication of *Shirakaba,* see Usui Yoshimi, *Kindai bungaku ronsō* (Tokyo, 1956), I, 107–149. According to Usui, it was not until 1919 that the literary

position of the Shirakaba-ha was firmly recognized in literary circles. Nevertheless, those who had been dissatisfied with the intellectual predominance of the naturalists, especially the younger and more idealistic intellectuals, welcomed the Shirakaba-ha with enthusiasm. The naturalists contemptuously referred to the Shirakaba-ha by reversing the syllables of *shirakaba* (white birch), as *bakarashi* (stupid), because of the latter's naive approach to life. See also Honda Shūgo, *Shirakaba-ha no bungaku* (Tokyo, 1955), pp. 12–39; Usui Yoshimi, "Shirakaba-ha no bungaku," *NB*, XII, 3; Kuno Osamu and Tsurumi Shunsuke, *Gendai Nihon no shisō* (Tokyo, 1956), pp. 2–28.

2. The literary and personal diversity within the group cannot be overemphasized. Satomi Ton, for example, started *Ningen* (Man) in 1920 with Yoshii Isamu and Kume Masao. On the Satomi-Shiga squabble, less intellectual than personal, see "Satomi Ton e" (To Satomi Ton), *Shiga Naoya zenshū*, Kaizōsha ed. (Tokyo, 1937), IX, 473–487. Despite their radical differences in personality and literary subject matter, Mushakōji's moral straightforwardness and Satomi's ideal of *magokoroshugi* (faithfulness) have the same air of moral concern, absent among the naturalists.

3. On the Shirakaba-ha as an ideological basis of Taishō democracy, see, e.g., "Shirakaba-ha no jindōshugi" (The humanitarianism of the Shirakaba-ha), *KNS*, I, 237–242; "Taishō kōki" (The latter part of the Taisho period), *GNB*, Appendix, I, 243–253; Yoshida Seiichi, *Meiji Taishō bungaku-shi* (Tokyo, 1956), pp. 279–309. Yoshida is explicit in equating "the humanism, pantheism, and individualism of the Shirakaba-ha with the ideological basis of the democratic thoughts expounded by such intellectuals as Yoshino Sakuzō"; "Risōshugi shichō" (The trend of idealism), *ibid.*, p. 287. Yoshida also speaks of the popularity among the intellectuals of neo-Kantianism during the decade following the emergence of the Shirakaba-ha. For the same view, see Yamazaki Masakazu, *Kindai Nihon shisō tsū-shi* (Tokyo, 1960), pp. 185–209; Miyakawa Tōru, *Kindai Nihon shisō no kōzō* (Tokyo, 1956), pp. 177–211. Miyakawa and Yamazaki take the view that Yoshino Sakuzō, the Shirakaba-ha, and the neo-Kantians in theory advocated Taishō democracy. Kamiyama Shumpei (in "Burujoa jiyūshugi no shisō," *KNS*, IV, 75–93), and Miyajima Hajime argue instead that the intellectual trends represented by Nishida Kitarō and the naturalists ideologically formed the liberal and democratic movements in late Meiji and Taishō Japan. Epistemologically, however, it is necessary to recognize the similarities that exist between what both the naturalists and Shirakaba-ha writers considered to be "realism" and the mental attitude philosophically articulated by Nishida.

4. See Kawazoe, *Nihon shizenshugi*, pp. 125–126; Honda,

Shirakaba-ha, pp. 193–201. Here, these two critics deal with the different attitudes with which such intellectuals as Natsume, Nagai, Arishima, Mori, and Shimamura reacted to their experiences in the United States and Europe. For "the psychic breakdown of the Japanese" that Natsume speaks of, see *Sōseki,* XIII, 378, 352–380.

5. Mushakōji and Arishima both were actively interested in social problems. It will be shown, however, that their concern was more aesthetic, therefore isolated, than political.

6. For an analytical piece on this problem, see Kuno Osamu, Fujita Shōzō, and Tsurumi Shunsuke, *Sengo Nihon no shisō* (Tokyo, 1959), pp. 72–107.

7. The biographical information was taken from the pertinent volumes of *GNB.*

8. Nakano Yoshio, *Gendai no sakka* (Tokyo, 1955), pp. 58–59.

9. Usui, "Shirakaba-ha," pp. 18–19.

10. See Nakano Yoshio, p. 12, for a description of Shiga Naoya's interest in Kunikida Doppo.

11. Among those who later joined the group were Kondō Keiichi, Inukai Takeshi, Ozaki Kihachi, and Kurata Hyakuzō. Inukai was the son of Inukai Tsuyoshi, one-time prime minister of Japan.

12. Mushakōji Saneatsu, in *Shirakaba* (July 1911).

13. For the biography of Arima Yoriyasu, see *Tenkō,* II, 121–147. Between 1924 and 1925, as a member of the Diet, Arima proposed reforms of the House of Peers and opposed the Peace Preservation Law of 1925. Also see Arima's own autobiographical notes in Arima Yoriyasu, *Shichijūnen no kaiko* (Tokyo, 1951); see also his *Seikai dōchū-ki* (Tokyo, 1949). For the complete biblography of Arima's own works and of works about him, see *Tenkō,* pp. 149–150.

14. For the intellectual biography of Prince Konoe Hirobumi, see Tsurumi Shunsuke, "Yokusanundō no sekkei-sha" (The architect of the imperial assistance movement), *Tenkō,* pp. 53–111. In 1924 Konoe wrote a book on the relationship between politics and the second chamber of parliament in different countries and pleaded for the need for democratizing the institution. Tsurumi shows the different stages through which Konoe went before he finally became committed to modern Japanese politics. One lasting influence on this indecisive political figure was his interest in literature.

15. *Shiga Naoya zenshū,* Iwanami ed. (Tokyo, 1955), XII, 165–166.

16. Minobe Ryōkichi, pp. 26, 27.

17. Arishima Takeo, "Sengen hitotsu" (One manifesto), and "Shiyū nōjō kara kyōsan nōen e" (From private farm to communal farm), *GNB,* XI, 420–425.

18. Usui, *Kindai bungaku ronsō,* pp. 144–147.

19. Quoted in Honda, *Shirakaba-ha,* p. 68. Note the familiar usage, *san* (Mr.).

20. Yamakawa Hitoshi, "Atarashiki mura," *Shakaishugi-sha no shakai kan* (Tokyo, 1919). Here Yamakawa, an early Japanese Marxist, criticizes the so-called bourgeois socialists or humanitarian radicals, such as Arishima, Tolstoy, Bergson, Kawakami Hajime, Fukuda Tokuzō, and Yamaji Aizan. This particular expression is quoted in Honda, *Shirakaba-ha,* p. 39.

21. See Shiga Naoya, "Nenpu", *GNB,* XX, 428. In 1932 Shiga had a spate of correspondence with Kobayashi Takiji, which is included in *Shiga,* IX, 495–502. There is a letter written to Kobayashi's mother after Kobayashi was killed.

22. *Shiga,* diary (Sept. 14, 1912), XII, 272.

23. *Shirakaba* (Dec. 1912).

24. *Sanshirō,* in *Sōseki,* V, 25.

25. "Taishō gannen nikki" (Diary of the first year of Taishō), in *Ōgai,* XXI, 52–53. Mori's historical novels which emerged after Nogi's death included such iconoclastic works as *Abeichihizoku* (The Abes), in *ibid.,* vol. 5.

26. Mushakōji Saneatsu, "Kojinshugi no tame ni" (For individualism), in Yamamuro Shizuka, ed. *Mushakōji Saneatsu* (Tokyo, 1961), pp. 9–18.

27. Usui, *Shirakaba-ha,*" pp. 23–28; "Sōsaku yodan" (Random comments on my work), *Shiga,* IX, 505–560.

28. See "The Recovery of the Unconscious," in Hughes, pp. 105–160. For biographical information, see footnotes throughout this chapter of Hughes'.

29. Shiga Naoya, "Waga seikatsu shinjō" (The principles of my life), *GNB,* XX, 222.

30. Watsuji Tetsurō, "*Mono no aware* ni tsuite," *GNB,* XCIV, 169–173. Watsuji Tetsurō was one of the first to welcome the Shirakaba-ha writers. See Usui, *Kindai bungaku ronsō,* I, 111–116.

31. "*Mono no aware* ni tsuite," *GNB,* XCIV, 170b-c., 169a.

32. Erich Heller, *The Disinherited Mind* (New York, 1959), p. 74. See also *Jakob Burckhardt:Gesamtausgabe* (Stuttgart, Berlin, and Leipzig, 1930), VIII, 231.

33. Heller, p. 74.

34. Watsuji, "*Mono no aware* ni tsuite," *GNB,* XCIV, 171c. *Mono* is considered as both *es* and *alles.*

35. *Ibid.,* pp. 171a, 172b–173c.

36. Georg Lukacs, *Existentialisme ou marxisme?,* tr. Shirotsuka Noboru et al. (Paris, 1947), pp. 93–105.

37. *Shirakaba* (Feb. 1911).

38. *Nigotta atama* (Muddled head), in *Shiga*, I, 296.

39. Nakano Yoshio, p. 12.

40. *Shirakaba* (Feb. 1912), quoted in Honda, *Shirakaba-ha*, p. 43.

41. *Shirakaba* (July 1910).

42. On the theoretical break Mushakōji made with Tolstoy through his acquaintance with Maeterlinck, see Honda, *Shirakaba-ha*, pp. 92–101.

43. Shiga, Nagayo, Arishima, Mushakōji, and Kurata were all interested in Christianity. Only Arishima made a serious commitment to it, however, while Kurata, a younger member, was a Buddhist and his works reflect this religious inclination. Mushakōji wove a kind of pantheism into his works.

44. Quoted in Abe Tomoji, "Nagayo Yoshio ron," *GNB*, XXVIII, 404.

45. See Nakano Yoshio, p. 8. Shiga considers Uchimura as one of the most critical influences on the formation of his personality. For Shiga's relation to Uchimura, see Nakamura Mitsuo, *Shiga Naoya* (Tokyo, 1958), pp. 37–63.

46. See "Uchimura Kanzō sensei no omoide" (The memories of Mr. Uchimura Kanzō), *Shiga*, IX, 206–210.

47. Nagayo Yoshio, *Seidō no Kirisuto*, *GNB*, XXVIII, 5–44.

48. *Ibid.*, p. 44a.

49. *Shirakaba* (June 1913), quoted in Honda, *Shirakaba-ha*, pp. 89, 98.

50. Nagayo Yoshio, *Seidō no Kirisuto*, p. 23c, also pp. 19a.–21b, 34c–35c.

51. Honda, *Shirakaba-ha*, p. 98. One's happiness is defined as "internal" and independent of one's relationship to the outside world.

52. Quoted in Honda, *Shirakaba-ha*, p. 85.

53. *Sōseki*, XIII, 477–513. For Natsume's thoughts on egoism, see Ino Kenji, "Sōseki," *NB*, vol. 15, Kataoka, Yoshikazu, *Natsume Sōseki* (Tokyo, 1955).

54. Howard Hibbett, "The Portrait of the Artist in Japanese Fiction," *Far Eastern Quarterly*, 14.3:351 (1955).

55. On this idea there are many pieces, written particularly by Mushakōji and Nagayo. See, e.g., Yamamuro, *Mushakōji*, pp. 139–196. The five essays included here deal with Mushakōji's *a priori* and tenacious optimism concerning the harmony between men and society.

56. Nagayo Yoshio, *Takezawa-sensei to yuu hito*, *GNB*, XXVIII, 146a-c. This is a summary translation of a rather lengthy discussion on philosophy.

57. Mushakōji Saneatsu, *Shinri-sensei* (Tokyo, 1952), pp. 229–233.

58. Honda, *Shirakaba-ha,* p. 74.

59. Nagayo Yoshio, *Mōmoku no kawa* (The blind river; Tokyo, 1914), quoted in Abe Tomoji, "Nagayo Yoshio ron," *GNB,* XXVIII, 402c.

60. Quoted in Honda, *Shirakaba-ha,* p. 74.

61. *Shirakaba* (Nov. 1911–Feb. 1912). On this controversy, see Usui, *Kindai bungaku ronsō,* pp. 129–132; Honda, *Shirakaba-ha,* pp. 50–52.

62. Søren Kierkegaard, "Of the Difference between a Genius and an Apostle," tr. A. Dru, in *Present Age,* quoted in Shklar, p. 82.

63. Shklar, pp. 79–96.

64. Odagiri Hideo, *Nihon kindai bungaku-shi* (Tokyo, 1953), III, 15. For the relationship between the individual and family or between the family and the state, see e.g., Ishida, pp. 150–215, 231–240; Isono Fujiko, "Ie to jiga-ishiki" (Family and the consciousness of self), *KNS,* VI, 69–109.

65. Mombushō, *Kokutai no hongi* (Tokyo: Mombushō, 1937).

66. *Nijūdai ichimen,* in *Shiga,* II, 44.

67. Mushakōji, *Shinri-sensei,* p. 7.

68. Shiga Naoya, *Ōtsu Junkichi, GNB,* XX, 222.

69. *Wakai,* in *Shiga,* VI, 1–158.

70. *Anya kōro (Shiga,* vols. 7 and 8), esp. VIII, 459–461.

71. Nagayo Yoshio, *Yasei no yūwaku,* in *GNB,* XXVIII, 188–257, esp. 256c–257b.

72. See "Gendai Nihon no kaika" (Enlightenment of modern Japan), in *Sōseki,* XIV, 279.

73. "Shōtaku" (A mistress's house), *(Nagai) Kafū,* X, 23.

74. Ebina Danjō, *Kirisutokyō shinron* (Tokyo, 1918). Here Ebina speaks of the need for saving Christianity from corruption, for which Europe is to blame, through Japanese ethical superiority. See also "Kyōgi hen" (Section on doctrine), in *Uemura (Masahisa) zenshū* (Tokyo, 1933–1934), vol. 4.

75. Usui, "Shirakaba-ha" p. 40.

76. Aono Suekichi, *Bungaku gojūnen* (Tokyo, 1957), pp. 39–40.

77. Usui, "Shirakaba-ha," p. 40.

78. Watsuji Tetsurō, *Koji junrei* (Tokyo, 1947), p. 296.

79. *Ibid.,* pp. 207, 295; *Nihon seishin-shi kenkyū* (Tokyo, 1926), pp. 2–3, 36, 232. Watsuji's political ideals are found in ancient Japan and reflect the Shirakaba's adoration of the absence of any form of serious conflict. He even suggests an admiration for communist society. The basis upon which Watsuji suggests his emotional affinity with communism is not political but historical romanticism.

80. Usui, "Shirakaba-ha," p. 36.

81. Watsuji Tetsurō, *Gūzō saikō* (Tokyo, 1918), pp. 10, 11, 13.

82. Watsuji was one of the first to introduce such European intellectuals as Kierkegaard and Nietzsche. See *Miki Kiyoshi chosakushū* (Tokyo, 1946–1951), XV, 169.

83. Watsuji, *Gūzō saikō*, pp. 268–272, 8.

84. In this, Yanagi Muneyoshi was particulary influential. Japanese folk art owes much of its present status to his work. See Yanagi Muneyoshi, *Mingei towa nanika* (Tokyo, 1941), pp. 175–199; also his *Nihon no mingei* (Tokyo, 1960), pp. 8–9. Note the author's adoration of "what is natural" in Japanese folk art.

85. See "Aogusachō" (Notes of inexperience), *Shiga*, IX, 86–90, 98–99.

86. Quoted in Abe Tomoji, "Nagayo Yoshio ron," *GNB*, XXVIII, 401c, from *Yūshi no tabi-nikki* (Travel diary of a wanderer; Tokyo, 1939).

87. "Satomi Ton," *GNB*, XXV, 403a-c.

88. *Nihon hyōron* (The Japanese review; 1940), quoted in Kuno and Tsurumi, p. 16. See also *Yomiuri* (Jan. 1, 1942).

89. Kuno Osamu and Tsurumi Shunsuke, pp. 2–28.

90. Kuno, Fujita and Tsurumi, p. 78. In 1948 a group of intellectuals formed an organization called Kokoro (The heart) and started a journal with the same name. The members were the liberals of the prewar years in Japan and included such men as Shiga Naoya, Satomi Ton, Kojima Kikuo, Yanagi Muneyoshi, Mushakōji Saneatsu, Nagayo Yoshio, Watsuji Tetsurō, Takamura Kōtarō, Amano Teiyū, and Abe Yoshishige. There are many others representing other intellectual and literary groups, and even some scientists. "Nihon no hoshushugi: Kokoro gurūpu" (Japanese conservatism: The Kokoro group), in Kuno, Fujita, and Tsurumi, pp. 72–107, deals specifically with this group and, therefore, not with the Shirakaba-ha exclusively.

91. *Ibid.*, p. 80.

VI. ARISHIMA TAKEO

1. Arishima Takeo was born in Tokyo in 1878. He entered Sapporo nōgakkō in 1896 and was graduated from the same institution in 1901. In 1900 he was baptized through the influence of Uchimura Kanzō. Unlike his fellow Shirakaba writers he neither finished the Peers' School nor chose Tokyo University. In 1903 he was asked to be a tutor to the crown prince, but declined this offer and instead went to the United States where he attended Haverford College (M.A. in history), and Harvard University. Between 1907 and 1908 he was in Europe and met Kropotkin, in whom he had been already interested.

Thereafter, until 1915, he was an instructor at Hokkaidō University (which originally had been Sapporo nōgakkō).

2. Fujita Shōzō, "Taishō demokurashī no ichidanmen" (One aspect of Taishō democracy), *Gendai rinri* (Tokyo, 1959), XI, 150–155. This is the best treatment of Arishima, despite the fact that in my opinion he carries his enthusiasm for Arishima a little too far. Honda, "Arishima Takeo ron," in his *Shirakaba-ha*, pp. 147–214.

3. Arishima Takeo, *Oshiminaku ai wa ubau* (Relentlessly love steals), in *GNB*, XXI, 370a.

4. "Mushakōji-kei e" (To Mushakōji), *ibid.*, p. 415c.

5. One might note an epistemological similarity between Uchimra and Arishima. Both removed themselves from the task of actually bringing about the apocalyptic future in which they believed. Uchimura thought that he was perhaps one of the elect and, though anxious, was hopeful that he might be chosen for salvation with the second coming of Christ. Arishima, on the other hand, thought that the elect were already chosen by history (the working class) and believed he had no place among them.

6. Karaki Junzō, "Kaisetsu" (Explanatory notes), in *GNB*, XXI, 432a. Arishima Takeo, *Aru onna* (A certain woman), in *ibid.*, pp. 5–206.

7. "Kaisetsu" (Explanatory note), *ibid.*, p. 432b.

8. Arishima Takeo, "Bungaku wa ikani ajiwau bekika" (How should literature be appreciated?; Nov. 1919), quoted in Karaki, "Kaisetsu," p. 432b.

9. Arishima Takeo, "Daigen" (Solicitor; July 1919), quoted in Karaki, "Kaisetsu," pp. 432b-c.

10. Arishima's diary for July 21, 1908; quoted in Karaki "Kaisetsu," p. 433b. In May of the same year he noted in his diary that he was reading one of Shimazaki's novels, *Haru*, and was "deeply moved."

11. "*Haru* okugaki" (Postscript to *Haru*), *Shimazaki zenshū*, XVIII, 184.

12. Arishima's diary for March 28, 1916; quoted in Karaki, "Kaisetsu," p. 433a. A part of this is quoted in Honda, *Shirakaba-ha*, p. 180.

13. Arishima Takeo, *Aru onna*, in *GNB*, XXI, 7a, 29a–b.

14. *Ibid.*, p. 61a–c.

15. Quoted in Honda, *Shirakaba-ha*, p. 194.

16. *GNB*, XXI, 370c.

17. *Ibid.*, p. 372a.

18. Honda, *Shirahaba-ha*, pp. 147–148.

19. Arishima, *Oshiminaku ai wa ubau*, *GNB*, XXI, 391a, 388a.

20. *Ibid.*, pp. 387c–389b. "What I want should be identical with

that which society wants, for, unquestionably, I am a particle of society."

21. *Ibid.*, pp. 385c–392a.

22. *Ibid.*, pp. 397b–c.

23. *Ibid.*, p. 407a–b.

24. *Ibid.*, pp. 396a, 408c.

25. *Ibid.*, pp. 409a,c, 414c.

26. *Ibid.*, pp. 376a–377a.

27. Socialism and anarchism are "the total answer" of the individual's needs. *Ibid.*, e.g., p. 409a.

28. *Ibid.*, pp. 424a, 424b.

29. *Ibid.*, pp. 422b–425a.

30. *Ibid.*, p. 425a.

31. For Mushakōji's optimism in his venture, see Mushakōji Saneatsu, "Atarashiki mura ni tsuite no taiwa" (A dialogue on the new village), in *GNB*, XIX, 356–372. Here, in the form of a dialogue, he explains his motive and aspirations in experimental living and is altogether indifferent to the circumstances surrounding his venture.

32. Arishima Takeo, "Mushakōji-kei e," *GNBZ*, XXI, 415b–416a.

33. *Ibid.*, pp. 416a–417b.

34. "Nōjō kaihō tenmatsu" (An account of the liberation of the farm), *ibid.*, p. 425a.

35. "Sengen hitotsu," *ibid.*, pp. 417b–c, 418a.

36. *Ibid.*, p. 419a–c.

37. *Ibid.*, p. 418b.

38. *Ibid.*, p. 418c.

39. Hirotsu Kazuo, "Arishima Takeo shi no kyūkutsu na kangaekata" (Arishima Takeo's punctilious manner of thinking), in Hirano Ken et al., *Gendai Nihon bungaku ronsō-shi*, I, 16a–b.

40. Arishima Takeo, "Hirotsu shi ni kotau" (An answer to Mr. Hirotsu), in Hirano Ken et al., *Gendai Nihon bungaku ronsō-shi*, I, 18a.

41. Katagami Noboru, "Kaikyū geijutsu no mondai" (The problems of class art), in Hirano Ken et al., *Gendai Nihon bungaku ronsō-shi*, I, 21b–31b.

42. Sakai Toshihiko, "Arishima Takeo shi no zetsubō no sengen" (Arishima Takeo's declaration of despair), in Hirano Ken et al., *Gendai Nihon bungaku ronsō-shi*, 35a–36b.

43. Kawakami Hajime, "Kojinshugi-sha to shakaishugi-sha" (Individualist and socialist), in Hirano Ken et al., *Gendai Nihon bungaku ronsō-shi*, I, 37a–b, 44b, 45a.

44. On Kawakami Hajime, see Furuta Hikaru, *Kawakami Hajime*

(Tokyo, 1959). For a bibliographical guide to this intellectual's life, see *ibid.*, pp. 256–260.

45. *GNB*, XXI, 425a.

VII. AKUTAGAWA RYŪNOSUKE

1. The subtitle of this chapter is taken from an essay on Akutagawa written in 1929 by Miyamoto Kenji. The Japanese title is "Haiboku no bungaku."

2. For the plight of bourgeois literature, see Ōya Sōichi, "Bungakushiteki kūhakujidai" (An empty period in Japanese literature), *GNB*, XCIV, 278. In this essay Ōya speaks of the general decline in the productivity of established writers. The quotation here is taken from *ibid.*, p. 279c. The only three Taishō survivors, according to Ōya, were Shimazaki, Tokuda, and Masamune. He also speaks of the death of Akutagawa as the twilight of the bygone artists (*ibid.*, p. 280c).

3. For a complete bibliography on Akutagawa's life, art, and death, see Yoshida Seiichi, ed., *Akutagawa Ryūnosuke kenkyū* (Tokyo, 1958), pp. 377–395. Among the contemporary comments on Akutagawa's suicide, Kawabata Yasunari's "In one word, Akutagawa fell into Strindberg's hell, longing for Goethe's paradise," seems most graphic. Kawabata has another article on Akutagawa: "Akutagawa Ryūnosuke to Kikuchi Kan," in *Kawabata Yasunari zenshū* (Tokyo, 1954), XVI, 313–338. The best biography of Akutagawa is Yoshida Seiichi, *Akutagawa Ryūnosuke* (Tokyo, 1958).

4. *Tanizaki Junichirō sakuhinshu*, Sogensha ed. (Tokyo, 1956–1958), vol. 9.

5. "Seihō no hito" (A man from the West), *Akutagawa Ryūnosuke zenshū*, Iwanami ed. (Tokyo, 1954–1955), XII, 25a–26a.

6. "Aru kyūyū e okuru shuki" (A note to an old friend), *ibid.*, XV, 173b–174a.

7. "Seihō no hito," *ibid.*, XII, 25a.

8. "Taishō hachinendo no bungeikai" (The world of literature in Taishō 8), *ibid.*, XIII, 108–109.

9. "Shuju no kotoba" (Words of a dwarf), *Akutagawa zenshū*, XII, 77a.

10. *Ibid.*, pp. 207b, 227a.

11. "Kekkonmae no hyōban" (A reputation before the marriage), *ibid.*, VIII, 135b; also "Shuju no kotoba," *ibid.*, XII, 100b, 103a.

12. *Ibid.*, 61a.

13. "Hana," *ibid.*, I, 44–52; "Imogayu," *ibid.*, pp. 85–105; *Jigoku hen*, in *ibid.*, II, 132–169.

14. *Ibid.*, II, 169a.

15. *Ibid.*, VIII, 131b–132a.

16. "Shuju no kotoba," *ibid.*, XII, 56a–107b.

17. "Bungeiteki na, amarini bungeiteki na" (Artistic, all too artistic), *ibid.*, p. 109b.

18. "Jōzetsu roku" (Random chatter), in *Tanizaki sakuhinshū*, IX, 115b. See also Satō Haruo, *Waga Ryūnosuke-zō* (Tokyo, 1959), pp. 91–116. Satō speaks of the theoretical consistency of Tanizaki and the clumsy logic of Akutagawa; he does not see the ironic similarities of these two writers.

19. "Bungeiteki na, amarini bungeiteki na," *Akutagawa zenshū*, XII, 109b, 112a.

20. "Jōzetsu roku" in *Tanizaki sakuhinshū*, IX, 116a–117a.

21. "With Mr. Masamune, I, too, believe that human suffering is unbearable under any social system." "Bungeiteki na, amarini bungeiteki na," *Akutagawa zenshū*, XII, 124a.

22. *Ibid.*, XIII, 124a–125b; Nezu Kenzō, "Anatōru Furansu o tooshite mita Akutagawa Ryūnosuke" (Akutagawa Ryūnosuke through Anatole France), *Akutagawa kenkyū*, pp. 154–161, esp. 156a–157a.

23. *Akutagawa zenshū*, XII, 96b.

24. "Shuju no kotoba," *ibid.*, XII, 97a.

25. *Ibid.*, p. 176b.

26. Cf. Karl Löwith, *Von Hegel zu Nietzsche* (Stuttgart, 1958), p. 194.

27. "Bungeiteki na, amarini bungeiteki na," *Akutagawa zenshū*, XII, 177a.

28. "Hekiken" (Prejudiced view), *ibid.*, p. 191a. See also "*Shinchō*: Iwayuru puroretaria bungaku to sono sakka ni tsuite tou" (*Shinchō*: Questions about the so-called proletarian literature and its authors), *ibid.*, XIV, 126. As early as 1923 Akutagawa acknowledged the inevitable rise of socialist literature. But he pleaded that neither it nor bourgeois literature should be allowed to exercise a tyranny capable of suffocating freedom of thought. "Puroretariabungei no kahi" (The advisability of proletarian arts), *ibid.*, XIII, 36–37.

29. Edmund Wilson, "T. S. Eliot," *Axel's Castle* (New York: Scribner, 1931), pp. 93–131. Cf. also Wilson's comments on symbolism, *ibid.*, pp. 1–25.

30. *Anchū montō* (The dialogue in darkness), in *Akutagawa zenshū*, VIII, 102a–b.

31. *Ibid.*, pp. 102b–103b.

32. "Shuju no kotoba," *ibid.*, XII, 67a.

33. *Anchū montō, ibid.,* VIII, 102a.

34. *Anchū montō, ibid.,* VIII, 101a–b, 104b, 102a, 104a.

35. "Otomi no teisō," *ibid.,* VI, 30–43; "Mikan," *ibid.,* III, 95–99; "Oitaru Susanōno Mikoto," *ibid.,* IV, 151–156; "Nezumi-kozō-Jirokichi," *ibid.,* IV, 17–35.

36. *Kappa, ibid.,* VII, 228a.

37. *Ibid.,* VI, 241a, 241b.

38. 'Shuju no kotoba," *ibid.,* XII, 98b; also *Kappa, ibid.,* VII, 227a.

39. *Ibid.,* VII, 197b, 228b, 205a.

40. *Ibid.,* pp. 220a, 220b.

41. *Ibid.,* pp. 216a–b, 216b.

42. *Ibid.,* pp. 213b–214a.

43. *Ibid.,* pp. 208a, 233a, 234b, 235b.

44. *Ibid.,* VIII, 138a.

45. "Shuju no kotoba," *ibid.,* XII, 67a. See also *ibid.,* p. 99a: "The ancients confessed to God, and the modern men confess to society. Perhaps it is that, except for fools and scoundrels, every one cannot bear the burden of life without confessing to something."

46. *Ibid.,* pp. 98b–90b.

47. Akutagawa's associates were friends of his with whom he revived the old university literary magazine, *Shinshichō* (The new intellectual tides) at Tokyo Imperial University, and included Kume Masao, Kikuchi Kan, Yamamoto Yūzō, to name only the most conspicuous few. Earlier the same journal had as editors such intellectuals as Tanizaki Junichirō and Osanai Kaoru (1881–1928), who started the new theater movement and in his lifetime raised the level of theater in Japan. On *Shinshichō,* see "Yamamoto Yūzō, Toyoshima Yoshio, Kume Masao," *Kawabata zenshū,* XVI, 339–360.

48. "Aru kyūyū e okuru shuki," *Akutagawa zenshū,* XV, 170b, 173b.

49. For comments on Akutagawa's death, see Yoshida Seiichi, *Akutagawa,* pp. 268–271; Ōyama Ikuo, "Akutagawa Ryūnosuke shi no shi to sono geijutsu" (Akutagawa Ryūnosuke's death and his art), in Yoshida, *Akutagawa kenkyū,* p. 229a–b; "Taishō kōki," *GNB,* Appendix, I, 301a–303a, 313a–316a.

50. *Asahi* (July 27, 1927).

51. *Akutagawa Ryūnosuke annai* (Tokyo, 1955), pp. 112a, 163b.

52. *Ibid.,* pp. 118b, 171b.

53. Aono Suekichi, "Akutagawa Ryūnosuke shi to shinjidai" (Akutagawa Ryūnosuke and the new era), in Yoshida *Akutagawa kenkyū,* pp. 82b–83a.

54. Both Genkakusambō, in *Akutagawa zenshū,* VII, 171–188, and *Haguruma* (The cogwheel), in *ibid.,* VIII, 59–95, are representative

works of his nightmarish world, neatly articulated and well composed. The latter work, however, has much less artistic unity than the former, which is an autobiographical description of his final days.

55. Quoted in Aono, "Akutagawa Ryūnosuke shi to shinjidai," p. 84a.

56. For Akutagawa's letter to Aono see Akutagawa zenshū, XVIII, 207b–208a.

57. Aono, "Akutagawa Ryūnosuke shi to shinjidai," pp. 83b, 85b.

58. Miyamoto Kenji, "Haiboku no bungaku," in GNB, XCIV, 293c–294b, 284b–c, 289c, 290a.

VIII. PROLETARIAN LITERATURE

1. Note, e.g., the sympathetic but detached way in which Nagai recorded the death of Akutagawa—Nagai Kafū nikki (Tokyo, 1958–1959), II, 128 (entry for July 24, 1927).

2. Nagai is one of few literary figures to record the economic crisis of Japan without political references—ibid., pp. 115–116. The state of the parliamentary system is studied in Maejima Shōzō, Nihon fashizumu to gikai (Kyoto, 1956), pp. 5–84. For the economic and social background of the decline of the parliamentary system, see Shinobu, Taishō seiji-shi, pp. 141–285, 541–693 (on the rice riots), 1327–78.

3. Many other organizations were formed by students and young intellectuals during the years immediately following World War I. The influence of Yoshino Sakuzō, Fukuda Tokuzō, Takano Iwasaburō, and Makino Eiichi ought to be noted in the formations of these groups. See Tenkō, I, 69–70. The Shinjinkai's manifesto is quoted in ibid., p. 71b.

4. Akamatsu Katsumaro, the son-in-law of Yoshino Sakuzō, was a member of the Japanese Communist Party from the time of its founding in 1922 to its dissolution in February 1924. He became interested in the party through his work in the labor movement of the early 1920s.

5. Both Akamatsu and Asou Hisashi, the leading spirits of the Shinjinkai, became actively antiparliamentary during the 1930s. In a round-table discussion conducted by Bungeishunjū in February 1940, Akamatsu expressed his thoughts on parties. "If we value realities in contemporary politics, society advances more rapidly than the parties can follow. Therefore, we are in a hurry." (Quoted in Tenkō, I, 76b.) Asou (who came to help Prince Konoe when the latter tried to form a single party for Japan in 1940) visualized the possibility of a revolution based on an alliance between the working class and the

emperor. (*Ibid.*, pp. 96b–97a.) Elsewhere Akamatsu wrote: "Democracy equalizes and vulgarizes humanity. Democracy liberates the private man, but cannot liberate the true man. I do not know a more adequate expression to criticize modern democracy than the expression, 'the liberation of the private man.' The private man's liberation is the liberation of the animal nature in man." (Akamatsu Katsumaro, *Kindai minshushugi hihan*, quoted in *Tenkō*, I, 87b.)

6. Documented in *Tenkō*, I, 72b; see also p. 86a. Here the ascetic character of the movement is recorded. The parents of both Akamatsu and Asou were socially active. The father of Miyazaki Ryusuke, another active member of the Shinjinkai, was a close friend of Huang Hsing, a Chinese revolutionary.

7. Tai Ro Hikanshō Dōshikai. The federation demanded "the immediate and unconditional evacuation of the Japanese army from Siberia, the immediate commencement of commercial trade with the Russians, assistance to be given to the starving masses in Russia, and finally the immediate recognition of the peasants' and workers' Russia." (*Tenkō*, I, 89a)

8. The federation included many radicals who were not socialists.

9. "Jikyoku o kataru" (Discussion on the present day situation), *Kaizō* (Mar. 1937). In this round-table discussion Akamatsu argues that the militarists have a better political sense than the parliamentarians. He even gives an apologia for the idea of assassination. Hamada Kunimatsu, the boldest of the last parlimentarians to fight against the antiparliamentary forces of Showa Japan, vehemently denounces Akamatsu for the latter's crude refutation of the meaning of party politics.

10. During the 1930s it was Kawai Eijirō, professor of economics at Tokyo University, who championed the ethical ideals implied in the democratic theory of Yoshino Sakuzō and others. The very abstraction he made of the ideals of "individualism and freedom" irritated both the Marxists and the rightists. On this subject, see Minobe Ryōkichi, pp. 214, 231–237; also Kawai Eijirō, *Tōmasu Hiru Gurīn no shisō taikei* (Tokyo, 1938), pp. 355–373. Kawai notes that one kind of "freedom" is individual freedom in civil and legal relations. Unfortunately, Kawai proceeded to deal with Green's critical comments on Kant and Hegel, rather than to elaborate on the idea of freedom in the legal and civil context neglected by the Japanese intellectuals.

11. Wilson, *Axel's Castle*, p. 102: "The present is more timid than the past"; the bourgeois are afraid to let themselves go." On the bourgeoisie's fear, see Edmund Wilson, *A Literary Chronicle: 1920–1950* (Gloucester, Mass., n.d.) pp. 92–97, 128–133. Speaking of Mencken and Dos Passos, Wilson observes that these writers, recog-

nizing the illness of their society, would not accept the ideal of transcending the given.

12. For bibliographical information, see Asou Isoji et al., *Nihon bungaku kenkyū nyūmon* (Tokyo, 1956), pp. 362–367.

13. A Marxist or a Communist in Japan is referred to as *aka* (red). Being so labeled, especially before the war, meant virtual alienation from one's common social surroundings. See Kuno and Tsurumi, pp. 30–31.

14. Three earlier issues of *Tanemakuhito* had appeared in February 1921. Throughout these first three issues, Komaki Oumi wrote commentaries on the Third International. The present study refers to the second series of the journal (Oct. 1921–Sept. 1923). Contributors included such nonsocialist writers as Arishima Takeo and Anatole France. For the character of the journal, see Watabe Yoshimichi et al., p. 119.

15. *NPB*, I, 324b. *Tanemakuhito* (Oct. 1921). The statement is printed on the back of the cover.

16. Quoted in Sobue et al., p. 7.

17. On the literary role of these groups, see Takami, *Shōwa bungaku*, pp. 23–43.

18. Hirabayashi Hatsunosuke, "Yuibutsushikan to bungaku" (The concept of dialectical materialism and literature), *GNB*, LXXVIII, 9a–b.

19. *Ibid.*, pp. 9b–10a.

20. Hirano Ken, "Kaisetsu," *GNB*, LXXVIII, 410b. The appreciation of Hirabayashi within the history of the proletarian literary movement is best expressed by Kurahara Korehito: "Not only did he [Hirabayashi] insist on the historical nature . . . of art, but also he already propagated the idea of 'art as an instrument of the class.'" Quoted in *ibid.*, p. 409a–b. Kurahara, however, depreciates Hirabayashi's remarks, which come close to advocating the independent role of art within the proletarian movement.

21. Hirabayashi, "Yuibutsushikan to bungaku," *GNB*, LXXVIII, 10a.

22. Hirabayashi Hatsunosuke, "Bungei-undō to rodō-undō," (The literary movement and the labour movement), *GNB*, LXXVIII, 14c. In this essay, Hirabayashi argues that the literary movement is a part of the whole proletarian movement. Here we see the author's energetic desire to organize the proletarian writers. See "Daiyonkaikyū no bungaku" (The literature of the fourth estate), *ibid.*, pp. 10b–13b. In this essay, Hirabayashi further articulates the class nature of art and, in addition, argues that the intellectuals' pretension of rising above the class situation is no more than an illusion (*ibid.*, p. 11b).

23. Kikuchi Kan (1888–1948), author and founder of *Bungeishunjū*, wrote in "Geijutsu hontai-ron" (On the essence of art), *Shinchō* (May 1922): "I cannot believe that art has any connection with the classes. The artistic element in literature is constant, independent of its relation to its class origin." He also wrote in *Waga bungeijin* (My literary associates): "For those artists [the proletarian writers], isn't it their urgent responsibility to go out to streets armed with bombs, instead of staying in the easy profession of writing novels and art criticism?" Both remarks are quoted in Yamada Seizaburō, *Puroretaria bungakushi* (Tokyo, 1954), I, 325–326. Earlier, in a literary controversy called "Naiyō teki kachi-ronsō" (content value controversy), Kikuchi defended the literary position that life in itself has artistic value. "Art is the common record," he wrote, "of the common life of the common man." His opponent, Satomi Ton, a member of the Shirakaba-ha, saw that Kikuchi argued in fact for the "sterile naturalist tendency" within the Japanese literary world. Satomi defended the artistic qualities to be added to life experiences which, in and of themselves, are devoid of art. Hirano Ken et al., *Gendai Nihon bungaku ronsōshi* (Tokyo, 1957), I, 47–46. Intellectually and in terms of their literary method, the proletarian writers and Kikuchi are closer to each other than they are to such figures as Satomi, Akutagawa, and Tanizaki. Satomi's remark that Kikuchi was defending the naturalist position indicates the similarities between the naturalists and the proletarian writers, especially those of the earlier period before the graduates of Tokyo University joined the proletarian movement after the mid-1920s. The latter considered the earlier proletarian writers to be the "unconscious offshoots" of bourgeois literature. Despite the distastefulness of the common, it does contain an element of truth. Yamada, II, 114; Kaji Wataru, "Iwayuru shakaishugi bungaku o kokufuku seyo" (Overcome the so-called socialist literature), *Musanshimbun* (Feb. 5, 1927).

24. *Pravda* (July 10, 1923); *Sochineniya*, XXI, 3–12. Trotsky's approach to art after the revolution is discussed in Isaac Deutscher, *The Prophet Unarmed* (London, 1959), pp. 165–200, under the suggestive chapter heading, "Not by Politics Alone."

25. Another proletarian writer, Maedagawa Kōichirō, wrote more explicitly about the independence of art. It was Maedagawa's *a priori* belief that proletarian art would take over the world of art without the leadership of politics. See "Bundan no seitōka o nanzu" (An attack on politicizing the literary world), *NPB*, I, 359–361. The proletarian writers made a distinction between proletarian art and the proletarian-art movement. The former, according to them, was a natural growth of the industrialization of ʻJapan, while the latter

would either collaborate with or work as a wing of the proletarian movement as a whole. Nishida Masaru, "Taishō-ki no puroretaria bungaku" (The proletarian literature of the Taishō era), *Nihon kakumei bungaku,* pp. 237–263, describes how the writers with a working-class background gradually made literary debuts without conscious political orientation.

26. Aono Suekichi, "Shirabeta geijutsu" (Art based on research), *GNB,* LXXVIII, 69c, 71a–b.

27. Hirano, "Kaisetsu," *ibid.,* p. 411a. Hirano writes: "Aono introduced the element that might appear nonliterary to the established literary concepts, and insisted on the special character of proletarian literature."

28. Aono Suekichi, "Shizenseichō to mokutekiishiki" (Natural growth and consciousness of purpose), *ibid.,* pp. 78a–b.

29. *Ibid.,* p. 80b–c.

30. *Bungeisensen* (June 1924), in *NPB,* II, 193b.

31. *Ibid.,* pp. 191–193.

32. "Nihon puroretaria bungei renmei kitei sōan" (Draft of the provisions of the Japan Proletarian Literary Federation), *ibid.,* p. 206b.

33. For this stage of Yamakawa's socialist thought, see Yamakawa Hitoshi, *Musankaikyū no seiji-undō* (Tokyo, 1924). He attributes the successful preservation of the working-class movement from bourgeois liberal thought and bourgeois political power to the negative attitude which the labor movement in Japan took toward bourgeois politics. The book is a collection of essays, written between 1922 and 1924, which defend the idea of mobilizing the unorganized proletarian sectors of Japanese society. For a good summary of the book, see Watabe et al., p. 159.

34. Fukumoto Kazuo (published under his penname, Hōjō Kazuo), *Hōkō tenkan* (Tokyo, 1927), p. 31. Matsuzawa Hiroaki, "Marukusushugi ni okeru shisō to shūdan" (Thought and groups in Marxism), *KNS,* V, 233–248, esp. p. 234, where the author documents how the party movement became intellectualistic in its recruitment of members.

35. Hayashi Fusao, *Bungakuteki kaisō* (Tokyo, 1958). The first section of the work deals with his experiences with the Shinjinkai, the more radical organizations such as the NAPF (*ibid.,* pp. 59–60), and the trial and his apostasy. Tsurumi Shunsuke, "Kōki Shinjinkai" (The latter phase of Shinjinkai), *Tenkō,* I, 114–134, analyzes the process through which Hayashi became a defector. On pp. 127–134 Tsurumi deals with the six factors he thinks contributed to Hayashi's apostasy.

36. Tani Hajime, "Wagakuni puroretaria bungaku no hatten" (The development of the proletarian movement in our country), *Bungeisensen* (Oct. 1926). Quoted in Sobue et al., p. 24.

37. Takami, *Shōwa bungaku*, I, 116–125.

38. Thoes who resigned included such figures as Nakanishi Inosuke and Muramatsu Masatoshi. Almost all of them were anarchists. Yamada Seizaburō wrote in the December issue of *Bungeisensen* that, although thé journal had opened its pages to anyone who was anti-bourgeois, such a policy could no longer be tolerated. Quoted in Takami, *Shōwa bungaku*, p. 118. The view reflects the theoretical position of the party.

39. Sobue et al., p. 24.

40. *Bungeisensen* (Feb. 1927). The translation here summarizes the article, "Shakaishugi bungei undō" (The socialist-literary movement), *NPB*, II, 220–222.

41. *Ibid.*, pp. 222a–222b.

42. Kaji Wataru, "Iwayuru shakaishugi bungaku o kokufuku seyo," *Musanshimbun* (Feb. 5, 1927), *NPB*, II, 224b, 225a.

43. Hayashi Fusao, "Tēze ni kansuru gokai ni tsuite" (On the misunderstandings concerning the theses), *Bungeisensen* (March 1927). Quoted in Sobue et al., p. 28.

44. Nakano Shigeharu, "Kesshō shitsutsu aru shōshimin-sei" (The crystalization of the petit-bourgeois nature), *Bungeisensen* (March 1927).

45. Quoted in Sobue et al. Nakano's article is also discussed in Yamada, pp. 119–120. Yamada writes (p. 120): "We cannot deny that his [Nakano's] position found the purpose of art in the narrow confines of indoctrination and propaganda. In this sense, he stands on the same ground as Kaji."

46. See Nakano Shigeharu, "Geijutsu ni kansuru hashirigakiteki oboegaki" (Hastily written notes on art), *GNB*, LXXVIII, 255–259, esp. 257a–c. In this well-known essay, written in October 1927, Nakano writes that "our art—the art of the workers themselves—should publicize the shame of our country." Here, Nakano is not nearly as simple-minded about the role of an artist within the proletarian movement as either Kaji or Tani. Nonetheless, they would agree that art could not stand alone.

47. Kuno and Tsurumi, pp. 40–41, describe the revolutionary mood prevailing among party members. Matsuzawa's articles heavily rely on the documentation made by the Ministry of the Interior on party members who were questioned. For the theoretical background of this mood, see, e.g., Noro Eitarō, *Nōgyō senryaku senjutsu mondai* (Tokyo, 1948), pp. 5–14.

48. "Iwayuru shakaishugi bungei o kokufuku seyo," *NPB, II,* 224b.
49. Yamada, II, 124.
50. Watabe et al., pp. 203, 232. *Puroretaria geijutsu* (July 1927–April 1928).
51. Miyamoto Kenji, "Haiboku no bungaku," *GNB,* XCV, 284c. Miyamoto enumerates the reactions to Akutagawa's death of such leftist writers as Aono, Hayashi, and himself.
52. *Nihon mondai ni kansuru hōshinsho ketsugishū* (Tokyo: Nihon Kyōsantō shiryō iinkai, 1950), pp. 28–35; Watabe et al., pp. 210–212.
53. See the item in *Nihon kindaishi jiten* (Dictionary of modern Japanese history; Tokyo, 1958), pp. 532b–533a. Even now, Fukumoto-ism is considered a dangerous deviation.
54. *GNB,* XXXVIII, 184–222.
55. On this episode, see Sobue et al., pp. 31–33.
56. *Zenei* (Jan. 1928–April 1928).
57. The December issue of *Bungeisensen* was devoted to criticism of Fukumotoism. Included were articles by such *rōnō* critics as Inomata Tsunao (1889–1942), Aono, and Yamakawai.
58. Sobue et al., p. 32.
59. Kurahara Korehito, "Musan kaikyū geijutsu-undō no shindan-kai," *Zenei* (Jan. 1928), in *NPB,* II, 245b, 246a.
60. *Ibid.,* p. 253a.
61. Sobue et al., p. 33.
62. Kobayashi Takiji, "Sen-kyūhyaku-nijū-hachi, san, jūgo" (March 15, 1928), *GNB,* XXXVIII, 113–144.
63. NAPF (March 1928–Nov. 1931). The new federation divided its cultural activities into five independent organizations (literature, theater, art, music, and movies). For a bibliographical guide, see Watabe et al., pp. 154, 203, 232.
64. For the theoretical difference between the *rōnō* group and the NAPF, which reflects the difference between the ideological position of the social democrats led by Yamakawa and that of the Japanese Communist Party, see Tōyama Shigeki, *Meiji ishin* (Tokyo, 1953), pp. 11–20, esp. p. 20 for a bibliography. From the theoretical positions of the *rōnō* group and the NAPF, it is understandable why the two appreciated differently the role of bourgeois artists. The former believed that they had come into their own after the Restoration, while the latter, considering Japan the weakest spot in the imperialist ring circling the socialist world, feared any form of bourgeois influence.
65. Included in Nakano Shigeharu and Odagiri Hideo, *Nihon puroretaria bungaku hattatsu-shi shiryō* (Tokyo, 1948), III, 23–37.
66. Aono Suekichi, "Shakai bungei ni tsuite no jihyo," *Bungeisensen* (May 1928), included in Nakano and Odagiri, III, 52.

67. E.g., Hayama Yoshiki, *Inbaifu* (A whore). The representative literary works of the proletarian writers are collected in Nakano and Odagiri, vols. 1–8 throughout.

68. Kaji Wataru, "Shōshiminsei no chōryō ni kōshite" (Against the rampancy of petty-bourgeois tendencies), *Senki* (July 1928), included in *ibid.*, III, 55–75. Here Kaji is less militant than he was earlier, when he wrote a series of articles for *Musanshimbun*. Still, his theme is the rejection of what is considered artistic in art, as a bourgeois "residue."

69. Marukusushugi bungei hihyō no kijun" (Standard of criticism of Marxist literature), *GNB*, LXXVIII, 151a, 154a.

70. "Kurahara Korehito nenpu," *ibid.,* p. 422b.

71. Kawakami Hajime, *Jijyoden* (Tokyo, 1949), II, 145–146; Furuta, pp. 189–190.

72. "Shōshiminsei no chōryō ni kōshite," in Nakano and Odagiri, *NPBHS*, III, 59–60; "Musanha bungeika tōronkai" (Proletarian writers: A forum), *NPB*, II, 281a–b, 283b–284a.

73. See the record of correspondence between Kurahara and Kobayashi in *Kobayashi Takiji zenshū* (Tokyo, 1959), II, 494–497, 501–503.

74. Kurahara Korehito, "Sayoku seisanshugi" (Leftist liquidationism), *Senki* (Oct. 1928), included in Nakano and Odagiri, III, 89, 90.

75. *Ibid.,* pp. 90, 100–101, 103.

76. Between April 1929 and March 1930, twenty-nine percent of the short stories and novels published in *Kaizō* and *Chūōkōron* were written by writers belonging either to the NAPF or to the *rōnō* group. During the following twelve months, the percentage rose to forty-three percent. For more detailed statistics, see Yamada, pp. 269–270. For the more representative works written during the period under discussion, see *ibid.*, pp. 270–272. For the statistics on *Senki,* see Nakano and Odagiri, III, 294–295.

77. Kurahara Korehito, "Hihyōka tōmen no nimmu" (The present task of a critic), *Senki* (Feb. 1929). In this article (Nakano and Odagiri, pp. 165–166) Kurahara defines the role of the literary critics on behalf of the central executive committee of the NAPF.

78. Hirano et al., *Gendai Nihon bungaku ronsō-shi,* I, 370–371.

79. In October 1924 fourteen young writers led by Yokomitsu started a journal entitled *Bungeijidai* (The literary age), in conscious opposition to the Marxists. To the extent that they had been dissatisfied with their predecessors, the naturalists and the Shirakaba-ha, the two schools shared a common antitraditional outlook. The Shinkankaku-ha, however, felt that it was through stylistic reform and departure from realism that they could improve the state of

literature. Hirano et al., *Gendai Nihon bungaku ronsō-shi*, I, 366b–367b; Takami, *Shōwa bungaku*, pp. 99–102.

80. "Hihyōka tōmen no nimmu," in Nakano and Odagiri, III, 166–167.

81. See Kobayshi Hideo, "Sakkaron" (On the authors), *GNB*, XLII, 271–273.

82. Between 1924 and 1929 he was not involved in the proletarian literary movement, although his literary associates included such *rōnō* writers as Aono Suekichi and Fujimori Seikichi. See "Hirabayashi Hatsunosuke nenpu," *GNB*, LXXVIII, pp. 414b–415b.

83. Hirabayashi Hatsunosuke, "Seijiteki kachi to geijutsuteki kachi" (Political and artistic value), *ibid.*, p. 60b. Here Hirabayashi summarizes the argument of Kurahara and Katsumoto Seiichirō, who, according to him, "monolithically" identified the artistic and social values of a work of art.

84. Kurahara Korehito, "Geijutsusakuhin no kachi" (The value of an art work), *Asahi* (Nov. 26, 1928), included in Nakano and Odagiri, III, 202–204. Kurahara cautions, however, that the value of a work of art cannot be "considered simply from a utilitarian point of view."

85. "Seijiteki kachi to geijutsuteki kachi," *GNB*, LXXVIII, 62a.

86. Nakano Shigeharu, "Geijutsu ni seijiteki kachi nante monowanai" (In art there is no such thing as political value), *ibid.*, p. 629b–c.

87. *Kobayashi*, II, 440, 662–633. Here Kobayashi writes in two letters to Shiga that he no longer has enough time to exercise his literary skill. Kobayashi's letters and diary are the explicit statement of the need for autonomy of even a dedicated Marxist writer.

88. Kobori Jinji, "Puroretaria geijutsu undō riron" (Theory of the proletarian art movement), included in Nakano and Odagiri, III, 187–200. The article was originally published in July 1927. On the class background of the *rōnō* writers, see, e.g., Odagiri Hideo, "Kaisetsu," *GNB*, XXXVIII, 413a–417a. In the *rōnō* interpretation of Marxism, the degree to which the working class had matured was higher than that in the interpretation of party circles. See *ibid.*, p. 196.

89. From the NAPF directives published in 1930. Quoted in Maruyama Shizuka, *Gendai bungaku kenkyū* (Tokyo, 1956), pp. 189–190.

90. The first paragraph of the action directives of the NAPF, published in the Sept. 1930 issue of *NAPF* (vol. 1, no. 1), conveys this acute sense of crisis and defines the coming years as the "age of war and revolution." "The moment we now face," the directives read, "proves itself to be the age of the disintegration of world capitalism

. . . the increasing danger of the new imperialist war, the progressive event of the Chinese Revolution . . . the fierce revolt of the workers and peasants in Japan against the capitalistic rationalization of industry . . . In short, the age is that of war and revolution." Nakano and Odagiri, III, 314.

91. Theoretically, the Japanese Communist Party took the position that it would give no assistance to those movements opposed to the historical disintegration of the present state. Hence the Manchurian incident was a landmark in the process of the collapse of capitalism in Japan. See Kuno and Tsurumi, p. 51. The authors considered the strategy of the Communist Party to be merely based on "the formalistic logic of total negation." Kazahaya Yasoji, *Kakumeika, Noro Eitarō no koto* (Tokyo, 1948), pp. 82–83; Kuno and Tsurumi, pp. 167–168. As one of the five crucial reasons for the final atrophy of the liberal and the constitutional movement in Japan, the authors mention the absence of collaboration between the socialist camps and the liberals. In this the Communist Party is above all to blame, for the liberals were left alone, while the other socialist camps made a working agreement with the rightist elements.

92. Maruyama Shizuka, pp. 220–222.

93. Kurahara Korehito, "Puroretaria geijutsu undō no soshiki mondai" (Organizational problems in the proletarian art movement), *GNB*, LXXVIII, 191a–b.

94. Maruyama Shizuka, p. 221. The reference is made to Kurahara Korehito, "Geijutsuteki hōhō ni tsuite no kansō" (Some impressions on artistic methods), *ibid.,* pp. 226a, 233c–234a.

95. It is not that they never mentioned their predecessors. Rather, they placed them only in a negative context. "The past art works have a value only to the extent that they can assist in some way the victory of the proletariat." *Ibid.,* p. 190b.

96. See, e.g., Tsurumi Shunsuke, "Kyomushugi no keisei" (The formation of anarchism), *Tenkō,* I, 289–315. Tsurumi deals with the life of Haniya Yutaka, a former Marxist, in terms of how he became an apostate and came to formulate his own nihilist philosophy. This is the best article in *Tenkō.*

97. "Burujoa shuppan ni taisuru wareware no taido wa kō de nakereba naranu" (Our attitude toward bourgeois publications must be as follows), in Nakano and Odagiri, III, 383–394.

98. "Sensō hantai ni kansuru ken" (Concerning an objection to the war), *ibid.,* p. 185.

99. "Burujoa shuppan ni taisuru wareware no taido wa kō de nakereba naranu," *ibid.,* p. 392.

100. *Ibid.,* pp. 387–388.

101. "Kurahara Korehito nenpu," *GNB*, LXXVIII, 422b.
102. Kurahara Korehito, "Puroretaria geijutsu undō no soshiki mondai," *ibid.*, pp. 191c–202b.
103. For the controversy, see Sobue et al., p. 49.
104. Kurahara Korehito, "Geijutsuteki hōhō ni tsuite no kansō," *ibid.*, pp. 202c–236a.

CONCLUSION

1. *Kōjin*, in *Soseki*, VIII, 318.
2. *Shirakaba* (Apr. 1913), quoted in Honda, *Shirakaba-ha*, p. 87.
3. "*Momo no shizuku*, igo," *Shimazaki zenshū*, XVII, 214.
4. Raymond Aron, *The Opium of the Intellectuals*, tr. T. Kilmartin (New York, 1955), p. 324.

Bibliography

Abe Jirō 阿部次郎. *Santarō no nikki* 三太郎の日記 (The diary of Santarō). Tokyo, 1918.

Akamatsu Katsumaro 赤松克磨. *Nihon shakai undō-shi* 日本社会運動史 (A history of the Japanese social movement). Tokyo, 1949.

Akutagawa Ryūnosuke annai 芥川龍之介案内 (Introduction to Akutagawa Ryūnosuke). Tokyo, 1955.

Akutagawa Ryūnosuke zenshū 芥川龍之介全集 (The complete works of Akutagawa Ryūnosuke). 17 vols.; Tokyo, 1954–1955.

Amano Keitarō 天野敬太郎. *Kawakami Hajime hakase bunken-shi* 河上肇博士文献志 (A bibliography of Dr. Kawakami Hajime's works). Tokyo, 1956.

Amano Teiyū 天野貞祐. *Gakusei ni ataeru sho* 学生に与える書 (Book for students). Tokyo, 1939.

Aono Suekichi 青野季吉. *Bungaku gojūnen* 文学五十年 (Fifty years in the literary world). Tokyo, 1957.

——— ed. *Gendai bungakuron taikei* 現代文学論大系 (A compilation of essays in literary criticism), vols. 2–4. Tokyo, 1954–1955.

Arahata Kanson 荒畑寒村. *Kanson jiden* 寒村自伝 (The autobiography of Arahata Kanson). Tokyo, 1960.

Arima Yoriyasu 有馬頼寧. *Seikai dōchūki* 政界道中記 (A note on the political world). Tokyo, 1949.

——— *Shichijūnen no kaiko* 七十年の回顧 (A reflection on my seventy years). Tokyo, 1951.

Aron, Raymond. *The Opium of the Intellectuals,* tr. T. Kilmartin. New York, 1955.

Asou Isoji 麻生磯次 et al. *Nihon bungaku kenkyū nyūmon* 日本文学研究入門 (An introduction to the study of Japanese literature). Tokyo, 1956.

Becker, Carl. *The Heavenly City of the Eighteenth-Century Philosophers.* New Haven, 1932.

Berdyaef, N. *Slavery and Freedom.* New York, 1950.

Burckhardt, Jakob. *Gesamtausgabe,* vol. 8. Stuttgart, Berlin, and Leipzig, 1930.

Cary, Otis. *A History of Christianity in Japan.* New York, 1909.

Deutscher, Isaac. *The Prophet Unarmed.* London, 1959.

Ebina Danjō 海老名弾正. *Kirisutokyō shinron* 基督教新論 (A new theory of Christianity). Tokyo, 1918.

Elliott, William Y. *The Pragmatic Revolt.* New York, 1928.

Fujioka Junkichi 藤岡淳吉 et al. *Nihon kyōsantō tēze* 日本共産党テーゼ (The Japanese Communist Party thesis). Tokyo, 1951.

Fukumoto Kazuo 福本和夫. *Hōkō tenkan* 方向転換 (The policy change). Tokyo, 1927.

Funayama Shin'ichi 船山信一. *Nihon no kannen ronsha* 日本の観念論者 (The idealists of Japan). Tokyo, 1956.

Furuta Hikaru 古田光. *Kawakami Hajime* 河上肇. Tokyo, 1959.

Gendai bungaku kōza 現代文学講座 (Series on modern Japanese literature), vols. 5 and 6 (The Taishō era). Tokyo, 1960.

Gendai Nihon bungaku zenshū, see *GNB.*

Gendai rinri 現代倫理 (Modern ethics), vol. 11 *(Japan),* esp. the essays by Maruyama Masao 丸山真男 and Fujita Shōzō 藤田省三. Tokyo, 1959.

Gendai shisō 現代思想 (Modern thoughts), vols. 3, 5, and 11. Tokyo, 1957.

GNB : Gendai Nihon bungaku zenshū 現代日本文学全集 (A complete compilation of modern Japanese literature). 97 vols. and 3 appendix vols,; Tokyo, 1953–1957. Each volume contains some biographical data on the author or authors whose representative works make up the volume.

Hall, A. R. *The Scientific Revolution.* New York, 1958.

Hani Gorō 羽仁五郎. *Nihon ni okeru kindai shisō no zentei* 日本に於ける近代思想の前提 (Preludes to modern thought in Japan). Tokyo, 1949.

Hartz, Louis. *The Liberal Tradition in America.* Boston, 1955.

Hasegawa Izumi 長谷川泉. *Kindai Nihon bungaku hyōron-shi* 近代日本文学評論史 (A history of Japanese literary criticism). Tokyo, 1958.

—— *Kindai Nihon bungaku no tembō* 近代日本文学の展望 (A survey of modern Japanese literature). Tokyo, 1960.

—— and Yoshimoto Takaaki 吉本隆明. "Kindai hihyō no tenkai 近代批評の展開 (The development of modern criticism); in *Nihon bungaku-shi,* vol. 14.

Hashikawa Bunzō 橋川文三. *Nihon rōman-ha hihan josetsu* 日本浪曼派批判序説 (An introduction to a critique of the Japanese romanticists). Tokyo, 1960.

Hauser, Arnold. *The Social History of Art.* 4 vols.; New York, 1958.

Hayashi Fusao 林房雄. *Bungakuteki kaisō* 文学的回想 (Literary recollections). Tokyo, 1958.

Hegel, G. W. F. *Philosophy of History,* tr. J. Sibree, as quoted in S. Sabine, *A History of Political theory.*

—— *The Philosophy of Hegel,* ed. and tr. Carl J. Friedrich. New York: Modern Library, 1953.

Heller, Erich. *The Disinherited Mind.* New York, 1959.

Himerareta Shōwa-shi 祕められた昭和史 (Hidden stories in Shōwa history); a special issue of *Chisei* 知性 (The intellect; Tokyo, November 1956).

Hirano Ken 平野謙. *Gendai no sakka* 現代の作家 (The contemporary writers). Tokyo, 1956.

—— *Shimazaki Tōson* 島崎藤村. Tokyo, 1957.

—— "Jinsei-ha to geijutsu-ha" 人生派と芸術派 (The life school and the art school); in *Nihon bungaku-shi,* vol. 15.

—— et al. *Gendai sakka ronsō-sho* 現代作家論爭書 (Modern literary controversies), vol. 3. Tokyo, 1955.

—— *Gendai Nihon bungaku ronsō-shi* 現代日本文学論爭史 (A history of modern Japanese literary controversies: A compilation of the original sources). 3 vols.; Tokyo, 1957.

Honda Shūgo 本多秋五. *Shirakaba-ha no bungaku* 白樺派の文学 (The literature of the Shirakaba). Tokyo, 1955.

—— *Tenkō bungaku-ron* 転向文学論 (A study of the literature of the apostates). Tokyo, 1957.

Hughes, H. Stuart. *Consciousness and Society.* New York, 1958.

Ienaga Saburō 家永三郎. *Nihon kindai shisō-shi kenkyū* 日本近代思想史研究 (A study of modern Japanese thought). Tokyo, 1953.

―――― *Minobe Tatsukichi no shisō-shiteki kenkyū* 美濃部達吉の思想史的研究 (Minobe Tatsukichi: A study in intellectual history). Tokyo, 1964.

Inagaki Tatsurō 稲垣達郎. *Shakaishugi bungaku* 社会主義文学 (Socialist literature). Tokyo, 1959.

Ino Kenji 猪野謙二. *Kindai Nihon bungaku-shi kenkyū* 近代日本文学史研究 (A study of the history of modern Japanese literature). Tokyo, 1953.

―――― *Nihon bungaku no kindai to gendai* 日本文学の近代と現代 (The modern and the contemporary in Japanese literature). Tokyo, 1958.

―――― *"Sōseki"* 漱石; in *Nihon bungaku-shi,* vol. 15.

Ishida Takeshi 石田雄. *Meiji seiji shisō-shi kenkyū* 明治政治思想史研究 (A study of Meiji political thought). Tokyo, 1954.

Itō Shirō 伊藤至郎. *Ōgai ronkō* 鷗外論稿 (A study of Mori Ōgai). Tokyo, 1941.

Itoya Toshio 糸屋寿雄. *Taigyaku jiken* 大逆事件 (The treason incident). Tokyo, 1960.

Iwanaga Yutaka 岩永胖. *Tayama Katai kenkyū* 田山花袋研究 (A study of Tayama Katai). Tokyo, 1956.

Iwaya Daishi 巌谷大四. *Hijyōji Nihon bundan-shi* 非常時日本文壇史 (A history of the Japanese literary world during the war). Tokyo, 1958.

Kagawa Toyohiko 賀川豊彦. *Shisen o koete* 死線を越えて (Beyond death); in *Kagawa Toyohiko zenshū* 賀川豊彦全集 (The complete works of Kagawa Toyohiko), vol. 14. Tokyo, 1964.

Kamei Katsuichirō 亀井勝一郎. *Shimazaki Tōson* 島崎藤村. Tokyo, 1938.

―――― *Shimazaki Tōson* 島崎藤村. Tokyo, 1957.

―――― *Kodai chishiki kaikyū no keisei* 古代知識階級の形成 (The development of the ancient Japanese intellectuals). Tokyo, 1960.

―――― and Maruyama Shizuka 丸山静. "Minzoku to bungaku" 民族と文学 (The race and literature); in *Nihon bungaku-shi,* vol. 15.

Kant, Immanuel. *The Philosophy of Kant,* ed. and tr. Carl J. Friedrich. New York: Modern Library, n.d.

Karaki Junzō 唐木順三. *Mori Ōgai* 森鷗外. Tokyo, 1949.

Karasawa Tomitarō 唐澤富太郎. *Gakusei no rekishi* 学生の歴史 (A history of students). Tokyo, 1955.

—— *Kyōshi no rekishi* 教師の歴史 (A history of teachers). Tokyo, 1955.

—— *Kyōkasho no rekishi* 教科書の歴史 (A history of textbooks). Tokyo, 1958.

Kataoka Yoshikazu 片岡良一. *Natsume Sōseki* 夏目漱石. Tokyo, 1955.

—— *Shizenshugi kenkyū* 自然主義研究 (A study of naturalism). Tokyo, 1957.

—— *Nihon rōmanshugi bungaku kenkyū* 日本浪漫主義文学研究 (A study of Japanese romantic literature). Tokyo, 1958.

Katō Shūichi 加藤周一. "Ōgai" 鷗外; in *Nihon bungaku-shi*, vol. 15.

Kawabata Yasunari zenshū 川端康成全集 (The complete works of Kawabata Yasunari), vols. 8 and 16. Tokyo, 1954.

Kawai Eijirō 河合栄次郎. *Tōmasu Hiru Gurīn no shisō taikei* トーマス・ヒル・グリーンの思想体系 (The thought of Thomas Hill Green). Tokyo, 1938.

Kawakami Hajime 河上肇. *Bimbō monogatari* 貧乏物語 (A tale of the poor). Tokyo, 1947.

—— *Jijyoden* 自叙伝 (Autobiography). 5 vols.; Tokyo, 1949.

Kawazoe Kunimoto 川副國基. *Nihon shizenshugi no bungaku* 日本自然主義の文学 (Japanese naturalist literature). Tokyo, 1957.

—— and Ino Kenji. *Shizenshugi no bungaku* 自然主義の文学 (Japanese naturalist literature); in *Nihon bungaku-shi*, vol. 11. Tokyo, 1958.

Kazahaya Yasoji 風早八十二. *Kakumeika, Noro Eitarō no koto* 革命家野呂栄太郎のこと (A revolutionary, Noro Eitarō). Tokyo, 1948.

Kindai Nihon bungaku jiten 近代日本文学辞典 (A dictionary of modern Japanese literature). Tokyo, 1957.

Kindai Nihon shisō-shi kōza, see *KNS*.

Kishimoto Eitarō 岸本英太郎 et al. *Katayama Sen* 片山潜. 2 vols.; Tokyo, 1960.

Kita Ikki chosakushū 北一輝著作集 (The writings of Kita Ikki). Tokyo, 1959.

KNS : Kindai Nihon shisō-shi kōza 近代日本思想史講座 (A series on modern Japanese intellectual history), vols. 1, 3–7. Tokyo, 1958–1960.

Kobayashi Takiji zenshū 小林多喜二全集 (The complete works of kobayashi Takiji). 5 vols.; Tokyo, 1959.

Kokutai no hongi 国体の本義. (The essence of polity). Tokyo: Mombushō 文部省 (Ministry of Education), 1937.

Kōtoku Shūsui sensho 幸徳秋水選書 (Selections from Kōtoku Shūsui). Tokyo, 1950.

Kōtoku Shūsui: Nikki to shokan 幸徳秋水: 日記と書簡 (Kōtoku Shūsui: Diary and letters), ed. Shioda Shōbei 塩田庄兵衛. Tokyo, 1954.

Kōza kindai shisō-shi 講座近代思想史 (Modern Japanese intellectual history), vol. 9: *Nihon ni okeru seiyō kindai shisō no juyō* 日本における西洋近代思想の受容 (Acceptance of modern Western ideas in Japan). Tokyo, 1959.

Krieger, L. *The German Idea of Freedom.* Boston, 1957.

Kubokawa Tsurujirō 窪川鶴次郎. *Nihon kindai bungei shichō-ron* 日本近代文芸思潮論 (A discussion of modern Japanese literary trends). Tokyo. 1956.

—— *Ishikawa Takuboku* 石川啄木; vol. 4 of *Gendai sakkazō zenshū* 現代作家像全集 (Modern literary figures). Tokyo, 1958.

—— et al., eds. *Nihon no puroretaria bungaku* 日本のプロレタリア文学 (A compliation of Japanese proletarian literature). Tokyo, 1956.

Kunikida Doppo shū 國木田独歩集 (Selections from Kunikida Doppo); vol. 15 of *Gendai Nihon bungaku zenshū.* Tokyo, 1927.

Kuno Osamu 久野收 and Tsurumi Shunsuke 鶴見俊輔. *Gendai Nihon no shisō* 現代日本の思想 (Modern Japanese thought). Tokyo, 1956.

—— Fujita Shōzō 藤田省三, and Tsurumi Shunsuke. *Sengo Nihon no shisō* 戦后日本の思想 (Postwar Japanese thought). Tokyo, 1959.

Kurahara Korehito 藏原惟人 et al. *Nihon puroretaria bungaku annai* 日本プロレタリア文学案内 (An introduction to Japanese proletarian literature). 2 vols.; Kyoto, 1955.

Kuyama Yasushi 久山康 et al. *Kindai Nihon to Kirisutokyō* 近代日本とキリスト教 (Modern Japan and Christianity). Tokyo, 1956.

Löwith, Karl. *Von Hegel zu Nietzsche.* Stuttgart, 1958.

Lukacs, Georg. *Existentialisme ou Marxisme,* tr. Shirotsuke Noboru et al. Paris, 1947.

Maejima Shōzō 前島省三. *Nihon fashizumu to gikai* 日本ファシズムと議会 (Japanese fascism and the Diet). Kyoto, 1956.

Mannheim, Karl. *Ideology and Utopia.* New York, 1936.

Maruyama Masao 丸山真男. *Gendai seiji no shisō to kōdō* 現代政治の思想と行動 (Thought and behavior in modern politics). Tokyo, 1956 (vol. 1) and 1957 (vol. 2).

—— *Nihon seiji shisō-shi kenkyū* 日本政治思想史研究 (A study of the history of Japanese political thought). Tokyo, 1956.

—— "Kindai Nihon no shisō to bungaku" 近代日本の思想と文学 (The thought and the literature of modern Japan); in *Nihon bungaku-shi*, vol. 15.

Maruyama Shizuka 丸山靜. *Gendai bungaku kenkyū* 現代文学研究 (A study of contemporary literature). Tokyo, 1956.

Masamune Hakuchō 正宗白鳥. *Sakka-ron* 作家論 (Notes on writers). Tokyo, 1948.

—— *Shizenshugi seisui-shi* 自然主義盛衰史 (A history of Japanese naturalism). Tokyo, 1948.

—— *Uchimura Kanzō* 内村鑑三. Tokyo, 1948.

Mead, G. H. *Thought and Movement in the Nineteenth Century*. Chicago, 1936.

Miki Kiyoshi 三木清. *Dokusho to jinsei* 讀書と人生 (Books and life). Tokyo, 1948.

Miki Kiyoshi chosakushū 三木清著作集 (The writings of Miki Kiyoshi). 16 vols.; Tokyo, 1946–1951.

Minobe Ryōkichi 美濃部亮吉. *Kumonsuru demokurashī* 苦悶するデモクラシー (Suffering democracy). Tokyo, 1959.

Minobe Tatsukichi 美濃部達吉. *Kempō satsuyō* 憲法撮要 (An outline of the constitution). Tokyo, 1923.

Miyajima Hajime 宮島肇. *Meijiteki shisōkazō no keisei* 明治的思想家像の形成 (The development of a Meiji thinker). Tokyo, 1960.

Miyakawa Tōru 宮川透. *Kindai Nihon shisō no kōzō* 近代日本思想の構造 (The structure of modern Japanese thought). Tokyo, 1956.

—— *Miki Kiyoshi* 三木清. Tokyo, 1958.

Miyanishi Kazumi 宮西一積. *Nihon bungaku no shisō-shi* 日本文学の思想史 (A history of Japanese literary thought). Tokyo, 1958.

—— *Kindai shisō no Nihonteki tenkai* 近代思想の日本的展開 (The development of modern thought in Japan). Tokyo, 1960.

Muroo Saisei 室生犀星. *Akutagawa Ryūnosuke no hito to saku* 芥川龍之介の人と作 (Akutagawa Ryūnosuke: The man and his works). Tokyo, 1943.

Mushakōji Saneatsu 武者小路実篤. *Shinri sensei* (Mr. Truth). Tokyo, 1952.

(Nagai) Kafū zenshū (永井) 荷風全集 (The complete works of Nagai Kafū). Chūōkōron ed.; 24 vols.; Tokyo, 1948–1953.

Nagai Kafū nikki 永井荷風日記 (The diary of Nagai Kafū). 7 vols.; Tokyo, 1958–1959.

Nakajima Kenzō 中島健蔵. *Senzen senchū bungaku* 戦前戦中文学 (Prewar and wartime literature); in *Nihon bungaku-shi,* vol. 13. Tokyo, 1959.

Nakamura Mitsuo 中村光夫. *Fūzoku shōsetsuron* 風俗小説論 (On the genre novel). Tokyo, 1950.

―――*Tanizaki Jun'ichirō ron* 谷崎潤一郎論 (A study of Tanizaki Jun'ichirō). Tokyo, 1952.

―――*Shiga Naoya ron* 志賀直哉論 (A study of Shiga Naoya). Tokyo, 1954.

―――*Gendai sakka-ron* 現代作家論 (Thoughts on contemporary writers). Tokyo, 1958.

―――*Shiga Naoya* 志賀直哉. Tokyo, 1958.

―――*Nihon no kindaika to bungaku* 日本の近代化と文学 (Literature and modernization in Japan); in *Nihon bungaku-shi,* vol. 14. Tokyo, 1959.

Nakamura Shin'ichirō 中村眞一郎. *Akutagawa Ryūnosuke no sekai* 芥川龍之介の世界 (The world of Akutagawa Ryūnosuke). Tokyo, 1956.

―――et al. *Nagai Kafū kenkyū* 永井荷風研究 (Studies on Nagai Kafū). Tokyo, 1956.

Nakano Shigeharu 中野重治, and Odagiri Hideo 小田切秀雄. *Nihon puroretaria bungaku hattatsu-shi shiryō* 日本プロレタリア文学発達史資料 (Materials on the development of the Japanese proletarian literature). Tokyo, 1948.

Nakano Yoshio 中野好夫. *Gendai no sakka* 現代の作家 (Contemporary authors). Tokyo, 1955.

NB : Nihon bungaku-shi 日本文学史 (A history of Japanese literature). 16 vols.; Tokyo, 1958–1959.

Neumann, Franz. *The Democratic and the Authoritarian State.* New York, 1957.

Nezu Masashi ねずまさし. *Hihan Nihon gendai-shi* 批判日本現代史 (A critique of modern Japanese history). Tokyo, 1958.

Nihon bungaku-shi, see *NB.*

Nihon kindaishi jiten 日本近代史辞典 (Dictionary of modern Japanese history). Tokyo, 1958.

Nihon kyōsantō kōryō mondai bunken shū 日本共産党綱領問題文献集 (A compilation of materials on the problem of the Japanese Communist Party program). Tokyo: Seiji mondai kenkyū kai 政治問題研究会 (Institute for Political Research), 1957.

Nihon kyōsantō-shi 日本共産党史 (A history of the Japanese Communist Party). Tokyo: Nihon kyōsantō chūō iinkai 日本共産党中央委員会

(Central Committee of the Japanese Communist Party), 1932.

Nihon mondai ni kansuru hōshinsho ketsugishū 日本問題に関する方針書決議集 (A compilation of the Comintern's resolutions and policy directives on Japan). Tokyo: Nihon kyōsantō shiryō iinkai 日本共産党資料委員会 (Committee on the Sources of the Japanese Communist Party), 1950.

Nihon puroretaria bungaku taikei, see *NPB.*

Nishida Kitarō zenshū 西田幾太郎全集 (The complete works of Nishida Kitarō). Iwanami ed.; 12 vols. and 6 appendix vols.; 1948–1953.

Nishida Kitarō. *Zen no kenkyū* 善の研究 (Studies in goodness). Iwanami paperback ed.; Tokyo.

Nishida Masaru 西田勝. *Nihon kakumei bungaku no tembō* 日本革命文学の展望 (A view of the revolutionary literature in Japan). Tokyo, 1958.

Nishio Minoru 西尾実. *Sakuhin kenkyū: Ōgai no rekishi shōsetsu* 作品研究・鷗外の歴史小説 (A study of the historical novels of Mori Ōgai). Tokyo, 1953.

Nock, Arthur D. *Conversion.* New York, 1933

Noro Eitarō 野呂栄太郎. *Nōgyō senryaku senjutsu mondai* 農業戦略戦術問題 (The problems of agrarian strategy). Tokyo, 1948.

NPB: *Nihon puroretaria bungaku taikei* 日本プロレタリア文学大系 (A compilation of Japanese proletarian literature). 9 vols.; Kyoto, 1954–1955.

Odagiri Hideo 小田切秀雄. "Shishōsetsu" 私小説 (The I-novel); in *Nihon bungaku-shi,* vol. 12. Tokyo, 1958.

Ōgai zenshū 鷗外全集 (The complete works of Mori Ōgai). Iwanami ed.; Tokyo, 1954–1956.

Ōi Tadashi 大井正. *Nihon kindai shisō no ronri* 日本近代思想の論理 (The logic of modern Japanese thought). Tokyo, 1958.

Okazaki Yoshie 岡崎義恵. *Nihon geijutsu shichō* 日本芸術思潮 (Trends in aesthetic thought in Japan). Tokyo, 1943.

Okino Iwasaburō 沖野岩三郎. *Kirisutokyō jūdanmen* キリスト教縦断面 (The phases of Christianity). Tokyo, 1920.

Ōkuma Nobuyuki 大熊信行. *Kokka aku* 国家悪 (The evils of the state). Tokyo, 1957.

Ono Shigeki 小野茂樹. *Wakaki hi no Kunikida Doppo* 若き日の國木田独歩 (The early years of Kunikida Doppo). Tokyo, 1959.

Ōsugi Sakae zenshū 大杉栄全集 (The complete works of Ōsugi Sakae). 8 vols.; Tokyo, 1923.

Ōta Saburō 太田三郎. "Hon'yaku bungaku" 翻訳文学 (Literature in translation); in *Nihon bungaku-shi,* vol. 14.

Ōuchi Hyōe 大内兵衛. *Watakushi no rirekisho* 私の履歴書 (My life history). Tokyo, 1951.

Ōyama Ikuo zenshū 大山郁夫全集 (The complete works of Ōyama Ikuo), vols. 1 and 2. Tokyo, 1947.

Sabine, George. *A History of Political Theory.* New York, 1954.

Saigusa Hiroto 三枝博音. *Nihon no yuibutsuron-sha* 日本の唯物論者 (The Japanese materialistic philosopher). Tokyo, 1956.

Saigusa Yasutaka 三枝康高. *Nihon rōman-ha no undō* 日本浪漫派の運動 (The Japanese romantic movement). Tokyo, 1959.

Sakakibara Yoshibumi 榊原美文. *Shōyō, Futabatei* 逍遙・二葉亭; in *Nihon bungaku-shi,* vol. 11.

Sasabuchi Tomoichi 笹淵友一. *Rōmanshugi bungaku no tanjō* 浪漫主義文学の誕生 (The birth of the romantic literature). Tokyo, 1958.

Sasaki Kiichi 佐々木基一. "Shinkankakuha oyobi sore igo" 新感覚派及びそれ以后 (The new Sensibility school and after); in *Nihon bungaku-shi,* vol. 15.

Satō Haruo 佐藤春夫. *Waga Ryūnosuke-zō* 我が龍之介像 (My image of Akutagawa Ryūnosuke). Tokyo, 1959.

Schumpeter, Joseph. *Socialism, Capitalism and Democracy.* New York, 1950.

Senuma Shigeki 瀬沼茂樹. *Hyōden, Shimazaki Tōson* 評伝・島崎藤村 (A biography of Shimazaki Tōson). Tokyo, 1959.

———— *Kindai Nihon no bungaku* 近代日本の文学 (Modern Japanese literature). Tokyo, 1959.

———— "Taishō demokurashī to bungaku" 大正デモクラシーと文学 (The Taishō democracy and Literature); in *Nihon bungaku-shi* vol. 15.

Shiga Naoya zenshū 志賀直哉全集 (The complete works of Shiga Naoya). Kaizōsha ed., Tokyo, 1937; Iwanami ed. 17 vols.; Tokyo, 1955.

Shigefuji Takeo 重藤威夫. *Makkusu Uēbā kenkyū* マックス・ウェーバー研究 (A study of Max Weber). Tokyo, 1949.

Shimamura Hōgetsu 島村抱月. *Kindai bungei no kenkyū* 近代文藝の研究 (Studies on modern literature). Tokyo, 1909.

Shimazaki Tōson dokuhon 島崎藤村読本 (A reader on Shimazaki Tōson). Tokyo 1958.

Shimazaki Tōson zenshū 島崎藤村全集 (The complete works of Shimazaki Tōson). Shinchō-sha 新潮社 ed.; 19 vols.; Tokyo, 1950.

Shinobu Seizaburō 信夫清三郎. *Taishō Seiji-shi* 大正政治史 (Taishō political history). Tokyo, 1954.

—— *Taishō demokurashi* 大正デモクラシー (Taishō democracy). 3 vols.; Tokyo, 1958.

Shioda Ryōhei 塩田良平. "Koten to Meiji igo no bungaku" 古典と明治以后の文学 (The classics and post-Meiji literature); in *Nihon bungaku-shi,* vol. 14.

Shklar, Judith. *After Utopia*. Princeton, 1957.

Sobue Shōji 祖父江昭二 et al. "Puroretaria bungaku" プロレタリア文学 (Proletarian literature); in *Nihon bungaku-shi,* vol. 13.

Sorel, Georges, *Reflections on Violence,* tr. T. E. Hulme and J. Roth. Glencoe, Ill., 1950.

Sōseki zenshū 漱石全集 (The complete works of Natsume Sōseki). 20 vols.; Tokyo, 1928–1929.

Sumiya Mikio 隅谷三喜男. *Kindai Nihon no keisei to kirisutokyō* 近代日本の形成とキリスト教 (Christianity and the development of modern Japan). Tokyo, 1950.

—— *Katayama Sen* 片山潜. Tokyo, 1960.

Tabata Shinobu 田畑忍. "Uchimura Kanzō ni okeru heiwashugi shisō no tenkai" 内村鑑三における平和主義思想の展開 (The development of pacifism in Uchimura Kanzō); *Shisō,* no. 353 (Nov. 1953).

Takahashi Yoshitaka 高橋義孝. *Mori Ōgai* 森鷗外. Tokyo, 1946.

Takami Jun 高見順. *Shōwa bungaku seisui-shi* 昭和文学盛衰史 (A history of the vicissitudes of Shōwa literature). 2 vols.; Tokyo, 1958.

—— et al. "Kakumei no bungaku to bungaku no kakumei" 革命の文学と文学の革命 (Revolutionary literature and the literary revolution); in *Nihon bungaku-shi,* vol. 12.

Tanaka Sōgorō 田中惣五郎. *Kita Ikki* 北一輝. Tokyo, 1951.

—— *Kōtoku Shūsui* 幸徳秋水. Tokyo, 1955.

—— *Yoshino Sakuzō* 吉野作造. Tokyo, 1958.

Tanizaki Jun'ichirō sakuhinshū 谷崎潤一郎作品集 (The works of Tanizaki

Jun'ichirō). Sōgensha ed.; Tokyo, 1956–1958.

Tanizaki Jun'ichirō zenshū 谷崎潤一郎全集 (The complete works of Tanizaki Jun'ichirō). Chūōkōron; 30 vols.; Tokyo, 1958–1959.

Tayama Katai 田山花袋. *Tōkyō no sanjūnen* 東京の三十年 (Thirty years in Tokyo). Tokyo, 1921.

―――― *Shōsetsu no sahō* 小説の作法 (The writing of novels). Tokyo, 1933.

Tenkō 転向 (Apostasy). 3 vols.; Tokyo: Shisō no kagaku kenkyū-kai 思想の科学研究会 (Society for Studying the Science of Thought), 1959–1962.

Terada Tōru 寺田透. "Kindai bungaku to Nihongo" 近代文学と日本語 (Modern literature and the Japanese language); in *Nihon bungaku-shi,* vol. 13.

Togawa Yukio 戸川行男. *Ansatsusha* 暗殺者 (The assassins). Tokyo, 1958.

Tōyama Shigeki 遠山茂樹. *Meiji ishin* 明治維新 (The Meiji Restoration). Tokyo, 1953.

―――― et al. *Kindai Nihon shisō-shi* 近代日本思想史 (A history of modern Japanese thought), vols. 1 and 2. Tokyo, 1956.

―――― *Shōwa-shi* 昭和史 (A history of the Shōwa period). Tokyo, 1959.

Uchida Jōkichi 内田穣吉. *Nihon shihonshugi ronsō* 日本資本主義論争 (Controversies over Japanese capitalism). 2 vols.; Tokyo, 1949.

Uchimura Kanzō zenshū 内村鑑三全集 (The complete works of Uchimura Kanzō). Iwanami ed.; 20 vols.; Tokyo, 1932–1933.

Uemura (Masahisa) zenshū 植村 (正久) 全集 (The complete works of Uemura Masahisa). 8 vols.; Tokyo, 1933–1934.

Usui Yoshimi 臼井吉見. *Kindai bungaku ronsō* 近代文学論争 (Modern literary controversies), vol. 1. Tokyo, 1956.

―――― "Shirakaba-ha no bungaku" 白樺派の文学 (The literature of the Shirakaba); in *Nihon bungaku-shi,* vol. 12.

Watabe Yoshimichi 渡部義通 et al. *Nihon shakaishugi bunken kaisetsu* 日本社会主義文献解説 (A commentary on Japanese socialist source materials). Tokyo, 1958.

Watkins, Frederick. *The Political Tradition of the West : A study in the Development of Modern Liberalism.* Cambridge, Mass., 1948.

Watsuji Tetsurō 和辻哲郎. *Gūzō saikō* 偶像再興 (The restoration of idols). Tokyo, 1918.

—— *Nihon seishin-shi kenkyū* 日本精神史研究 (Studies in Japanese intellectual history). Tokyo, 1926.

—— *Son'nō shisō to sono dentō* 尊皇思想とその伝統 (The *Son'no* idea and its tradition). Tokyo, 1943.

——*Koji junrei* 古寺巡礼 (A pilgrimage to old temples). Tokyo, 1947.

Weber, Marianne. *Max Weber: Ein Lebensbild*. Tübingen, 1926.

Wilkins, E. H. *A History of Italian Literature*. Cambridge, Mass., 1954.

Wilson, Edmond. *A Literary Chronicle: 1920–1950*. Gloucester, Mass., n.d.

—— *Axel's Castle*. New York. Scribner Library, 1931.

Yamada Seizaburō 山田清三郎. *Puroretaria bungaku-shi* プロレタリア文学史 (A history of proletarian literature). 2 vols.; Tokyo, 1954.

Yamaji Aizan 山路愛山. *Gendai Nihon kyōkai shiron* 現代日本教会史論 (A historical essay on modern Japanese Christian churches). Tokyo, 1906.

Yamakawa Hitoshi 山川均. *Shakaishugisha no shakai kan* 社会主義者の社会観 (The social view of a socialist). Tokyo, 1919.

—— *Musankaikyū no seiji-undō* 無産階級の政治運動 (The political movement of the proletariat). Tokyo, 1924.

Yamamuro Shizuka 山室靜. *Hyōden, Mori Ōgai* 評伝・森鷗外 (A biography of Mori Ōgai). Tokyo, 1960.

—— ed. *Mushakōji Saneatsu* 武者小路実篤. Tokyo, 1961.

Yamazaki Masakazu 山崎正一. *Kindai Nihon shisō tsū-shi* 近代日本思想通史 (A general history of modern Japanese thought). Tokyo, 1960.

Yanagi Muneyoshi 柳宗悦. *Mingei towa nanika* 民芸とは何か (What is folk art?). Tokyo, 1941.

—— *Nihon no mingei* 日本の民芸 (Japanese folk art). Tokyo, 1960.

Yanagida Izumi 柳田泉. *Meiji shoki no hon'yaku bungaku* 明治初期の翻訳文学 (Translated literature in the early Meiji period). Tokyo, 1935.

—— *Tayama Katai no bungaku* 田山花袋の文学 (The literature of Tayama Katai). 2 vols.; Tokyo, 1957.

—— *Keimō-ki bungaku* 啓蒙期文学 (The literature of the enlightenment); in *Nihon bungaku-shi*, vol. 13.

Yanaihara Tadao 矢内原忠雄. *Yo no sonkei suru jimbutsu* 余の尊敬する人物 (Personalities I admire). Tokyo, 1948.

Yoshida Seiichi 吉田精一. *Tembō: Gendai Nihon bungaku* 展望・現代日本文学 (A view of contemporary Japanese literature). Tokyo, 1941.

——— *Kindai Nihon rōmanshugi kenkyū* 近代日本浪漫主義研究 (A study of modern Japanese romanticism). Tokyo, 1943.

——— *Meiji Taishō bungaku-shi* 明治大正文学史 (A history of Meiji Taishō literature). Tokyo, 1956.

——— *Kindai Nihon bungaku-shi, Meiji Taishō hen* 近代日本文学史・明治大正篇 (A history of modern Japanese literature, Meiji and Taishō). Tokyo, 1957.

——— *Akutagawa Ryūnosuke* 芥川龍之介. Tokyo, 1958.

——— "Rōmanshugi no seiritsu to tenkai" 浪漫主義の成立と展開 (The birth and growth of romanticism); in *Nihon bungaku-shi,* vol. 11.

——— *Shizenshugi no kenkyū* 自然主義の研究 (Studies of Japanese naturalism). 2 vols.; Tokyo, 1958.

——— *Kindai Nihon bungaku gaisetsu* 近代日本文学概説 (A general introduction to modern Japanese literature). Tokyo, 1959.

——— *Mori Ōgai kenkyū* 森鷗外研究 (Studies on Mori Ōgai). Tokyo, 1960.

———, ed. *Akutagawa Ryūnosuke kenkyū* 芥川龍之介研究 (Studies on Akutagawa Ryūnosuke). Tokyo, 1958.

Glossary

Abe Isoo, 安部磯雄

Abe Tomoji 阿部知二

Abeichizoku 阿部一族

Ai to ninshiki tono shuppatsu 愛と認識との出発

Aizu Tsuneji 会津常治

Aka to kuro 赤と黒

"Akutagawa Ryūnosuke shi no shi to sono geijutsu" 芥川龍之介氏の死とその藝術

"Akutagawa Ryūnosuke shi to shinjidai" 芥川龍之介氏と新時代

"Anatōru Furansu o tooshite mita Akutagawa Ryūnosuke" アナトール・フランスを通して見た芥川龍之介

Anchū mondō 暗中問答

Anezaki Masaharu 姉崎正治

Anya kōro 暗夜行路

"Aogusachō" 青臭帳

Aoyama Hanzō 青山半藏

Arashi 嵐

Arishima Ikuma 有島生馬

Arishima Takeo 有島武郎

"Arishima Takeo shi no kyūkutsu na kangaekata" 有島武郎氏の窮屈な考え方

"Arishima Takeo shi no zetsubō no sengen" 有島武郎氏の絶望の宜言

Aru ahō no isshō 或阿呆の一生

"Aru kyūyū e okuru shuki" 或る旧友へ送る手記

Aru onna 或る女

Asahi 朝日

Asou Hisashi 麻生久

Atarashiki mura 新しき村

"Atarashiki mura ni tsuite no taiwa" 新しき村に就ての對話

"Atarashiki sekai no tame no atarashiki geijutsu" 新しき世界のための新しき藝術

"Awaremubeki mono" 憐むべきもの

"Azamukazaru no ki" 欺かざるの記

"Bashō no isshō" 芭蕉の一生

"Beruguson to Soreru" ベルグソンとソレル

bōkoku 亡国

"Boku wa seishin ga suki da" 僕は精神が好きだ

Bokushi ni natte kara 牧師になってから

bonyari shita fuan ぼんやりした不安

"Bundan no seitōka o nanzu" 文壇の政党化を難ず

"Bungaku wa ikani ajiwau bekika" 文学は如何に味はふべきか

"Bungakushiteki kūhakujidai" 文学史的空白時代

"Bungei undō to rōdō undō" 文芸運動と労働運動

Bungeijidai 文藝時代

Bungeisensen 文藝戦線

Bungeishunjū 文芸春秋

Bungeitekina amarini bungeitekina 文藝的な，餘りに文藝的な

Buraku kaihō dōmei 部落解放同盟

"Burujoa jiyūshugi no shisō" ブルジョア自由主義の思想

"Burujoa shuppan ni taisuru wareware no taido wa kō de nakereba naranu" ブルジョア出版に對する我々の態度はかうでなければならぬ

bushidō 武士道

Chikamatsu 近松

"Chishiki kaikyū ni atau" 知識階級に與ふ

chokusetsu kōdō 直接行動

Chūōkōron 中央公論

"Dai naru katei" 大なる過程

"Daigen" 代言
"Daiyonkaikyū no bungaku" 第四階級の文學
Demokurashī デモクラシー
"Dendō no seishin" 傳道の精神
Denen no yūutsu 田園の憂欝
"Denmaruku koku no hanashi" デンマルク国の話
Dokuritsu kyōkai 獨立教會
dokuritsu-shin 独立心

"Epesosho kenkyū" エペソ書研究
eta 穢多
Fujimori Seikichi 藤森成吉
Fukko-ha 復古派
fukoku kyōhei 富國強兵
Fukuda Tokuzō 福田徳三
Fukuin to sekai 福音と世界
Fukuzawa Yukichi 福沢諭吉
Furansu monogatari ふらんす物語
Futabatei Shimei 二葉亭四迷
Futon 蒲団

Gakumon no susume 学問のすすめ
Gakushūin 学習院
"Gariraya no michi" ガリラヤの道
"Geijutsu hontai-ron" 藝術本體論
"Geijutsu ni kansuru hashirigakiteki oboegaki" 藝術に關する走り書的覺え書
"Geijutsu ni seijitekikachi nante mono wa nai" 藝術に政治的價値なんてものはない
"Geijutsusakuhin no kachi" 藝術作品の價値
"Geijutsuteki hōhō ni tsuite no kansō" 藝術的方法についての感想
"Gendai Nihon no kaika" 現代日本の開化
"Genjitsu bakuro no hiai" 現實暴露の悲哀
Genkakusambō 玄鶴山房
Gondō Seikei 權藤成卿

Hagakure 葉隱

Hagiwara Kyōjirō 萩原恭次郎
Haguruma 齒車
"Haiboku no bungaku" 敗北の文學
Hakai 破戒
"Hakai hyō" 破戒評
"Hana" 鼻
"Hanabi" 花火
"Handō no genshō" 反動の現象
Haniya Yutaka 埴谷雄高
Haru 春
Haru o machitsutsu" 春を待ちつゝ
"*Haru* okugaki" 「春」奥書
Hasegawa Tenkei 長谷川天渓
Hataraku mono kara miru mono e 働くものから見るものへ
Hayama Yoshiki 葉山嘉樹
heimen byōsha 平面描寫
Heimin shimbun 平民新聞
"Heiwa naru" 平和成る
"Heiwa no shukufuku" 平和の祝福
"Hekiken" 僻見
"Hibi no shōgai" 日々の生涯
"Hihyōka tōmen no nimmu" 批評家当面の任務
Hirabayashi Hatsunosuke 平林初之輔
Hirabayashi Taiko 平林たい子
Hirata Atsutane 平田篤胤
Hirotsu Kazuo 広津和郎
"Hirotsu shi ni kotau" 広津氏に答ふ
"Hisenshugisha no senshi" 非戰主義者の戰死
"Hōgetsu no niseshizenshugi" 抱月の偽自然主義
Hōjō Kazuo 北條一雄
"Hokuchi kigen" 北地危言
Honda Yōichi 本田庸一

"Ichinichi" 一日
Ie 家
"Ie to jiga-ishiki" 家と自我意識

"Iesu no shūmatsu kan: Mataiden dai nijuyon shō no kenkyū" イエスの終末観；馬太傳第二十四章の研究

"Igaku no setsu yori idetaru shōsetsu ron" 醫學の説より出でたる小説論

Iikura dayori 飯倉だより

Ikanishite yo wa shōsetsuka to narishika 如何にして予は小説家となりしか

Ikeda Sumihisa 池田純久

"Imogayu" 芋粥

Inbaifu 淫賣婦

Inoue Kaoru 井上馨

Inoue Tetsujirō 井上哲次郎

Inukai Takeshi 犬養健

Ishihara Ken 石原謙

ishin 維新

Isono Fujiko 磯野富士子

Iwano Hōmei 岩野泡鳴

"Iwayuru shakaishugi bungei o kokufuku seyo" 所謂社会主義文芸を克服せよ

"Iwayuru shakaishugi bungaku o kokufuku seyo" 所謂社會主義文學を克服せよ

Izumi Kyōka 泉鏡花

"Jidai heisoku no genjō" 時代閉塞の現狀

Jigoku hen 地獄變

Jiji shimpō 時事新報

"Jikoshuchō no shisō toshite no shizenshugi" 自己主張の思想としての自然主義

"Jikoshugi no shisō toshite no shizenshugi" 自己主義の思想としての自然主義

"Jikyoku o kataru" 時局を語る

"Jinsei mondai kaishaku no hōhō" 人生問題解釋の方法

jissekai 實世界

jiyū minken undō 自由民權運動

"Jiyū no maebure" 自由の前觸れ

Jogaku zasshi 女學雜誌

"Jōzetsu roku" 饒舌錄

junsui keiken 純粹經驗

"Junsuikeiken sōgo no kankei oyobi renraku ni tsuite" 純粋經驗相互の關係
及連絡に付いて

"Kagawa Toyohiko ron" 賀川豊彦論
Kaihō 解放
Kaijin 礦人
"Kaikyū geijutsu no mondai" 階級藝術の問題
"Kaisetsu" 解説
Kaizō 改造
Kaji Wataru 鹿地亘
"Kakumei no kenkyū" 革命の研究
Kambara Tai 神原泰
Kamiyama Shumpei 神山春平
Kamono Mabuchi 賀茂眞淵
Kanikōsen 蟹工船
Kappa 河童
Katagami Noboru 片上伸
Kataoka Kenkichi 片岡健吉
Katayama Koson 片山孤村
Katō Hiroyuki 加藤弘之
Katō Kazuo 加藤一夫
Katsumoto Seiichirō 勝本清一郎
keibaku kaikoku 敬幕開國
keishiki-naiyō-ronsō 形式内容論争
Keizaigaku kenkyū 経済學研究
"Kekkonmae no hyōban" 「結婚前」の評判
"Kentai" 倦怠
"Kesshō shitsutsu aru shōshimin-sei" 結晶しつつある小市民性
Kikuchi Kan 菊地寛
kindai-jin 近代人
Kindai minshushugi hihan 近代民主々義批判
kindai-shisō 近代思想
"Kinji zakkan" 近時雑感
"Kiregire ni kokoro ni ukanda kanji to kaisō" きれぎれに心に浮んだ感じと
回想
"Kirisuto sairin no yokkyū: Roma sho hasshō jūyon, nijūsan setsu no kenkyū"

基督再臨の欲求：羅馬書八章十四—廿三節の研究
"Kirisuto shinto no nagusame" 基督信徒の慰
"Kirisutokyō to aikokushin" キリスト教と愛國心
Kirisutokyō to shakaishimpo 基督教と社會進步
"Kirisutokyō to shakaishugi" 基督教と社會主義
Kitamura Tōkoku 北村透谷
Kobayashi Hideo 小林秀雄
Kobori Jinji 小堀甚二
kōbugattai 公武合體
Kōgiroku 講議錄
Kojima Kikuo 小島喜久雄
"Kojinshugi no tame ni" 個人主義のために
"Kojinshugi to seijiundō" 個人主義と政治運動
"Kojinshugi-sha to shakaishugi-sha" 個人主義者と社會主義者
"Kōki Shinjinkai" 後期新人會
"Kokian ki" 古稀庵記
Kokka shakaishugi 國家社會主義
"Kokka to katei to kojin" 國家と家庭と個人
"Kōkoku to bōkoku" 興國と亡國
kōkokushidan 興國史談
Kokoro 心
Kokugaku 國学
Komaki Oumi 小牧近江
Konoe Fumimaro 近衛文麿
kuge 公卿 (公家)
Kume Masao 久米正雄
"Kumiai undō to kakumei undō" 組合運動と革命運動
Kurahara Korehito 蔵原惟人
Kuraku 苦樂
Kurata Hyakuzō 倉田百三
Kuroiwa Ruikō 黒岩涙香
Kushida Tamizō 櫛田民藏
kyōgen 狂言
"Kyōgi hen" 教義篇
Kyōiku jiron 教育時論
"Kyōkai shomondai" 教會諸問題

"Kyomushugi no keisei" 虚無主義の形成

Maedagawa Kōichirō 前田河廣一郎
magokoroshugi まごころ主義
"Maihime" 舞姫
Makino Eiichi 牧野英一
Mannyōshū 万葉集
"Marukusushugi bungei hihyō no kijun" マルクス主義文藝批評の基準
"Marukusushugi ni okeru shisō to shūdan" マルクス主義における思想と集団
Matsukata Masayoshi 松方正義
Matsumura Kaiseki 松村介石
Matsuzawa Hiroaki 松澤弘陽
"Meiji Nihon ni okeru Purotesutanto kyōkai" 明治日本におけるプロテスタント教会
"Mikan" 蜜柑
"Minshū geijutsu no gikō" 民衆藝術の技巧
"Minshushugi no jakumetsu" 民主主義の寂滅
"Mirai-ha no shōri" 未来派の勝利
"Mirukoto to kakukoto" 見ることゝ書くこと
Mishima Yukio 三島由紀夫
Miyake Setsurei 三宅雪嶺
Miyamoto Kenji 宮本顕治
Miyazaki Ryūsuke 宮崎龍介
Momo no shizuku 「桃の雫」
Mōmoku no kawa 盲目の川
Mon 門
mono no aware もののあはれ
Morita Sōhei 森田草平
Morito Tatsuo 森戸辰男
Motoori Norinaga 本居宣長
mu 無
"Mudabana" むだ花
mukyōkaishugi 無敎會主義
"Mukyōkaishugi no zenshin" 無敎會主義の前進
"Mune o hirake" 胸を開け
Muramatsu Masatoshi 村松正俊

"Musan kaikyū geijutsu-undō no shindankai" 無産階級藝術運動の新段階
"Musanha bungeika tōronkai" 無産派文芸家討論会
Musanshimbun 無産新聞
Musashino 武藏野
"Mushakōji-kei e" 武者小路兄へ
mushisō mukaiketsu 無思想無解決

Nagayo Yoshio 長與善郎
"Naiyō teki kachi-ronsō" 内容的價値論爭
Nakae Chōmin 中江兆民
Nakajima Nobuyuki 中島信行
Nakanishi Inosuke 中西伊之助
nenpu 年譜
Nezu Kenzō 根津賢三
"Nezumi-kozō-Jirokichi" 鼠小僧次郎吉
Nigotta atama 濁った頭
"Nihon dasshutsuki" 日本脱出記
Nihon hyōron 日本評論
"Nihon no hoshushugi: Kokoro gurūpu" 日本の保守主義：「心」グループ
"Nihon no shisō" 日本の思想
Nihon puroretaria bungei remmei 日本プロレタリア文藝聯盟
"Nihon puroretaria bungei remmei kitei sōan" 日本プロレタリア文芸聯盟
  規定草案
Nihon shakaishugi dōmei 日本社會主義同盟
Niijima Jō 新島襄
Nijūdai ichimen 二十代一面
Ningen 人間
Nishida Sotohiko 西田外彦
"Nisshin sensō no gi" 日清戰爭の義
"Noa no daikōzui o omou" ノアの大洪水を思ふ
Nochi no Shinkatamachi yori 後の新片町より
Nogi Maresuke 乃木希典
"Nōjō kaihō tenmatsu" 農場開放顛末
Noma Hiroshi 野間宏

Ohara Kokingo 大原小金五

"Oi naru kenzensei" 大いなる健全性
"Oitaru Susanōno Mikoto" 老いたる素盞鳴尊
Okakura Tenshin 岡倉天心
"Okubyōmono" 臆病者
Ōsaka heimin shimbun 大阪平民新聞
Osanai Kaoru 小山内薫
ōseifukko 王政復古
Oshiminaku ai wa ubau 惜しみなく愛は奪ふ
"Otomi no teisō" お富の貞操
Ōtsu Junkichi 大津順吉
Ōya Sōichi 大宅壯一
Ozaki Kihachi 尾崎喜八
Ozaki Kōyō 尾崎紅葉

"Paionia no akusen" パイオニアの惡戰
"Puroretaria bungei no kahi" プロレタリア文藝の可否
Puroretaria geijutsu プロレタリア藝術
"Puroretaria geijutsu undō no soshiki mondai" プロレタリア藝術運動の組織
問題
"Puroretaria geijutsu undō riron" プロレタリア藝術運動理論

Risōdan 理想團
"Risōkoku wa nan de aru ka" 理想國は何である乎
"Risōshugi shichō" 理想主義思潮
Rōdō bungaku 勞働文學
"Rōdō undō to chishiki kaikyū" 勞働運動と知識階級
"Rōdō undō to rōdō bungaku" 勞働運動と勞働文學
Rōdō geijutsuka remmei 勞働藝術家聯盟
rōnō-ha 勞農派
"Russō no *Zange* chū ni miidashitaru jiko" ルツソオの「懺悔」中に見出し
たる自己

Saigyō 西行
"Saihō no hito" 西方の人
Saikaku 西鶴
"Saikin shisōkai no keikō" 最近思想界の傾向

Saionji Kimmochi 西園寺公望

Sakai Toshihiko 堺利彦

"Sakkaron" 作家論

Sakura no mi no jukusuru toki 櫻の實の熟する時

"Sanjō no suikun ni tsuite: torinozokubeki mittsu no gokai" 山上の垂訓について：取除くべき三つの誤解

Sanshirō 三四郎

Sapporo Nōgakkō 札幌農學校

Sasaki Sōichi 佐々木惣一

Satomi Ton 里見弴

"Sayoku seisanshugi" 左翼清算主義

"Sei no kakujū" 生の擴充

"Sei no sōzō" 生の創造

Seidō no kirisuto 青銅の基督

"Seijiteki kachi to geijutsuteki kachi" 政治的價値と藝術的價値

"Seinen shōkō to kakushin shisō" 青年將校と革新思想

"Seisho kenkyūsha no tachiba yori mitaru Kirisuto no sairin" 聖書研究者の立場より見たる基督の再臨

Seisho no kenkyū 聖書之研究

"Seisho no shōmei: Kirisuto sairin ni kansuru omonaru seigo" 聖書の證明：基督再臨に關する主なる聖語

"Sengen hitotsu" 宣言一つ

"Senji ni okeru hisenshugisha no taido" 戰時に於ける非戰主義者の態度

Senki 戰旗

"Sensō hantai ni kansuru ken" 戰爭反對に關する件

Shakai bungei kenkyūkai" 社會文藝研究会

"Shakai bungei ni tsuite no jihyo" 社會文藝についての時評

"Shakai no kyūsai" 社會の救濟

"Shakai seisaku to shakaishugi" 社會政策と社會主義

Shakai shimbun 社會新聞

"Shakaishugi bungei undō" 社會主義文芸運動

Shakaishugi kenkyū 社會主義研究

Shakaishugi mondai 社會主義問題

"Shakaiteki risōron" 社會的理想論

"Shakaitō museifutō bunretsu no kekka" 社会黨無政府黨分裂の結果

shasei 寫生

"Shichifuku no kai" 七福の解

"Shidō" 士道

Shimada Saburō 島田三郎

shimmin 臣民

"Shin no dendōshi" 眞の傳道師

Shinchō 新潮

"*Shinchō*, iwayuru puroretaria bungaku to sono sakka ni tsuite tou" 「新潮」所 謂プロレタリア文學と其作家に就いて問ふ

"Shinja to gensei: Mataiden goshō jūsan jūroku setsu no kenkyū" 信者と現世: 馬太傳五章十三—十六節の研究

Shinkankaku-ha 新感覺派

Shinkatamachi yori 新片町より

Shinsei 新生

Shinshakai 新社會

Shinshichō 新思潮

"Shirabeta geijutsu" 調べた藝術

Shirakaba-ha 白樺派

"Shirakaba-ha no jindō shugi" 白樺派の人道主義

Shirakawa Jirō 白河次郎

Shirayanagi Shūko 白柳秀湖

Shisei ni arite 市井にありて

"Shishōsetsu to shinkyō shōsetsu" 私小説と心境小説

Shisō 思想

"Shitsubō to kibō: Nippon koku no sendo" 失望と希望: 日本國の先途

"Shiyū nōjō kara kyōsan nōen e" 私有農場から共産農園へ

"Shizen kara geijutsu o eru: 'Shingikō to iukoto' eno kaitō" 自然から藝術を 得る:「新技巧といふこと」への回答

"Shizenseichō to mokutekiishiki" 自然生長と目的意識

"Shizenseichō to mokutekiishiki sairon" 自然生長と目的意識再論

"Shizenshugi dakkyakuron" 自然主義脱却論

"Shokan oyobi kansō" 所感及び感想

"Shōsetsu no jissai-ha o ronzu" 小説の實際派を論ず

"Shōshiminsei no chōryō ni kōshite" 小市民性の跳梁に抗して

"Shōtaku" 妾宅

"Shuju no kotoba" 侏儒の言葉

shūshin 修身

sonnō jōi 尊王壤夷
Sorekara それから
"Sōsaku yodan" 創作餘談
Sōsekai 想世界
Suematsu Kenchō 末松謙澄
Suzuki Bunji 鈴木文治
Suzuki Fujiya 鈴木富士彌

Tai Ro hikanshō dōshikai 対露非干渉同志會
taiseihōkan 大政奉還
"Taishō demokurashī no ichidanmen" 大正デモクラシーの一断面
"Taishō gannen nikki" 大正元年日記
"Taishō hachinendo no bungeikai" 大正八年度の文藝界
"Taishō kōki" 大正後期
taishūka 大衆化
Taiyō 太陽
Taiyō no nai machi 太陽のない街
Takamura Kōtarō 高村光太郎
Takano Iwasaburō 高野岩三郎
Takezawa-sensei to yuu hito 竹澤先生といふ人
"Takuboku ni kansuru danpen" 啄木に關する斷片
Tamura Naoomi 田村直臣
Tanaka Shōzō 田中正造
Tanemakuhito 種蒔く人
Tani Hajime 谷一
"Tanjū sūteki" 膽汁數滴
"Tanjū yoteki" 膽汁餘滴
Taoka Reiun 田岡嶺雲
Tayama Rokuya 田山錄彌
Tazoe Tetsuji 田添鐵二
"Tetsu" 鉄
"Tēze ni kansuru gokai ni tsuite" テーゼに関する誤解について
Tōhō no mon 東方の門
Tokai no yūutsu 都會の憂鬱
Tokuda Shūsei 德田秋聲
Tokunaga Sunao 德永直

Tokutomi Roka 德富蘆花
"Torotsukī no kyōdōsensenron" トロツキイの共同戦線論
Tōseikatsusha 黨生活者
Tōshūsai Sharaku 東洲齊寫樂
Toyama Shōichi 戸山正一
Toyoshima Yoshio 豊島與志雄
Tsuboi Shigeji 壺井繁治

"Uchimura Kanzō no omoide" 内村鑑三先生の想い出

Waga bungeijin 我が文藝人
"Waga seikatsu shinjō" 我が生活信條
"Wagakuni puroretaria bungaku no hatten" 我國プロレタリア文學の發展
Wakai 和解
"Warazōri" 薬草履
Warera 我等
"Warera no Kirisutokyō" 我等の基督敎
Waseda bungaku 早稻田文學
"Wasedaha ron" 早稻田派論

"Yajū" 野獸
Yamaga Sokō zenshū 山鹿素行全集
Yamagata Aritomo 山縣有朋
Yamakawa Kikue 山川菊江
Yamamoto Yūzū 山本有三
Yasei no yūwaku 野性の誘惑
Yoake mae 夜明け前
Yokomitsu Riichi 横光利一
"Yokusanundō no sekkei-sha" 翼賛運動の設計者
Yomiuri 讀賣
"Yorozu" よろづ
Yorozuchōhō 萬朝報
Yoshii Isamu 吉井勇
"Yotei no kyōgi" 豫定の敎義
"Yuibutsushikan to bungaku" 唯物史觀と文學
"Yuiitsusha" 唯一者

"Yuiitsusha" 唯一者
Yūshi no tabi-nikki 遊子の旅日記

zettai mushinen 絶對無私念
"*Zoku shisaku to taiken* igo" 「續思索と體驗」以後

Index

Aka to kuro (Red and black), 180

Akamatsu Katsumaro, 177

Akutagawa Ryūnosuke: Christianity of, 5, 153-154, 166; art forms of, 67, 95, 154-155, 161; philosophy of, 152, 155-164, 172, 215; death of, 153, 154, 167-168, 172-174 *passim*, 178, 192; legacy of, 154; on Taishō authors, 154; his unpredictability-of-life theme, 156-157; in "plot controversy," 158; on Voltaire, 159; on socialist writers, 160-161; Aono on, 168-170; Miyamoto on, 170-171; "The life of Christ will forever move us," 153; *Kappa*, 155, 164-166; "Hana" (The nose), 156; "Imogayu" (Yam gruel), 156; *Jigoku hen* (The hell screen), 156-157; "Kentai" (Boredom), 157; *Aru ahō no isshō* (The life of a fool), 159; *Bungeitekina, amarini bungeitekina* (Artistic, all too artistic), 160; *Anchū montō* (The dialogue in darkness), 161-162; "Otomi no teisō" (The virginity of Otomi), 163; "Mikan" (Oranges), 163; "Oitaru Susanōno Mikoto" (The aged Prince Susanō), 163; "Nezumi-kozō-Jirokichi," 163; *Samusa* (The chill), 163-164; *Shuju no kotoba* (The words of a dwarf), 164, 166; "A Note to an Old Friend," 168; *Genkakusambō*, 169

Althusius, Johannes, 7

American Mission Boards, 26

Anarchism: place of politics in, 51; growth of, 51-60; anarchist-artists, 67-68; suppression of, 69; of Shirakaba-ha, 104-105. *See also* Ōsugi Sakae

Aono Suekichi: on Shirakaba-ha, 122; on Akutagawa, 168-170; on Arishima, 169-170; on proletarian artists, 183-185; on *Tanemakuhito*, 186; on Japanese Proletarian Literary Federation, 187; reflects Marxism, 187; in *rōnō* group, 192, 196-197; "Akutagawa Ryūnosuke and the New Era," 169; "Art Based on Research," 183; "The Natural Growth and Consciousness of Purpose," 184; mentioned, 188, 200

Aquinas, Thomas, 91

Arima Yoriyasu, Count, 103-104

Arishima Ikuma, 102, 119, 131

Arishima Takeo: background of, 102-103, 119-120; Ōuchi on, 105; Christianity of, 114, 129-130; historical sense of, 126; philosophy of, 128-144 *passim*, 150-151; compared to Shiga, 128-129, 135; Marxism of, 130, 139-146 *passim*, 150, 153, 177-178, 215; death of,

Arishima Takeo (*continued*)
139, 152, 168, 173; his "Community Farm," 140-141, 150; on Mushakōji's New Village Movement, 141-143; on capitalism, 142, 143; criticism of his manifesto, 146-149; *Aru onna* (A certain woman), 61, 130-132; "Dai naru kenzensei" (Grand healthiness), 133; *Oshiminaku ai wa ubau* (Relentlessly love steals), 133; "Okubyōmono" (The coward), 134-135; "Sengen hitotsu" (One manifesto), 141, 144, 147, 173; "From a private farm to a Communist Farm," 150; mentioned, 125, 154
Aron, Raymond, 216
Ashahi, 146, 202

Becker, Carl, 91
Berdyaev, Nicholas, 64
Bergson, Henri, 65, 150
Bodin, Jean, 5
Buddhism, 22, 156
Bungeisensen (The literary front), 185-186, 189-192 *passim*, 194-196 *passim*, 203
Bushidō, 3, 21-25 *passim*, 47
Byron, George, 90

Carlyle, Thomas, 33
Chiang Kai-shek, 125
Chikamatsu Monzaemon, 162, 209
Christianity: its role in the West, 4, 5; Uchimura's theology of, 14, 16, 18-36 *passim*, 41-42, 46, 48-50, 121, 176; *vs.* Marxism, 15; influences Japanese philosophy, 15-16; influences Japanese nationalism, 18; spreads in Japan, 27-28; Tanaka on, 38; influences Japanese socialists, 39; interests naturalists, 89-90, 114; interests Shirakaba-ha, 114
Chu Hsi school, see Confucianism
Chūōkōron (The central review), 141, 200

Comintern, 188, 193, 194
Communist Manifesto, 55, 202
Confucianism: influences Japanese ethics, 2, 4, 35, 37, 111; influence of Chu Hsi school of, 18, 22-23, 42, 91; Shiga on, 120
Congress of Great Asian Writers (*1943*), 83
Crick, B. R., 214

Dante, Alighieri, 48, 137, 156
Darwin, Charles: *The Origin of Species*, 92
Demokurashī (Democracy), 53, 176
Dewey, John, 97
Dostoevsky, Feodor, 92, 122, 208

Earthquake of *1923*, 52, 68, 153, 173, 186
Ebina Danjō, 37, 121
Edo culture, 47, 52, 97, 121
Eliot, T. S., 161
Ellis, Havelock: *Studies in the Psychology of Sex*, 131

Federation for Non-Intervention in Russia, 177
Federation of Vanguard Artists (Zenei Geijutsuka Dōmei), 194, 195
Filmer, Robert, 5
Flaubert, Gustave, 70, 196, 208
French Enlightenment, 17-18, 100-101, 175
French Revolution, 72, 101
Fujita Shōzō, 126
Fukumoto Kazuo, 188, 192
Fukumotoism, 188-194 *passim*, 198
Fukuzawa Yukichi, 27; *Gakumon no susume* (For the advancement of learning), 17
Furukawa Ichibei, 37-38
Futabatei Shimei, 209

Gakushūin Peers' School, 7, 102, 103, 114
Gard, Roger Martin du, 70
Goethe, Johann, 90, 110, 160, 162

Gondō Seikei, 59
Green, T. H., 10

Hagakure, 22
Hagiwara Kyōjirō, 180
Haiku, 95
Hall, A. R., 71
Hauser, Arnold, 71
Hayama Yoshiki, 197
Hayashi Fusao, 188-192 *passim*, 197, 204; "The Socialist Literary Movement," 190
Hedonists, 95, 112-113, 174
Hegel, Georg, 10, 47-49 *passim*, 63; "Problems of Raison d'État," 11
Heller, Erich: *The Disinherited Mind*, 110
Hibbert, Howard, 116
Hirabayashi Hatsunosuke, 180-183, 187, 201-202; "The Concept of Dialectical Materialism and Literature," 180
Hirabayashi Taiko, 203
Hirotsu Kazuo: "Arishima Takeo's Punctilious Manner of Thinking," 146
Honda Shūgo, 134
Honda Yōichi, 37

Ienaga Saburō, 46
Ino Kenji, 74
Inoue Kaoru, 27
Inoue Tetsujirō, 36; "Collision of Religion and Education," 34-35
Ishikawa Tabubokin, 80-81, 87; "Jidai heisoku no genjō" (On contemporary frustration), 80
Iwanaga Yutaka, 76-77
Iwano Hōmei, 84, 86
Izumi Kyōka, 146

Japanese Communist Party: opposed by Ōsugi, 63; intellectuals in, 177-179 *passim*, 198, 206; internal policy struggles of, 187-190, 193, 208; banned by government, 195
Japanese Proletarian Literary

Federation (Nihon Puroretaria Bungei Remmei), 186-187, 189, 192
Japanese Socialist Party: proclamation of, 39-40; strength of, 40; government opposition to, 40; Second Congress of, 56
Jiji shimpō (The daily times), 27, 146
Jiyū Minken Undō (Liberal People's Right Movement), 28

Kagawa Toyohiko, 57; *Shisen o koete* (Beyond death), 104
Kaihō (Liberation), 53
Kaijin (The destroyer), 180
Kaizō (Reform), 53, 144, 170, 200
Kaji Wataru, 189-191, 195, 197-201 *passim*, 212; "Overcome So-Called Socialist Literature," 190
Kambara Yasuo, 67
Kamei Katsuichirō, 74, 90, 189
Kanazawa Higher School, 7, 86
Kant, Immanuel, 67, 72
Katagami Noboru: "Problems of Class Art," 147
Kataoka Kenkichi, 28
Katayama Sen, 63
Katō Hiroyuki, 18
Katō Kazuo, 67-68
Katsu Kaishū, 43
Katsumoto Seiichirō, 212
Kawabata Yasunari, 201
Kawakami Hajime, 53, 59, 145-146, 198; *Bimbō monogatari* (A story of poverty), 104; "Individualist and Socialist," 149
Kawazoe Kunimoto, 87
Keiō University, 27
Keizaigaku kenkyū (Economic studies), 54
Kierkegaard, Søren, 117-118, 123, 150
Kita Ikki, 59
Kitamura Tōkoku, 87-89 *passim*, 168
Kobayashi Takiji, 107, 112, 179, 199, 203; *Toseikatsusha* (The

Kobayashi Takiji (continued)
life of a party member), 193-
194; 3/15/1928, 195; Kanikōsen
(A crab ship), 206
Kobori Jinji, 197, 203-206
Kojima Kikuo, 102
Kokka shakaishugi (National so-
cialism), 53
Kokutai no hongi (The essence of
the national polity), 119
Konoe Fumimaro, Prince, 103-104
Korea, 32
Kōtoku Shūsui, 52, 56, 82, 104
Kropotkin, Peter, 55, 105, 140, 144-
145, 149, 176
Kunikida Doppo, 84-86 passim, 89,
120, 131, 209; Musashino (The
Musashino Plain), 89
Kuno Osamu, 126-127
Kurahara Korehito: in proletarian
art movement, 192, 194-196, 198-
205 passim, 210- 212; on study-
ing past literature, 208; "New
Stages of the Proletarian Art
Movement," 194; "The Road to
Proletarian Realism," 196; "The
Organizational Problems of the
Proletarian Art Movement," 211;
"Thought on the Method of
Art," 212
Kuroiwa Ruikō, 41
Kusaka Eijirō, 189
Kushida Tamizō, 55
Kyōiku jiron (Journal of educa-
tion), 35
Kyoto, 103, 106, 107
Kyoto Imperial University, 13, 53,
104, 145, 198
Kyūshū, 105

Lenin, V. I., 82, 176, 185, 202
Lincoln, Abraham, 48, 176
Locke, John, 5
Lombroso, Cesare, 92, 131
Luxemburg, Rosa, 176

Maedagawa Kōichirō, 197
Maeterlinck, Maurice, 115, 122

Mannheim, Karl, 71
Mannyōshū, 209
Marinetti, F. T.: Manifesto of Futurism, 68
Maruyama Masao, 5, 23
Maruyama Motoyoshi, 67
Maruyama Shizuka, 208-209
Marx, Karl, 150, 161, 175-176, 204;
Capital, 145
Marxism: influences Nishida, 10;
vs. Christianity, 15; influences
Japanese philosophy, 15-16; at-
tracts intellectuals, 52-56; of
Ōsugi, 63-64; influences socialist
writers, 82, 100, 147-149, 153,
173-210, 215-216; of Arishima,
130, 139-145, 150, 153, 177-178,
215; receptiveness of Taishō era
to, 174-179; Third International,
180. See also Anarchism; Japanese Communist Party; Japanese Socialist Party
Masamune Hakuchō, 89, 90, 94-95
Matsukata Masayoshi, 103
Matsumura Kaiseki, 37
Maupassant, Guy de, 196
Meiji Gakuin (missionary school),
86
Meiji Restoration: character of,
2-7, 17; Imperial Household in,
4, 11-13 passim; Imperial Rescript of 1890 on Education, 4,
35; Imperial Constitution of
1889, 12, 57; influence of Uchimura on, 16-27; spread of Christianity in, 27-28; Sat-Chō oligarchy in, 42-43, 45; antimodernist movement in, 44; growth of
anarchism in, 51-69 passim; naturalism in, 70-98; relation of
Shirakaba-ha to, 101; institutions of aristocracy in, 106-107
Mill, John Stuart, 35
Miyamoto Kenji, 170-171; "Haiboku no bungaku" (The literature of defeatism), 170
Mono no aware (aesthetic category),
110-112

Mori Ōgai, 78-79, 54, 92, 108, 152; *Vita sexualis*, 78
Morito Tatsuo, 54-56, 105
Motoori Norinaga, 110-111
Mu philosophy, 10-11, 124
Musanshimbun (Proletarian news), 190, 194
Mushakōji Saneatsu: background of, 102-103, 142; on Japan, 103, 117, 125; New Village Movement of, 105-106, 141-143 *passim*, 148, 150; on Nogi's death, 107-108, 120; philosophy of, 112-113, 115-118 *passim*, 122, 126-128 *passim*, 162, 193, 215; on Tolstoy, 114-115; *Shinri-sensei* (Mr. Truth), 116, 120; mentioned, 133

Nagai Kafū: recreates Edo culture, 47, 52, 121; art of, 67, 95, 108, 121, 154; reacts to Akutagawa's death, 173-174; influences intellectuals, 209; *Furansu monogatari* (Tales from France), 46-47; "Hanabi" (Fireworks), 52
Nagayo Yoshio: background of, 102-103; philosophy of, 113-114, 117, 128, 162; influences on, 114; opposes violence, 125; *Seidō no Kirisuto* (Bronze Christ), 114, 115; *Takezawa-sensei to yuuhito* (The man called Mr. Takezawa), 116; *Yasei no yūwaku* (The temptation of the wild), 121
Nakae Chōmin, 17-18
Nakajima Noboyuki, 28
Nakano Shigeharu, 188, 191, 199, 202-205 *passim;* "In Art There Is No Such Thing as Political Value," 202
NAPF (Nippona Proleta Artista Federatio), 195-196, 200, 206-212
Natsume Sōseki: literary prominence of, 54, 152; on Shimazaki, 73; his feelings toward the West, 99, 121; reacts to Nogi's death, 108; philosophy of, 108, 115-116, 133, 136, 214; praises Akutagawa,

156, 167; influences intellectuals, 209; *Sorekara* (Thereupon), 115; *Kokoro* (The heart), 115; *Mon* (The gate), 115; *Kōjin* (Passersby), 214; mentioned, 103
Naturalists: in Europe, 70-73; critiques of, 78-81, 196; yield to socialist authors, 84-90 *passim*, 96, 99, 128; react to Christianity, 89-90; identify art with experience, 91-98; influenced by European writers, 92; literary dictum of, 94, 97; *vs.* Shirakaba-ha, 99, 107, 116; family concept of, 118-119; lose social position, 120; resemblance of Arishima's writings to, 130-131. *See also* Shimazaki; Tayama
Nietzsche, Friedrich, 123, 138, 160
Niijima Jō, 18
Nishida Kitarō: philosophy of, 7-14 *passim*, 124; influences young intellectuals, 8, 104; influences on, 10; *Zen no kenkyū* (Studies in goodness), 8; *Hataraku mono kara miru mono e* (From an observer to a doer), 9
Nogi Maresuke, General, 107-108, 120

Ōhara Kokingo, 17
Okakura Tenshin, 83
Ōsugi Sakae: anarchism of, 59-68 *passim*, 136-137, 180; influences on, 64-66 *passim;* death of, 68-69; legacy of, 69
Ōuchi Hyōe, 55-56, 105
Ozaki Kōyō, 92

Peers' School, *see* Gakushūin Peers' School
Perry, Matthew, 17
Plato, 12, 13, 118, 134
Pravda, 182, 194
Proletarian Art Foundation, 194-195
Puroretaria geijutsu, 192, 194, 195

Rembrandt, 149
Renan, Joseph: *Life of Christ*, 90
Risōdan (Idealists' Association), 41
Rōdō bungaku (Workers' literature), 53
Rōnō-ha writers, 192, 195, 197, 201, 203-204, 206
Rousseau, Jean, 18, 58, 127, 159, 176; *Confessions*, 90, 93
Russia, 34, 55, 117, 210
Russian Social Democrats, 210
Russo-Japanese War, 33, 39, 73

Saigyō, 94
Saikaku, 94
Saionji Kimmochi, Prince, 103
Sakai Toshohiko, 53, 147-149, 190
Satō Haruo: naturalism of, 96-98; *Denen no yūutsu* (The pastoral melancholy), 96-97; *Tokai no yūutsu* (The urban melancholy), 97
Satomi Ton, 102, 125, 129, 130-131
Scheler, Max, 127
Schleiermacher, Friedrich, 48
Schumpeter, Joseph, 62
Seisho no kenkyū (Biblical research), 33
Senki (The fighting flag), 195-197 *passim*, 199, 200, 203, 205, 208-210 *passim*, 212
Shakai Bungei Kenkyūkai (Society for the Study of Socialist Literature), 188-189
Shakai mondai kenkyū (Journal of social problems), 53
Shakaishugi kenkyū (Studies in socialism), 53
Shiga Naoya: background of, 102, 119; anarchism of, 104-105; his relations with Kobayashi, 107, 112, 203; on Nogi's death, 107; philosophy of, 109-110, 112-113, 116, 125; influenced by Uchimura, 114; on Confucianism, 120; compared to Arishima, 128-129, 135; his unfaithfulness

theme, 134; *Anya kōro* (Through the dark night), 120, 121; *Ōtsu Junkichi*, 120, 121; *Wakai* (Reconciliation), 120, 121; mentioned, 152
Shimada Saburō, 28
Shimamura Hōgetsu, 74, 75, 84-87 *passim*, 89, 94
Shimazaki Tōson: influenced by Zola, 74, 92; philosophy of, 77-78, 81-84 *passim*, 92-94, 97-98, 116, 215; background of, 84-86, 159; themes of, 88-89; Christianity of, 89-90; influenced by Rousseau, 93; Masamune on, 95; interested in criminal psychology, 131; his reaction to Akutagawa's death, 173-174; *Hakai* (Apostasy), 73-75, 78, 81; *Shinsei* (Regeneration), 75-76, 95; *Asahi*, 82; *Yoake mae* (Before the dawn), 82, 85, 97; *Toho no mon* (The gate of the east), 83; *Sakura no mino jukusuru toki* (The season when cherries ripen), 87, 90; *Ie* (The family), 93, 118, 120; *Haru* (The spring), 93; "Mirukoto to kakukoto" (To observe and to write), 93; mentioned, 102, 152
Shinchō, 169
Shinjinkai (New people's society), 176-177
Shinkankaku-ha (New Sensibility School), 201
Shinshakai (The new society), 53
Shintoism, 22
Shirakaba, 99, 102, 113, 122, 124, 130
Shirakaba-ha (White Birch Society): philosophy of, 99-101, 108-117; aristocratic origins of, 101-106; influenced by Tolstoy, 104, 114; anarchism of, 104-106; acceptance of, 107; *vs.* naturalism, 107; evaluated, 108, 125-128 *passim*; interested in Christianity, 114; genius concept of, 117-118, 215; family concept of,

118-121; contributions of, 121-125

Shirakawa Jirō, 46

Shishōsetsu (I-novel), 81, 116

Shisō (Thought), 67

Shklar, Judith, 118

Shōwa intellectuals, 168, 178

Sino-Japanese War, 32, 42

Sobue Shōji, 189, 195

Socialism, *see* Japanese Socialist Party; Marxism

Society for the Study of Marxist Art, 189, 191, 199, 203

Sorel, Georges, 65-66

Spencer, Herbert, 35

Springfield Republican, The, 33

Stirner, Max, 65, 104

Strindberg, August, 122-124 *passim*

Suematsu Kenchō, 40

Sumiya Mikio, 28

Suzuki Bunji, 63

Taishō era: role of intellectuals in, 1-2, 99; Nishida's importance in, 7-14; Ōsugi's influence in, 63; receptive to Marxism, 174-179

Tale of Genji, The, 111, 209

Tale of Heike, The, 209

Tanaka Seizō, 38

Tanemakuhito (Those who sow the seeds), 180, 183, 186

Tani Hajime, 188-189, 199, 212; "The Development of the Proletarian Movement in Our Country," 189

Tanizaki Junichiro: hedonism of, 67, 95, 154; on Marxist literature, 153; in "plot controversy," 158; reacts to Akutagawa's death, 173-174

Taoka Reiun, 45

Tayama Katai: theme patterns of, 76-77, 94, 97, 152; background of, 84-85; naturalism of, 88; reacts to Akutagawa's death, 173-174; *Futon* (Quilt), 75, 77; *Execution of a Soldier,* 76; *Death of Shigeemon,* 76; *Toki wa sugiyuku*

(The time passes), 85; *Sei* (Life), 118-119; mentioned, 81, 92

Tazoe Tetsuji, 56

Tokuda Shūsei, 81, 84-86 *passim,* 97

Tokugawa hegemony, 23, 38, 43, 57-58, 91

Tokunaga Sunao: *Taiyō no nai machi* (A town without a sun), 206

Tokyo, 7, 37, 69, 81, 87

Tokyo First Higher Middle School, 104

Tokyo Imperial University, 7, 27, 34, 53, 54, 86, 102-104 *passim,* 176, 188, 191

Tolstoy, Leo, 114-115, 122-124 *passim,* 208; *What Is To Be Done?,* 104

Toyama Shōichi: *Kirisutokyō to shakai-shimpo* (Christianity and social progress), 27-28

Troeltsch, Ernst, 20

Trotsky, Leon: "Not by Politics Alone Do We Live," 182

Tsuboi Shigeji, 180

Tsurumi Shunsuke, 126-127

Uchimura Kanzō: Christianity of, 14, 16, 18-36 *passim,* 41-42, 46, 48-50, 108, 121, 176; on *bushidō,* 21-22, 47; influenced by Confucianism, 22-23, 37, 42; on World War I, 29, 34; on menace of China, 32; pacifism of, 32-34, 40-41; on Rescript of *1890* on Education, 35-36; ideal human relationship concept of, 36-37; reports on copper-poisoning problem, 38-39; on capitalism, 39; on Sat-Chō government, 42-43, 45; antimodernism of, 44-47; *vs.* anarchists, 51; influences intellectuals, 114, 215; "The Death of a Pacifist in Battle," 33; "Christianity as a Solution for the Agrarian Crisis," 36-37; "Chris-

Uchimura Kanzō (*continued*)
tianity and Socialism," 40-41;
"What is Risōdan?", 41; "The
Reforms I Desire," 43-44; *Kōko-kushidan* (Historical study of
the birth of nations), 47-48;
mentioned, 89, 90,
Uemura Masahisa, 89, 121
United States, 19, 33
Uozumi Setsurō: "Jikoshugi no
shisō to shiteno shizenshugi"
(Naturalism as the idea of in-
dividualism), 80-81

Voltaire: *Candide,* 159

Warera (We), 53
Waseda University, 86, 87, 180, 183
Watsuji Tetsurō, 12-13, 110-112,
123-124, 209; "*Mono no aware* ni
tsuite" (On *mono no aware*),
110; "Koji junrei" (A pilgrimage
to old temples), 123; *Gūzō saiko*
(The idol restored), 123
Weber, Max, 25, 112, 193
Wilde, Oscar, 162; *The Soul of*

Man under Socialism, 104; *De
Profundis,* 104
Wordsworth, William, 89
Workers' and Peasants' Artist Fed-
eration (Rōnō Geijutsu Dōmei),
192, 194, 195
World War I, 29, 34, 52, 54, 63, 96
World War II, 38

Yamaga Sokō, 22
Yamagata Aritomo, 54
Yamakama Hitoshi, 53, 59, 187,
189-190, 194
Yamakawa Kikue, 63
Yamakawaism, 187-188, 193-195
passim
Yanagi Muneyoshi, 102, 123
Yokomitsu Riichi, 201
Yorozuchōhō, 38, 39, 41
Yoshino Sakuzō, 63, 82, 148, 177

Zen, 7-9
Zenei (Vanguard), 147-148, 176, 194
Zola, Emile: naturalism of, 70-71;
his influence in Japan, 73, 74,
90, 92, 196; Mori on, 79

Harvard East Asian Series

1. *China's Early Industrialization: Sheng Hsuan-huai (1844–1916) and Mandarin Enterprise.* By Albert Feuerwerker.

2. *Intellectual Trends in the Ch'ing Period.* By Liang Ch'i-ch'ao. Translated by Immanuel C. Y. Hsü.

3. *Reform in Sung China: Wang An-shih (1021–1086) and His New Policies.* By James T. C. Liu.

4. *Studies on the Population of China, 1368–1953.* By Ping-ti Ho.

5. *China's Entrance into the Family of Nations: The Diplomatic Phase, 1858–1880.* By Immanuel C. Y. Hsü.

6. *The May Fourth Movement: Intellectual Revolution in Modern China.* By Chow Tse-tsung.

7. *Ch'ing Administrative Terms: A Translation of the Terminology of the Six Boards with Explanatory Notes.* Translated and edited by E-tu Zen Sun.

8. *Anglo-American Steamship Rivalry in China, 1862–1876.* By Kwang-Ching Liu.

9. *Local Government in China under the Ch'ing.* By T'ung-tsu Ch'ü.

10. *Communist China, 1955–1959: Policy Documents with Analysis.* With a foreword by Robert R. Bowie and John K. Fairbank. (Prepared at Harvard University under the joint auspices of the Center for International Affairs and the East Asian Research Center.)

11. *China and Christianity: The Missionary Movement and the Growth of Chinese Antiforeignism, 1860–1870.* By Paul A. Cohen.

12. *China and the Helping Hand, 1937–1945.* By Arthur N. Young.

13. *Research Guide to the May Fourth Movement: Intellectual Revolution in Modern China, 1915–1924.* By Chow Tse-tsung.

14. *The United States and the Far Eastern Crises of 1933–1938: From the Manchurian Incident through the Initial Stage of the Undeclared Sino-Japanese War.* By Dorothy Borg.
15. *China and the West, 1858–1861: The Origins of the Tsungli Yamen.* By Masataka Banno.
16. *In Search of Wealth and Power: Yen Fu and the West.* By Benjamin Schwartz.
17. *The Origins of Entrepreneurship in Meiji Japan.* By Johannes Hirschmeier, S.V.D.
18. *Commissioner Lin and the Opium War.* By Hsin-pao Chang.
19. *Money and Monetary Policy in China, 1845–1895.* By Frank H. H. King.
20. *China's Wartime Finance and Inflation, 1937–1945.* By Arthur N. Young.
21. *Foreign Investment and Economic Development in China, 1840–1937.* By Chi-ming Hou.
22. *After Imperialism: The Search for a New Order in the Far East, 1921–1931.* By Akira Iriye.
23. *Foundations of Constitutional Government in Modern Japan, 1868–1900.* By George Akita.
24. *Political Thought in Early Meiji Japan, 1868–1889.* By Joseph Pittau, S.J.
25. *China's Struggle for Naval Development, 1839–1895.* By John L. Rawlinson.
26. *The Practice of Buddhism in China, 1900–1950.* By Holmes Welch.
27. *Li Ta-chao and the Origins of Chinese Marxism.* By Maurice Meisner.
28. *Pa Chin and His Writings: Chinese Youth Between the Two Revolutions.* By Olga Lang.
29. *Literary Dissent in Communist China.* By Merle Goldman.
30. *Politics in the Tokugawa Bakufu, 1600–1843.* By Conrad Totman.
31. *Hara Kei in the Politics of Compromise, 1905–1915.* By Tetsuo Najita.
32. *The Chinese World Order: Traditional China's Foreign Relations.* Edited by John K. Fairbank.
33. *The Buddhist Revival in China.* By Holmes Welch.
34. *Traditional Medicine in Modern China: Science, Nationalism, and the Tensions of Cultural Change.* By Ralph C. Croizier.

35. *Party Rivalry and Political Change in Taishō Japan.* By Peter Duus.

36. *The Rhetoric of Empire: American China Policy, 1895–1901.* By Marilyn B. Young.

37. *Radical Nationalist in Japan: Kita Ikki, 1883–1937.* By George M. Wilson.

38. *While China Faced West: American Reformers in Nationalist China, 1928–1937.* By James C. Thomson Jr.

39. *The Failure of Freedom: A Portrait of Modern Japanese Intellectuals.* By Tatsuo Arima.